American Protestant Thought
THE LIBERAL ERA

AMERICAN PROTESTANT THOUGHT:

THE LIBERAL ERA

EDITED BY

WILLIAM R. HUTCHISON

❧

HARPER TORCHBOOKS
Harper & Row, Publishers
New York and Evanston

AMERICAN PROTESTANT THOUGHT:
THE LIBERAL ERA

Introduction, Selected Reading List, editorial notes, and compilation copyright © 1968 by William R. Hutchison.

Printed in the United States of America.

First edition: HARPER TORCHBOOKS, 1968,
Harper & Row, Publishers, Incorporated,
49 East 33rd Street, New York, N.Y. 10016.

Library of Congress Catalog Card Number: 68-27286.

CONTENTS

I. The Setting

II. Characteristic Ideas

III. Implications

IV. Complications

V. Reconstruction

American Protestant Thought
THE LIBERAL ERA

INTRODUCTION

No single religious movement can claim a monopoly on the term "liberal." The essential liberal principle has been at work wherever men have sought to change accepted doctrines or institutions in such a way as to increase individual freedom. It has operated, therefore, in a variety of contexts and even within directly competing systems of religious thought. Such seventeenth-century dissenters as Roger Williams and Anne Hutchinson contributed to the liberal tradition despite purposes which in some respects seem very conservative indeed. A century later, liberalizing forces were at work in the religious rationalism that stressed human ability, yet were almost equally potent in the frontier revivalism that was the sworn enemy of this rationalism. Like most other powerful and lasting impulses, liberalism resists the nervous housecleaning that would identify it exclusively with any one of its historical embodiments.

But terms like "liberal" do acquire secondary meanings of a more restricted kind. Champions of republicanism become Republicans; the venerable unitarian doctrine of God becomes embodied as Unitarianism; and other principles such as congregationalism and "levelling" become so identified with particular historical movements that these terms in their generic forms nearly fall into disuse.

By a process of this sort, the words "Protestant liberalism" have come to refer especially to a set of religious ideas that flourished in Europe and America from the opening of the nineteenth century through the first quarter of the twentieth. The American liberal movement, phased somewhat later than the European, attained its greatest strength between the 1870's and the 1930's. It was shaped both by the culture of those decades and by a considerable legacy of earlier liberal ideas.

Notable among the inherited ideas was confidence about human nature and human prospects brought down essentially from the eighteenth-century Enlightenment. In religious as in secular liberalism, belief in progress varied greatly in form and intensity. It could appear as the expectation of a hard-won human victory, under God's Providence, over the forces of evil; or it could become a quite radical belief in man's automatic progress toward perfectibility. But preoccupation with problems of human nature and destiny, and relative optimism about their resolution, pervaded all of liberalism, and especially marked its American form.

Even more evident, however, because more directly controversial, were the liberals' characteristically advanced views on Biblical criticism and their readiness to question religious creeds and institutions. The latter-day liberals, like their eighteenth-century predecessors, tended to go beyond criticism of particular creeds to distrust of creeds in general. Though they criticized particular Biblical interpretations, their more fundamental aversion was to "Bibliolatry," to strict Biblical literalism. And their objection to certain sects was at least matched by their dislike for "sectarianism" itself.

Besides these traits of humanism and anti-formalism, a third strand of continuity between eighteenth- and nineteenth-century liberalism was the emphasis placed upon ethics. Liberals did not necessarily agree on specific questions of personal or social ethics; they were in fact less likely than conservatives to reach that kind of agreement. But they were virtually at one in their strong tendency to value moral accomplishment more than confessional regularity.

Other features of post-Civil War liberal thought derived from the romantic liberalism of the earlier nineteenth century, rather than from the rationalistic liberalism of the eighteenth. The most important heritage from this more recent era was a stress upon the immanence, or "indwelling," of God in man and nature. Romantic liberalism of the kind promoted by the Transcendentalists within Unitarianism and by Horace Bushnell in Congregationalism, had supported the rationalists in depicting a more benign God than that of Calvinist orthodoxy; but the romantics had broken sharply with rationalism by picturing an immanent God who was less remote, less "transcendent," than the God of either Calvinism or Deism. Liberalism after 1870 remained strongly committed to this conception of an immanent deity.

Philosophical Idealism and the so-called Higher Criticism were also legacies from the immediately preceding era. Idealism, since it located "reality" in the world of spirit far more than in the world of matter, helped liberals to minimize the importance of those physical or material objects of faith (such as the Christian miracles) in which they could no longer literally believe. The Higher Criticism served a correlative function by bringing the conclusions of historical and cultural analysis to bear upon Scripture, upon the traditional creeds, and upon religious institutions.

Such ideas and interests were not in all cases peculiar to religious liberals, or indebted exclusively to a liberal tradition. Anti-sectarianism, for example, together with a tendency to discount the value of detailed creeds or formal rituals, had appeared in frontier religious movements that were in most other respects inimical to liberalism. But, taken together, the characteristics listed above virtually defined Protestant liberalism in the era preceding the Civil War; and they were to remain important for the next several generations.

What, then, was distinctive about the liberals of the period after 1870? The first answer is that they were winning. Dissenters and declared liberals of earlier times, from the outcast Anne Hutchinson in the 1630's, through the handful of Deists around 1800, to the Unitarian and Congregational romantics of the 1850's, had all waged losing battles. Even those who had not experienced failure in their immediate communities had fallen far short of goals they had set for liberalizing other regions and denominations. Massachusetts liberals of 1825, for instance, had expected Unitarianism to spread "like a prairie fire" across America; but the fire had sputtered out west of Worcester and south of the Connecticut line, and had only with difficulty been re-lighted in more distant places.

Post-Civil War religious liberalism was another matter. While radical campaigns such as that of the extra-Christian Free Religious Association achieved, at best, modest organizational success in this later period, the milder liberal forces at work from within the churches enjoyed steady and rapid gains. Despite setbacks and heresy trials in most denominations, and a lack of any visible effect in some others, by the later nineteenth century Protestant liberalism was very much in the ascendant. The rise of fundamentalism, and of other highly defensive reactions, confirms rather then contradicts this judgment.

As a consequence of their widespread success, liberals found themselves able to work within the existing Protestant organizations, instead of forming their own Liberal Church. Their preference for doing this was in itself nothing new. The unitarian and universalist

Christians of an earlier era had also wished to reform existing structures from within. But these pioneering movements had found it
necessary to establish new denominations. And other pre-Civil War
liberals, in spite of limited changes within major denominations,
had found little welcome except in the Unitarian or Universalist
churches, or in the Society of Friends. But the disaffected liberal Christian of the 1880's could readily find a place among the Congrega-
tionalists or the Episcopalians; or, a few years later, among rapidly
liberalizing Northern Baptists, Methodists, or Disciples of Christ.

Liberals were not lacking in organizational interest. They strove
with wide success for control of churches, periodicals, denominations, and inter-church bodies; and by the 1920's they had made
liberalism the acknowledged point of view in approximately half the
Protestant theological seminaries.[1] But forming a separate organization was not the goal of this movement, and never became an urgent
necessity. A "liberal sectarianism" seemed a contradiction in terms;
and, unlike some of their predecessors, the men of this generation
were not forced to brazen out that particular contradiction.

Another distinguishing feature of post-1870 liberalism, besides its
unprecedented success in penetrating major denominations, was the
emergence within it of a form of argument that eventually would be
labelled "modernist." The term "modernism" is sometimes used to
denote the more extreme liberalism of any historical period, however
early. But such usage, like the common indiscriminate use of the
word "fundamentalist," is anachronistic and misleading. The term
"modernism" had no currency before the later nineteenth century;
more important, before about 1870 one finds few examples of the
kind of religious liberalism it denotes.

The hallmark of modernism is the insistence that theology must
adopt a sympathetic attitude toward secular culture and must consciously strive to come to terms with it. One may discover, or suspect, implicit forms of this attitude in earlier religious movements,
and indeed some excited polemicists of the liberal era tried to attach
the term, as a badge either of honor or of shame, to almost every
innovative movement in Christian history. But explicit modernism,
the frank argument for cultural accommodation that was voiced so

powerfully in the last third of the nineteenth century, had been only infrequently and meagerly stated before that time.

Earlier liberals in fact had often been clearly doubtful of the merits of religious adaptation to contemporary culture. The changes inspired by antinomians, seekers, separatists and other early dissenters, though strongly contributory to the liberal tradition, had been based almost wholly on Biblical criteria, not on any conscious striving for modernity. Similarly, in the eighteenth century the usual criteria for theological innovation had been the Bible, or a universal and primordial Reason, or a de-mythologized "religion of Jesus"; and here again modernity had been more often condemned than even implicitly admired. Although many eighteenth-century rationalists had shown enthusiasm for new philosophical formulations, others had feared "the perils of metaphysics" too much to go even that far. Intimations of "modernism," in any case, had been largely cancelled out by doubts about the institutions representing contemporary culture. Rationalistic liberals had adumbrated a glorious future that was to be realized less by embracing modern culture than by finding ways through its complex structures, or ways over the rubble of its doomed institutions. "Progress," when invoked, had customarily pointed backward to models of Edenic simplicity.

In the earlier nineteenth century, when intuition and "universal religious feeling" were becoming the new standards of religious innovators, a celebration of contemporary culture had indeed begun to work its way into liberal arguments, but its place there had been far from secure. In the thought of the Transcendentalist Theodore Parker, for example, arguments in praise of science and modernity stand like awkward boys in the company of an intuitionism that speaks a more ethereal and timeless language. Parker's apparent vacillation, often remarked upon, between a reliance upon intuition and a frenzied search for "facts of demonstration," is just one sign of a dilemma that runs all through the thought and rhetorical enthusiasms of mid-century liberal and radical religion.

In the postwar period, the militant radicals who in some ways were Parker's most direct descendants were heirs to only part of this Parkerite dilemma. Though the radicals continued to sense the strain between intuitionism and scientific modernism, they no longer felt compelled to relate either method to a defense of Christian faith. The dual task of fusing these approaches and then fitting the resulting philosophy to Christian apologetics fell, therefore, to liberals in the larger churches and in the conservative wing of Unitarianism.

As this story of gradual emergence should suggest, the argument for modernism did not drop suddenly from the sky, or rise from the pages of Darwin, in the 1870's. Nor was its later domination complete. Among those liberals who remained in the Christian fold, no absolutely unalloyed modernism appeared after 1870 or even, despite a common assumption, after 1910. The frequent attempts of religious historians to separate the Protestant progressives into sharply differentiated "liberal" and "modernist" teams have some use in retrospective theological polemics, but almost none in clarifying the way in which the modernist argument typically worked. In individual minds as well as in the movement as a whole, modernism worked by alliance with more traditional approaches. It follows, of course, that one looks in vain for a sudden qualitative change in liberalism to be linked laboriously to some "watershed" event such as the firing on Fort Sumter or Asa Gray's review of Darwin.

What did happen after 1870 was that Protestant liberals, as they moved through a period of unprecedented controversy and increasing influence, carried the modernist argument with them. It grew with their growth, and seemed to succeed with their success. Increasingly influenced by the newer outlook, liberals developed and applied the plea for cultural adaptation with a directness and expansiveness that had little precedent even in Unitarianism, and none at all in evangelicalism. The stridency of the modernist appeal in America seems, in fact, to have gone well beyond anything manifested in the liberal theology of the Continent.

By the 1890's, most of the Protestant liberals were ready to join wholeheartedly in the renewed self-congratulation and enthusiasm for modernity with which Americans generally were ringing in the new century. The liberalism of 1900, for all its continuities with the past, differed significantly from that of other times and places. One important reason was that the mark of modernism was by then clearly upon it.

Some adherents were led by this discernible change in liberalism, and in the cultural alembic affecting it, to feel that earlier influences had been of relatively little importance. William Jewett Tucker, in the first selection of the present anthology, argues that his immediate generation, the young liberals of the 1870's and 1880's, not only felt but acted upon a sense of drastically new occasions and new intellectual requirements. Yet neither he nor his colleagues really thought of their movement as *sui generis;* on the contrary, like most reformers who are determined to stop short of radicalism, they were transparently anxious to strengthen their credentials by proving how well liberalism accorded with tradition. It was the men of 1870–1890, to be sure, who were most eager to show themselves the true heirs of the early Christians, or of the "right" Church Fathers, or of the creedmakers at Westminster; but liberal spokesmen in the 1920's also lost few chances to seek out a modernist impulse in remote eras of Church history.[2]

Most liberals were equally ready to acknowledge their more recent mentors, both European and American. The European sources of which they were most conscious were those representing the massive tradition of the Romantic Enlightenment, the schools of philosophy, theology, and Biblical criticism inspired by Immanuel Kant and Friedrich Schleiermacher. The representatives of this tradition had sought to lift the discussion of ultimate questions out of the arena governed by sensory observation and scientific demonstration, an arena wherein such matters as the reality of God or of immortality could not, in their view, be settled. But at the same time they had accepted and developed the use of the scientific-historical method in such penultimate areas as the interpretation of Scripture and institutions. By the end of the nineteenth century, this way of arranging theological discourse had achieved its archetypal expression in the work of Albrecht Ritschl of Göttingen and the work of his pupil Adolf von Harnack at Berlin.

American liberalism enjoyed direct intensive contact with these European sources. Among the thirty most prominent liberals of the period between 1875 and 1915, over half had studied at German universities, and had incurred intellectual debts to a long list of scholars headed by Ritschl, Harnack, and R. H. Lotze of Göttingen.

[2] See, for example, Shailer Mathews' *The Faith of Modernism* (New York: The Macmillan Co., 1924).

Among second-rank American liberals the incidence of foreign study was somewhat lower, yet was almost twice that found in the leadership of conservative Protestantism in the same period.[3]

The pattern of foreign study is slightly less conspicuous if one focuses upon that portion of the liberal leadership whose training fell before the 1880's. Among these a majority, including such important figures as Theodore Munger and Washington Gladden, felt most directly indebted to the American Unitarian and Transcendentalist movements, to Horace Bushnell, and to a variety of British theological and literary figures led by Frederick D. Maurice, Frederick Robertson, and (at a further remove) Samuel Taylor Coleridge.

Both the younger and the older men acknowledged also a considerable, if more ambiguous, debt to teachers in American theological schools. Most frequently mentioned were such revisers of Calvinism as Henry Boynton Smith of Union Seminary and Samuel Harris of Andover. These were the transitional men, the latter-day Channings who had effected liberalizing changes in their own generation and who lived into the next in the memories and the respectful criticisms of students who had gone beyond them. One frequently finds appreciations of Harris or Smith tucked into articles that are dedicated to arguing the newness of the New Theology.

If partisans like Tucker sometimes exaggerated the sharpness of liberalism's break with the past, later detractors of the movement were to show an even greater tendency to over-dramatize its eventual "dissolution." The selection in this volume from the writings of Walter Marshall Horton, the Congregational theologian, indicates that liberals themselves shared the sense of cataclysmic decline in the years around 1930. But more adverse critics, going well beyond Horton, pictured liberalism as having fallen apart, much like the Calvinism allegorized in Holmes's *One-Hoss Shay*, "all at once and nothing first." That bit of historical imprecision, in one case as in the other, seriously strained the limits of poetic license; and many early neo-orthodox pronouncements about the end of lib-

[3] The statements in this and the two succeeding paragraphs are drawn from a comparative analysis, to be published elsewhere, of the careers and opinions of 150 liberals and 100 conservatives prominent between 1875 and 1915.

eralism have by now come to seem more illuminating as autobiography than as history. The renewed vigor of classic liberal
themes in the 1960's has even roused the thought, most therapeutic
for liberals after long losing bouts with paranoia, that their neo-
orthodox tormentors may themselves have been part of a very temporary adjustment within a continuing progressive movement.

Even if that view should be vindicated, however, the early Depression years will continue to stand in American religious history as
"the end of an era." Reinhold Niebuhr and his colleagues were unduly cataclysmic. Liberalism was not so dead as they thought it was.
Yet their personal sense of cataclysm, like that of the desperate men
who jumped from buildings, was itself a guarantee that the old
order was not going to be restored. Liberal theological ideas would
straggle back from the neo-orthodox wars, but they would find the
old homestead, the ideological environment in which classic liberalism had flourished, altered almost beyond recognition.

Between its rise in the 1870's and its gradual dissolution a half-
century later, liberalism passed through rather well-defined stages.
The early years, the 1870's and 1880's in particular, produced ini-
tiatory explorations and manifestoes of the kind reprinted in Part
II of this anthology. Some of these ground-breaking statements,
such as A. V. G. Allen's *Continuity of Christian Thought,* aroused
fear and opposition without provoking actual heresy trials; but
nearly all the others, from the writings of Beecher in the 1870's
to those of Bordon P. Bowne at the turn of the century, brought
upon their authors either heresy proceedings or equivalent challenges
to professorial appointment and membership in ministerial associations.

By the 1890's, in spite of further heresy trials, the liberal movement displayed an increased self-confidence. When Lyman Abbott,
editor of the powerful *Christian Union,* began in 1892 his series of
popular volumes relating Christianity and evolution, cynics remarked upon his ability to catch a prevailing wind in his own sail.
A kinder view is that, the opening battles having been fought and
a real penetration achieved in several denominations, the time had
come for the kind of popularization that Abbott did so well, just
as it had for the rather loose and "liberal" kind of systematizing

best seen in William Newton Clarke's *Outline of Christian Theology* (1898). The time had also come for serious attempts to work out liberalism's implications for missions, for personal and social ethics, for education, and for the rebuilding of Christian unity. (Examples appear in Part III below.)

The systematization and extension of liberal thought led to further questioning. System-building in a liberal movement causes discomfort among those adherents whose reaction was against systems in the first place; and diverse applications of an ideology make fertile ground for real disagreement about the ideology itself. Internal dissent arose within liberalism as early as the 1890's. Well before the first world war, as the middle third of the present anthology attests, prominent liberals were expressing dissatisfaction with the theology, with the philosophical Idealism that permeated it, and with the complacency that seemed to assume, in the face of growing social disruptions, that modern man with his modern religion had achieved the long-sought Kingdom. William Wallace Fenn, the Unitarian Dean of Harvard Divinity School, denounced the extravagances of Idealism, and George B. Foster at Chicago stirred a generation of students with a functional view of religion that raised tormenting questions about the remnants of Christian supernaturalism. Walter Rauschenbusch joined Washington Gladden and other liberals in castigating the social naïveté of sophisticated churches. And Newman Smyth, an elder statesman of the liberal movement, ·excused himself from certain current celebrations by writing eloquently, and without tears, about "the passing of the Protestant age of history."

The events of the 1920's brought consolidations in the liberal position, though they also augmented the strains of disunity working beneath the surface. Shailer Mathews' *Faith of Modernism,* the most impressive of a number of liberal restatements in the decade, furthered the assimilation of modernism into liberalism. In Mathews' work, as in that of Harry Emerson Fosdick and other leading liberal advocates of the 1920's, the imperatives of "modernism" were the same, after due allowance for changes in scientific and intellectual environment, as those asserted in typical liberal statements of fifty years earlier. Mathews' modernism prescribed that theology must take account of culture, but insisted also upon the final authority of the Christian message. "Modernists as a class," Mathews wrote, "are evangelical Christians. That is, they accept Jesus Christ as the revelation of a savior God. . . . [Their] starting point is the inherited orthodoxy."[4]

Further evidence of consolidation, and of the powerful position liberalism had achieved in American religion, appeared in a poll conducted by *Ministers' Monthly* in the mid-twenties. Theological seminaries were asked to state whether they were liberal or orthodox. With liberalism defined as substantially synonymous with modernism, and orthodoxy with fundamentalism, only 18 of the 91 seminaries polled found it unfitting or embarrassing to take a stand on one side or the other. Forty seminaries conceived of themselves as liberal, 33 orthodox. Eleven considered themselves to be occupying a middle ground. Only seven made the admission, almost too candid for a theological seminary, that they were unsure where they stood.[5]

But behind the battlements shored up in the 1920's, liberal self-criticism and differentiation continued, as the essays in this collection by Willard Sperry and Henry N. Wieman make evident. Even Fosdick, represented here in combat with the "acrid literalism" of the fundamentalists, could be roundly condemnatory of the "arid liberalism" which he said was the besetting sin of his own party.[6] In Wieman's writings, a new set of reservations about human perfectibility augmented the philosophical realism that insisted theology must start from the "hard facts" of a scientifically observable universe. "This is not a nice world," Wieman wrote, "and God is not a nice God."[7] The *Christian Century,* the leading liberal organ, gave a hearing to every sort of liberal self-criticism from charges of impotence in international affairs (as in the 1923 article "Save Your War Sermons") to analyses of liberalism's fatal alliance with stagnating bourgeois culture.

[4] *The Faith of Modernism,* pp. 34–5. In fact, in these same pages Mathews places modernism somewhat to the theological right of liberalism, on the ground that "liberalism" is a term frequently used for movements not fully committed to New Testament religion.
[5] Cited in *Methodist Quarterly Review,* 74 (July, 1925), 399.
[6] See his chapter on "The Dangers of Modernism" in *Adventurous Religion and Other Essays* (New York: Harper and Brothers, 1926), pp. 258–74.
[7] *The Wrestle of Religion with Truth* (New York: The Macmillan Co., 1927), p. 3.

The movement called neo-orthodoxy, which came to public attention in 1932–1934, was an orchestration, under the emotional impact of the Depression, of these critical motifs with themes of divine transcendence and human finitude that had been moving in continental theology for some fifteen years. The larger constituency of liberalism, which had ignored the forebodings of its leaders before 1930, was to be equally oblivious for at least a decade of the new, massive questioning of liberal assumptions. But to many of the theological intelligentsia, the coming of neo-orthodoxy was an abrupt and shattering experience, one which demanded either profound mental readjustment or an equally difficult acceptance of minority status. Men accustomed to the sensation of riding the wave now felt themselves crushed by it, and some responded with a severe defensiveness.

From the first, though, a number of liberals viewed neo-orthodoxy as a salutary corrective for a theology they still considered valid. John C. Bennett of Union Seminary sought in 1933 to distinguish the points on which liberalism needed correction from other elements "which we must not lose in the present stampede." Among the latter, according to Bennett, were the higher criticism of Bible and doctrine, the recognition of individual insight as a source of religious authority, the emphasis upon the Jesus of history, and the stressing of continuities between revelation and reason.[8] In the subsequent work of Walter Marshall Horton and others (see Parts IV and V below), the liberal themes remained vital despite substantial appropriations of neo-orthodox thought.

By the late 1950's an American theological community that had been startled, thirty years earlier, by the ferocity of Karl Barth's critique of liberalism, heard the Swiss theologian acknowledging that "we were at that time only partially in the right, even in reference to that theology which we inherited and from which we had to disengage ourselves."[9] They saw Barth returning, with a depth of appreciation that liberals themselves might well envy, to the study of that nineteenth-century theology which he still fundamentally rejected. The translation in 1959 of *Protestant Thought from*

---

[8] "After Liberalism—What?" *Christian Century, 50* (November 8, 1933), 1403–04.
[9] *The Humanity of God* (Richmond: John Knox Press, 1960), p. 42.

Rousseau to Ritschl coincided with, and augmented, a renewed American interest in the liberal tradition, and a gradual lifting of long-standing inhibitions against its being taken seriously. And within a very few years after that, younger radical theologians were refurbishing the argument which Barth had called the most valuable, if also the most dangerous, in the liberal repertoire: the insistence "that the guiding principle of theology must be confrontation with the contemporary age and its various problems."[10]

Some theological radicals of the mid-sixties felt passionately that the central problem to be confronted in their own age was that of "the death of God"; and it was this metaphor (promoted by some as more than a metaphor) that caught public attention. But along with the death-of-God theme and other borrowings from recent theologies of paradox, radical theology in the 1960's produced some rather clear echoes of traditional liberalism. These could be heard not only in the insistence upon confrontation with secular culture, but also in such specific resonances as the critique of religious language, the stress upon the humanity of Christ, and the increased interest in contextual or "situation" ethics. The advance party of the 1960's sometimes slighted their more remote mentors by presenting venerable liberal themes as if they were new discoveries. But this was scarcely surprising when the consciousness of a liberal tradition had been suppressed or attenuated for a generation. And the new radicals, who were not to be confused with their breathless biographers in the newsmagazines, at least equalled Tucker's generation, and surpassed Niebuhr's, in their readiness to acknowledge ideological forebears.

Since the selections gathered in this volume are manifestoes of the liberal movement, or express its most advanced thought, they are more explicit and more combative than the "typical" liberal sermon or article had any need of being. But in ideas, if not always in style or format, these are representative utterances. Each expresses views that were shared widely, either throughout the liberal movement or in one of its significant branches.

A major criterion of selection, along with the influence and

---

[10] *The Humanity of God*, p. 18.

representativeness of these authors, has been the relative unavailability of their writings. One might wonder why the editor, who has felt free to include some of the latter-day heirs of the liberal movement, has excluded its great precursors. The answer is that the precursors—Channing, Emerson, Parker, Bushnell—are all reasonably accessible ιn paperbound or at least in modern editions. Since the intention of the American Perspectives series has been to reprint significant but inacccessible historical materials, a starting-point in the 1870's seemed fitting.

The criterion of accessibility has also limited the coverage given in this volume to the Social Gospel. While theological and social liberalism are by no means coextensive, the Social Gospel, for at least half the liberals, arose as an irresistible corollary of their theological position. A larger place for it in this book could easily have been justified; but, as the Selected Reading List indicates, good editions in the 1960's have made the literature of social Christianity readily available.

Still other areas tangential to Protestant liberalism are large enough or distinct enough to require separate treatment. This is the case with the social doctrines of the neo-orthodox movement (to say nothing of neo-orthodoxy itself) and with the thought of those off-shoots of Protestant liberalism, such as Free Religion, that took leave of Christianity.

SELECTED READING LIST

Primary Materials: The student should consult the sources from which selections in this anthology are taken, and also the following key liberal writings:

Books

ABBOTT, Lyman. *The Theology of an Evolutionist.* Boston: Houghton Mifflin Co., 1897.

BEECHER, Henry Ward. *Evolution and Religion.* New York: Fords, Howard and Hulbert, 1885.

BRIGGS, Charles A. *Biblical Study*. New York: Charles Scribner's Sons, 1883.

CLARKE, William Newton. *An Outline of Christian Theology*. New York: Charles Scribner's Sons, 1898.

FOSDICK, Harry Emerson. *The Living of These Days*. New York: Harper and Brothers, 1956. Paperback edition, Harper & Row, 1967.

FOSTER, George B. *The Finality of the Christian Religion*. Chicago: University of Chicago Press, 1906.

GLADDEN, Washington. *Recollections*. Boston: Houghton Mifflin Co., 1909.

MACINTOSH, Douglas C. *Theology as an Empirical Science*. New York: The Macmillan Co., 1919.

McGIFFERT, Arthur C. *A History of Christian Thought*. New York & London: Charles Scribner's Sons, 1932–33. 2 vols.

MUNGER, Theodore T. *The Freedom of Faith*. Boston: Houghton Mifflin Co., 1883.

RAUSCHENBUSCH, Walter. *A Theology for the Social Gospel*. New York: The Macmillan Co., 1917. Paperback edition, New York: Abingdon Press, 1960.

Collections

AHLSTROM, Sydney E. (ed.). *Theology in America*. Indianapolis: Bobbs-Merrill Co., 1967.

CROSS, Robert D. (ed.). *The Church and the City, 1865–1910*. Indianapolis: Bobbs-Merrill Co., 1967.

HANDY, Robert T. (ed.). *The Social Gospel in America, 1870–1920*. New York: Oxford University Press, 1966.

SMITH, H. Shelton, Robert T. HANDY, and Lefferts A. LOETSCHER. *American Christianity*. Vol. II. New York: Charles Scribner's Sons, 1963.

Secondary Works

BARTH, Karl. *Protestant Thought: From Rousseau to Ritschl*. Translated by Brian Cozens. New York: Harper and Brothers, 1959.

BUCKHAM, John W. *Progressive Religious Thought in America*. Boston: Houghton Mifflin Co., 1919.

CAUTHEN, Kenneth W. *The Impact of American Religious Liberalism.* New York: Harper & Row, 1962.

FOSTER, Frank Hugh. *The Modern Movement in American Theology.* New York: Fleming H. Revell Co., 1939.

MAY, Henry Farnham. *Protestant Churches and Industrial America.* New York: Harper and Brothers, 1949. Paperback edition, Harper & Row, 1967.

MEYER, Donald B. *The Protestant Search for Political Realism, 1919–1941.* Berkeley: University of California Press, 1960.

NASH, Arnold S. (ed.). *Protestant Thought in the Twentieth Century.* New York: The Macmillan Co., 1951.

SMITH, H. Shelton. *Changing Conceptions of Original Sin.* New York: Charles Scribner's Sons, 1955.

WILLIAMS, Daniel Day. *The Andover Liberals.* New York: King's Crown Press, 1941.

I
THE SETTING

THE SENSE OF A NEW ENVIRONMENT

The autobiography of William Jewett Tucker, published in 1919, underlined the liberal contention that theology must respond directly to cultural change, and gave a detailed account of the intellectual and social impulses to which Tucker's generation had in fact responded.

Tucker was a highly qualified spokesman, having fought battles for liberalism in most of its leading areas of concern. In the 1880's he had attracted notice as an editor of the theologically liberal *Andover Review*. By the early nineties, he had won acquittal (along with four Andover Seminary colleagues) in an epoch-making trial for heresy, and had founded the Boston social settlement later known as South End House. From 1893 to 1909 he had been the innovating, successful, and politically outspoken President of Dartmouth College.

After his retirement Tucker turned to punditry, and his wise if ponderously phrased observations on world affairs appeared frequently in the *Atlantic Monthly* and elsewhere. The autobiography, coming in this period, offered an insider's reminiscence of the whole liberal effort, but especially of that portion of it which assumed a direct relationship between theological reform and social or political progressivism.

～ 1 ～
THE FORTUNE OF MY GENERATION
by William Jewett Tucker

The generation which was beginning to take shape and character when I came of age, was to have the peculiar fortune, whether to its disadvantage or to its distinction, of finding its own way into what we now call the "modern world." If I were to characterize the generation as I look back upon its course, I should say that it was by this necessity a self-educated generation. The great gift of educational value which came to it from the past, through the faithful transmission of the previous generation, was discipline, the intellectual and moral discipline of the old régime. The actual process of self-education began with its conscious entrance into the world of the new knowledge and of the new values, constantly opening before it. This process was progressive rather than cumulative. Men no longer estimated one another by the relative amount of their knowledge, but rather by their relative power of intellectual initiative, by their ability to enter the new fields of inquiry and research, and to occupy advanced positions.

I have referred to this peculiar condition or circumstance in which the lot of my generation was cast, as its fortune. It came, that is, in the order of time, and not, with a single exception, by the compulsion of some great inheritance, or by the setting apart to some specific duty. The stimulus, the incentive, the challenge was altogether in the situation itself. Men found themselves singularly stirred to think new thoughts and to attempt new methods of action. There was no manifest unity of purpose in the spirit of the age, but all movements, though often conflicting, were seen to make for progress. Gradually the desire and struggle for progress became the unifying purpose of the generation. The self-education of which I have spoken developed more and more in all departments of life into a passion for progress.

SOURCE: *My Generation: An Autobiographical Interpretation* (Boston: Houghton Mifflin Co., 1919), pp. 1–7, 13–14, 16–18.

The peculiar fortune of the generation becomes evident and clear as we give due account to its place in the order of time. It explains what was by far the most significant fact in its fortune, namely, its intellectual detachment in so large degree from the past. It is not difficult to place the cause, or to fix the date of the break between the old order of thought and the new, provided we make due allowance for the intervening period between the time when the break took place, and the time when it took effect. By common consent, the break came with the publication of *The Origin of Species*. This was in the fall of 1859. The significance, however, of the publication of the *Notes,* as Mr. Darwin modestly called the treatise, was not readily apprehended, doubtless in part because of the unassuming way in which it was put forth. The most that Mr. Darwin then claimed is summed up in the following words, of which the last sentence only is now really prophetic:

When the views entertained in this volume on the origin of species, or when analogous views are generally admitted, we can dimly foresee that there will be a considerable revolution in natural history. . . . In the distant future I see open fields for far more important researches. Psychology will be based on a new foundation, that of the necessary acquirement of each natural power and capacity by gradation. Light will be thrown on the origin of man and his history.

It was not till 1871 that Darwin published *The Descent of Man,* embodying his conclusions regarding the derivation of man's nature from lower and still lower forms of animal life.

An interesting reminiscence, showing the rather casual manner in which the earlier volume came to the notice of persons of culture in this country, has been given by the late Rev. Dr. Charles C. Caverno, of Lombard, Illinois. Dr. Caverno was at the time of the incident a young lawyer in Milwaukee, and was acting as chairman of a committee on the public library of the city. "Sometime in the winter of 1859–60," he says, "Ralph Waldo Emerson, who was then giving a course of lectures in Milwaukee, asked me if I could procure him a copy of a book on Species, which an Englishman had published lately, and he added, 'from what I have heard it is likely to make the dry bones rattle.' I have given," Dr. Caverno adds, "Mr. Emerson's description of the book he was after, for he gave no name of author or definite title of book."

However casual may have been the introduction of *The Origin of Species* among general readers of non-scientific habits, it was not long before it began to change the intellectual atmosphere. It gradually changed the point of view. Men began to see things differently. The intellectual detachment from the past was brought about chiefly through this change in the point of view—a change set forth with great clearness by Mr. Balfour in his analytic retrospect of the nineteenth century:

> No century has seen so great a change in our intellectual apprehension of the world in which we live. It is not merely that this century has witnessed a prodigious and unexampled growth in our stock of knowledge— for new knowledge might accumulate without end, and yet do nothing more than fill in, without materially changing the outline already traced by the old. Something much more important than this has happened. Our whole point of view has altered. The mental framework in which we arrange the separate facts in the world of men and of things is quite a new framework. The spectacle of the universe presents itself now in a wholly changed perspective. We do not see more, but we see differently.

Doubtless the intellectual detachment from the past was effected with less violence through changing the point of view, than would have been possible through any other method. And yet the result was not gained without opposition, and in some quarters sharp antagonisms. The scientific renaissance, if such we choose to term it, was not like the revival of letters in the fourteenth and fifteenth centuries, making itself felt through the diffusion of light and culture, and creating a more spiritual environment. In reality, it was not so much a renaissance as a revolution. It became articulate as a challenge, calling in question the established order of thought, and summoning men to new ways of thinking. The controversial aspect of the scientific renaissance or revolution became manifest more quickly and more seriously in Great Britain than in this country. This was due, I think, in no small measure to the presence of such pugnacious advocates of the new theories as Huxley and Tyndall, who found a welcome opportunity for controversy in the conservatism and conventionalism of the English Church. So sensitive were the religious interests which the controversy touched, that men quite remote from ecclesiastical or theological connections were drawn into it. As early as 1864 Disraeli, in a speech before a diocesan conference at Oxford, uttered his famous mot—"The question before us is this, Is man an ape or an angel? I, my lord, I am on the side of the angels." Within the next decade, Oxford was aflame with the controversial spirit which had spread in all directions. "Darwinism," says Mrs. Humphry Ward in her recent *Recollections,* "was penetrating everywhere; Pusey was preaching against its effects on belief; Balliol stood for an unfettered history and criticism, Christ Church for authority and creeds; Renan's *Origines* were still coming out, Strauss's last book also; my uncle [Matthew Arnold] was publishing *God and the Bible* in succession to *Literature and Dogma;* and *Supernatural Religion* was making no small stir."

That the controversy was carried on with less bitterness in this country was due in part, of course, to the preoccupation of mind with the affairs of the nation (1860-70), but still in part to the different religious or ecclesiastical conditions which obtained here. The difference in tone may also be attributed to the marked contrast in the temper of our leading scientists of the period—Agassiz, Gray, and Dana. There was a good deal of attempted sarcasm of the Disraeli order, which found expression in the pulpit, but the higher religious journals and reviews spoke with becoming restraint. Especially noticeable in this regard was a series of articles in the *Bibliotheca Sacra,* the leading theological review of the time, by Professor George Frederick Wright of Oberlin, then the young pastor of the Free Church in Andover, Massachusetts. These papers were characterized by a breadth and candor, and above all by a thorough comprehension of the real questions at issue, which make them still an example of fair-minded and intelligent discussion in place of controversy.

The secondary stages of the scientific controversy in this country were more marked than the earlier stages in their effect upon religion. The various phases of Biblical Criticism, which followed as a natural sequence from the application of the new scientific standards to the Bible, awakened more concern, and stirred more bitterness, than the new hypothesis regarding the origin of man. And the after-effect of the controversy upon the popular as well as upon the critical mind was for the time disturbing to religious faith. The wave of agnosticism which spread over the country necessitated various changes in the presentation of religious truth. A larger place was given in the teaching of the seminaries to the department of

Apologetics; more emphasis was placed by the pulpit upon conduct and duty; and gradually there was an appropriation of the new truths disclosed by science in the interest of ethics and of faith. As a general result, I think that it may now be said that the loss to religion of certain dogmatic but divisive beliefs found in due time its compensation, in the insistence placed upon the function of conscience in the interpretation, as well as in the enforcement of religion.

I have referred at some length to the religious controversy attending the scientific revolution, because it produced at first a greater effect as a disturbing force in religion than as a constructive force in education. Of this latter effect I shall have much to say in detail hereafter. The educational effect when it came was twofold: it brought in a vast amount of new subject matter, and it changed altogether the method of the higher education. Of these two effects, the latter was by far the more revolutionary. In fact, the scientific method my be said to have created some subjects in the curriculum of the colleges, to have recreated others, and to have changed the relative position of certain other subjects, as in the case of the ancient and modern languages. Within the range of college and university teaching, the greatest contribution of the scientific method was the graduate school. Various attempts of a partial nature had been made to anticipate this object, but the opening of Johns Hopkins in 1876 inaugurated the epoch of graduate instruction. Beyond this contribution was the establishment of the research foundation, separating investigation from teaching, in which Johns Hopkins led the way in the advanced study of medicine.

I have emphasized the fact that, with a single exception, the fortune of my generation was not predetermined by its inheritance. That exception however, though local, was of the highest consequence. Before it passed off the stage, the preceding generation in this country had reached the climax of its moral power in the struggle for the abolition of slavery. A part of its unfinished task went over to my generation. The whole spirit of the struggle went over as a moral heritage—the bequest of the Puritan conscience at the stage of its greatest activity. The bequest took precedence of the new gifts which marked the intellectual abundance of the modern age. It was not something to be accepted or denied: it was to be taken at its full value and put to immediate use. Due consideration must be given to this relation of the generation to its moral heritage, as the explanation in part of the slow awakening of intellectual life in this country to the scientific renaissance.

． ． ．

Men went about their work under a new sense of responsibility. Side by side with the work of national reconstruction, there was the vast work of reconstructing the economic, social, and religious life of the country, which was in one way or another every man's business. And for this task the earlier education, with its more rigid moral discipline, was still efficacious, in spite of its lessening intellectual authority. It remained, as I have intimated, a steadying force in the midst of the quickening but distracting influences which marked the incoming of the "modern era." In referring to the abolition of slavery as the unfinished task of Puritanism, I do not assert that the accomplishment of this end completes its task. But later movements of the moral order have not been so distinctively the work of Puritanism. What we have begun to term the social conscience is wider in its sources and broader in its workings than the anti-slavery conscience. The prohibition crusade, for example, is of the South more than of New England. Economic crusades have their origin most frequently in the West. The Puritan conscience may be expected to go over into the national blend of moral forces, with the prestige and influence attending its accomplished results.

In the further estimate of the causes which affected the fortune of my generation, according to its place in the order of time, I put without hesitancy the incoming of the new social order consequent upon the rise of industrialism. This incoming of the new social order was in reality a social revolution, though lacking most of the usual signs of violence. For it was nothing less than the change from the individualistic basis of society to the collective basis, or, if we do not allow the political implication of the term, to the socialistic basis. And the change came, not in any way of evolution from the existing theory or state of society, but altogether through the compulsion of outer forces. Individualism, as a working theory of society, was overwhelmed and put to confusion by the vast output of the material forces, which had been set in operation by the discoveries and applications of science. True, individualism itself was a contributory cause in this material expansion, perhaps the greatest, because furnishing the necessary initiative. But whatever may have been the relative part taken by the agencies already at work, the situation which they created forced the change. The old order could not bear the strain of modern industrialism.

· · ·

The religious effect of the social revolution was in some respects deeper and more far-reaching than the political effect. It changed the prevailing type of religion. Individualism had been the foundation of the Protestant faith, especially of Puritanism. Now men began to think in terms of social Christianity. "Even the Church," wrote Stanley Leathes in the introduction to *The Latest Age* in the series of Cambridge Histories, "even the Church has been infected; the modern priest is sometimes more concerned for the unemployed than for the unrepentant." This sarcasm hid a deep truth. Christianity had begun to concern itself with economic conditions. Poverty, if the result of unemployment, called for more than charity. The relief lay in social justice, a term which came into service to express the obligation of society to the unemployed or to the underpaid. New methods of meeting this obligation were adopted. Social settlements sprang up in the cities side by side with the religious mission and the charity organization. The Church became as conspicuously the agency for "social service" as it had been the "means of grace" in the work of individual salvation.

· · ·

Such was the fortune of my generation in respect to the time in which its lot was cast—a time of new and aggressive intellectual demands, of unfinished moral tasks, of widespread changes in the social order. As may be seen from this brief retrospect, it was not a time through which one could find his way clearly, either the way of knowledge or the way of duty. But it was from first to last, as I have said, a period of incentive and challenge. One felt all the while that he was living in the region of undiscovered truth. He was constantly made aware of the presence of some unsatisfied opportunity. When compared with the times which have burst upon us with such sudden and appalling fury, the times which I have described seem orderly and undisturbed; but when at last the true perspective of history is reached, I doubt not that they will regain their natural place in the opening era of the modern world.

II
CHARACTERISTIC IDEAS

~~~~~~

REJECTION OF BIBLICAL LITERALISM

The so-called Higher Criticism of Scripture, though perhaps not
the paramount issue between liberals and their foes, was surely the
issue that had greatest visibility and provoked the most bitter discussion. For that reason, as well as for reasons of scholarly eminence,
Charles A. Briggs will always be counted a major figure in American liberalism. The point sometimes made, that Briggs was liberal
only in Biblical interpretation, has about the same force as the plea
once entered for an extravagant woman: that she was extravagant
only with respect to money.

Because Briggs thought the theory of word-for-word Biblical in-
spiration a downright heresy, and said so with great vehemence,
Presbyterian conservatives tried to exclude him from the Robinson
Chair of Biblical Theology at Union Seminary, and did prevent
him from continuing in the Presbyterian ministry. Union stood by
Briggs, and in 1898 the Episcopal Church received him.

Through all this, the noted heretic remained conservative on
such doctrinal points as the deity of Christ, and on nearly all social
issues. But as the following selection shows, he was uncompromising
in his demand that the Bible and the creeds be exposed to modern
knowledge.

～2～
ORTHODOXY
by Charles A. Briggs

Orthodoxy is right thinking about the Christian Religion: not that Orthodoxy consists only in thinking, but that right thinking involves right teaching and right acting.

No thinking can be right that is not in accordance with the truth. Truth is the daughter of God. She is one, and she cannot be rightly known in parts or sections; for no one can rightly know the various parts who does not see them centering in their unity; and no one can rightly know their unity who does not comprehend the variety that springs therefrom. Hence all human orthodoxy is partial and incomplete. No one can be entirely orthodox, as no one can be altogether good, save God only.

Orthodoxy, so far as man is concerned, is relative and defective; it is measured by the knowledge that he has of the truth. Man's knowledge is not a constant quantity. It varies in different men, in different nations and societies, and still more in different epochs of history.

The Pharisees claimed to be orthodox, and in their pretended orthodoxy condemned the Savior of the world. The Greek Church claims to be orthodox, and has remained stationary in its stereotyped forms of thinking for centuries. The Roman Catholic Church parades its unity, catholicity, and orthodoxy, and yet it persecuted the pious and used every diabolical art to prevent the Reformation of the Church. The Lutheran scholastics claimed the possession of the pure doctrine, and in the name of orthodoxy made war upon the vital piety of Spener and the Pietists. The Reformed scholastics in the interest of orthodoxy divided the Church into hostile camps, and their successors have been busy sowing discord, making strife, battling with science, philosophy, art, and every form of human thinking, and thus rending the Church of Jesus Christ into numerous

SOURCE: *Whither? A Theological Question for the Times* (New York: Charles Scribner's Sons, 1889), pp. 6–15, 17–19. Footnotes omitted.

sects. Orthodoxy has been made the pretext for oppression and crime, the foe to progress in science and theology, the enemy of the truth in all ages. Orthodoxy is a good thing, one of the best things, but it has been put to shame by the great number of counterfeits that have circulated in the world.

It is necessary to distinguish between true orthodoxy and false orthodoxy—between orthodoxy and orthodoxism. Orthodoxism assumes to know the truth and is unwilling to learn; it is haughty and arrogant, assuming the divine prerogatives of infallibility and inerrancy; it hates all truth that is unfamiliar to it, and persecutes it to the uttermost. But orthodoxy loves the truth. It is ever anxious to learn, for it knows how greatly the truth of God transcends human knowledge. It follows the truth, as Ruth did Naomi, wherever it leads. It is meek, lowly, and reverent. It is full of charity and love. It does not recognize an infallible pope: it does not bow to an infallible theologian. It has one only teacher and master— the enthroned Savior, Jesus Christ—and expects to be guided by His Spirit into all truth.

Orthodoxy has a different meaning in different lands and different ages, depending partly on the stage of the education of our race, and partly upon the different race or national characteristics and the temperaments that distinguish mankind.

There must be some objective standard, some comprehensive statement by which the relative orthodoxy of men may be estimated and measured. The absolute standard of human orthodoxy is the sum total of truth revealed by God. God reveals truth in several spheres; in universal nature, in the constitution of mankind, in the history of our race, and in the sacred Scriptures, but above all in the person of Jesus Christ our Lord.

If a man has mastered this entire revelation of the truth, all that science, philosophy, history, the sacred Scriptures and Jesus Christ can give him, then, and then only, he may claim to be entirely orthodox. His orthodoxy has revealed its limit and its perfection. But until that desirable result has been attained, orthodoxy is variable and progressive; it is partial and incomplete, and must go on to reach perfection and completion. Hence, for all practical purposes, Orthodoxy and Progressive Orthodoxy are convertible terms.

That man or church whose orthodoxy does not make progress, ceases thereby to be orthodox, and from the necessities of the case becomes heterodox. He refuses to accept the truth that is offered him by the advances in science, philosophy, history, and the more exact study of the sacred Scriptures. He is heterodox, in that he falls short of the revealed truth that the truly orthodox have already accepted. He is also heterodox in all that he does accept and teach; for he keeps his thinking and teaching in the shadow of stereotyped forms of thought; he declines to bring his knowledge into the full light of the truth, which like the sun has risen higher toward its zenith; he prefers his darkness to the light of God; he fears to look the truth in the eyes, lest he should be convicted of error, and be compelled to change his position, his convictions and statements. Intellectual timidity and cowardice are not consistent with Christian orthodoxy. True orthodoxy is brave, manly, and aggressive; it marches forward.

Truth is so connected and interwoven in an organism that an advance in any department exerts an important influence upon the whole system. Any man or church that refuses to accept the discoveries of science or the truths of philosophy or the facts of history, or the new light that breaks forth from the Word of God to the devout student, on the pretence that it conflicts with his orthodoxy or the orthodoxy of the standards of his church, prefers the traditions of man to the truth of God, has become unfaithful to the calling and aims of the Christian disciple, has left the companionship of Jesus and His apostles and has joined the Pharisees, the enemies of the truth. He that is born of God heareth God's words. The man who has within him the spirit of truth, and is following the guidance of the divine Spirit of truth, will hail the truth and embrace it whether he has seen it before or not; and he will not be stayed by the changes, that he fears may be necessary, in his preconceptions or prejudices, or his civil, social, or ecclesiastical position. A traditional attitude of mind is one of the worst foes to orthodoxy.

We have an infallible standard of orthodoxy in the sacred Scriptures. God himself, speaking in His holy Word to the believer, is the infallible guide in all questions of religion, doctrine, and morals.

But the sacred Scriptures do not decide for us all questions of orthodoxy. They do not answer the problems of science, of philosophy, or of history. They do not cover the whole ground of theology. There are important matters in which the Christian religion enters into the spheres of science, philosophy, and history where the divine revelation given in these departments of knowledge is either presupposed by the sacred Scriptures, or else has been left by them for mankind to investigate and use in the successive constructions of Christian theology, which have gone on since the apostolic age, and which will continue until the end of the world.

The sacred Scriptures are not the only source of Christian theology; they were given in the midst of other sources of knowledge to enlighten us in the fields where these were insufficient. The New Testament does not give us the entire instruction of Jesus Christ, the sum total of apostolic doctrine.

The Bible does not decide all questions of religion. It does not decide the mode of baptism; it does not clearly determine whether infants are to be baptized; it does not definitely confirm the change from the Sabbath to the Lord's day; it does not determine the question of liturgical worship; it does not clearly fix the mode of church government. It leaves a great number of questions upon which Christians are divided undetermined.

The Bible does not decide all questions of doctrine. It does not give us the mode of creation, the origin of sin and evil, the psychological construction of human nature, the reasons of the divine election, the mode of life in the middle state. If the current systematic theology were reduced to its Biblical dimensions and then extended so as to cover the Biblical ground, it would be so different that few would recognize it.

The Bible does not decide all questions of morals. It does not decide against slavery or polygamy; it does not determine a thousand political and social questions that have sprung up in our day.

Doubtless there are general principles given in the Bible that may guide us to the solution of all these questions. But it is high time for men to cease confounding Biblical statements with the conclusions that they have drawn from these statements. The religion, doctrine, and morals of the Bible are very different from the current religion, doctrines, and morals of the Church, whether expressed by systematic statements, or in the lives and teachings of the people.

None of the older divines gave the human reason its proper place in religion and theology. They were all too much involved in the older methods of exegesis which sought to prove everything possible from the Bible. It was necessary that there should be a long conflict with Deism in order to eliminate *Natural Theology* as a distinct theological discipline; and then the long conflict with Rationalism in order to establish the place of *Speculative Theology*. The Bible does not war against the truths of nature, of the reason, or of history. It rather concentrates their instruction in its central Revelation.

The Scriptures shine with heavenly light in the midst of the sources of human knowledge. They cannot be understood alone by themselves. It is probable that the reason why the Scriptures have not been more completely mastered in our time, is that the divine truth revealed in other spheres has not been brought into proper relation with the Scriptures. The sacred Scriptures are for the whole world and for all time. As man grows in the knowledge of nature, of himself and of history, he will grow in the knowledge of the Scriptures.

The sources of knowledge are so interrelated that they cannot be entirely understood apart from the whole organism of truth. The Reformation would have been impossible without the new birth of learning that preceded it—the emancipation of the human spirit from the bondage of medieval scholasticism. The present advance in science is preparing the way for another reformation of the Church—it is emancipating us from the bondage of Protestant scholasticism.

We are well aware that there are some theologians, especially in America, who have claimed that their system of theology is altogether Biblical, and who have made it their boast that they have taught nothing new in theology. But, to say the least, these theologians are mistaken; they have deceived themselves, and they delude others. In fact they have restated the scholastic formulas of Protestantism; they have appropriated from other spheres of learning all the truth that seemed to suit their purpose and that could be used in their system. They have done precisely the same in their use of the sacred Scriptures.

Biblical theology is a recent branch of theological science that sprang from the necessity of distinguishing between the theology of the Bible and the theology of the theologians. Any one who has taken the trouble to compare the two has noticed the difference. He finds that each Biblical writer has his own range of ideas and each writing its own scope, and that it is necessary to gather this vast variety in a higher unity in order to comprehend the sum total of the theology of the Bible. He also sees that every age has its own circle of thought and every theologian his point of view and every Christian church its peculiar mission. The sum of Biblical theology is not represented in any creed or any theologian. Many Biblical doctrines were overlooked by the ancient and the medieval churches, and were first brought into their influential position at the Reformation. But the student of Biblical theology finds that the Reformers built also on too narrow ground, chiefly upon the epistles to the Romans and Galatians. There are not a few who still find the theology of Paul in the epistle to the Romans, and build their system upon that. But in fact, no one can understand the doctrine of Paul who has not advanced beyond the epistle to the Romans and apprehended the more developed Christology of the epistles of the imprisonment. Protestantism, by building too exclusively on Paul and on his earlier epistles at that, can never attain the climax of Christian orthodoxy until it enlarges its horizon by a more faithful use of the Pauline epistles of the imprisonment, and also of the theology of James, Peter, and John. Our orthodoxy cannot be Biblical orthodoxy until it has comprehended the sum total of the theology of the Bible both in its variety and unity. But even if this maximum were attained, the maximum of Christian orthodoxy would not be reached. Indeed the Bible itself cannot be thus mastered unless a corresponding advance is made in other departments. Even Christ does not open up the Scriptures to His people until they are prepared to understand and use the knowledge given to them.

Christian theology must be constructed by the induction of divine truth from all spheres of information. There is no system of theology which has not been influenced by the discoveries of science, the principles of philosophy, and the events of history, as well as by the temperaments and characteristic features of the individual writer, his nation and race.

As the Scottish commissioners to the Westminster Assembly well said:

> All the books of God are perfect, the book of life, the book of nature, the book of providence, and especially the book of Scripture, which was dyted by the Holy Ghost to be a perfect directory to all the churches unto the second coming of Jesus Christ, but so that it presupposeth the light and law of nature, or rules of common prudence, to be our guide in circumstances or things local, temporal, and personal.

But unfortunately there are not a few theologians who have mingled bad science, false philosophy, traditional history, and incorrect exegesis with the genuine truth of the Word of God; they have given forth this mixture of wood, hay, straw, and stubble with the fine gold, as the standard of orthodoxy, and have presumed to set it up as a bulwark against the vast and profound discoveries of modern science. We are not suprised that we are hearing shrieks and groans as we see these airy structures disappearing in the flames that have been kindled by the torch of Truth, who is tired of such foolery.

Such theologians have assumed an unfriendly attitude to science, philosophy, and history, and even the scientific study of the Scriptures. They have refused to taste the fruits of modern methods and modern learning. They have appropriated with marvelous caprice whatever seemed to suit their purpose. They have delighted in any little flaws and mistakes of scholars. They have stoutly resisted everything that was antagonistic to their traditional system. They have been impatient of new truths and branded them as "novelties." They have made Christian theology the enemy of human learning so far as they have been able to exert an influence. They have been the true successors of the Pharisees. They have zealously contended to do what the Roman Catholic hierarchy failed in doing. They have not succeeded in retarding human learning, but they have alienated a large proportion of the scholars of the world from the Christian Church. They have wrought serious damage to the science of Christian theology. Such pretended orthodoxy is real heterodoxy.

It is to blame for the dethronement of theology from its rightful position as the queen of the sciences. God has dethroned her for a season as He did Nebuchadnezzar, because she exalted herself against the truth of God, but after a season of humiliation she will be enthroned again.

* * *

The prejudices of traditionalism cannot stay the advancing truth of God. Every form of Christianity that has opposed the progress of doctrines in the past has been cast aside and left behind in the race. Are Protestantism, Calvinism, Puritanism, Presbyterianism, Methodism, and Anglo-Catholicism to have the same fate? They have all come to a halt in religious, doctrinal, and ethical progress. They have all alike become stereotyped in church order and types of doctrine. But there is a stir amid the dry bones. What is to come out of it all? Is there to be another Reformation that will throw them aside? Is there to issue forth a new orthodoxy leaving the reacting heterodoxy in its present lifeless position? Or will the vital forces that are at work in the Protestant Churches be sufficient to revive them and lead them on to a higher destiny? It would seem that the types of Protestantism have still a work to do in the world. We believe that the Churches of Protestantism are ripening for a better future in which all the Churches of the world will share.

God is speaking to His Church with an imperative voice and commanding it to go forward. The progress of learning in our day has been marvelous. The Bible itself has been flooded with the new light cast upon it from all directions by modern discoveries. The spirit of research animates a large number of professors and students of theology and Christian ministers and Christian people of all ranks. These are still in the minority.

There is a freer theological atmosphere in England and Scotland, but in Ireland and America Orthodoxism and Traditionalism are still predominant, and thinkers are obliged to work cautiously. But there are not a few in America who are striving earnestly to advance in Christian orthodoxy. Exegetical theology is passing through a transformation. The Bible is studied by theological students as never before. Historical theology is beginning to share in the same movement. Practical theology is also active and aggressive. Systematic theology alone is pulling back. But this will not endure. There are noble Christian theologians who are at work reconstructing the system of doctrine. The old traditional systems are the rallying points of Orthodoxism and Traditionalism. They do not realize the facts of the case. They do not see what is manifest to the rest of the world—that the Traditional Orthodoxy has been undermined and honeycombed by the recent Biblical and historical studies, as well as by the newer science and philosophy. Unless it can be strengthened by better exegesis and history and be more conformed to truth and fact, it will soon crumble and perish. We greatly need a system of theology that will embrace the results of modern learning.

Dogmatic Theology in Great Britain and America has been too long in the bondage of the seventeenth-century Scholasticism and the eighteenth-century Apologetics. The time has come for it to burst these bonds and march forward. It ought to run with all its might and march at the head of the column of modern learning. Christ is the king of the kingdom of truth, and His followers ought to be ashamed to drag His banner in the rear.

The battle against science, philosophy, exegesis, and history must come to an end. All truth should be welcomed, from whatever source, and built into the structure of Christian doctrine. The attitude of *Traditional Orthodoxy* should be abandoned as real heterodoxy, and the attitude of *Advancing Orthodoxy* assumed as the *true* orthodoxy.

CONFIDENCE IN MAN

Human nature has been the leading topic in half the debates marking liberal history, and has been on the hidden agenda in most others. But the form of the argument changes from one era to the next. Lyman Beecher's generation of evangelical liberals, which flourished in the 1820's, had shown confidence in human nature by contending for freewill doctrine; his children's generation took the freedom of the will for granted and went on to battle such Calvinist remnants as the belief in total depravity and the promise of automatic damnation for the heathen.

Yale's choice in 1871 of Henry Ward Beecher to give the first Lyman Beecher Lectures on Preaching was thus appropriate on a number of grounds. The younger Beecher, at a high point of fame and untarnished respectability, was America's leading preacher. But he was also, in more than the filial sense, one child of the old liberalism who had turned to the preoccupations of the new. He had expressed approval of Darwin as early as 1860, and had become quite explicit about the need for theological adaptation to contemporary culture. His rejection, already apparent in the Yale lectures, of certain "barbarous doctrines" of Calvinism, was to lead a decade later to his resignation under fire from the Congregational Association of New York.

～ 3 ～

THE STUDY OF HUMAN NATURE
by Henry Ward Beecher

My impression is that preachers are quite as well acquainted with human nature as the average of well-informed citizens, but far less than lawyers, or merchants, or teachers, or, especially, politicians. The preachers of America have been, I think, as intelligent and successful as any that ever lived. As a body of men they have been

SOURCE: *Yale Lectures on Preaching* (New York: J. B. Ford and Co., 1872), pp. 76–84, 87–90.

upright, discreet, and wise in the general management of the affairs of Christian churches. As a body, they have in their personal and administrative or pastoral relations been, on the whole, sagacious in matters pertaining to human nature. Nevertheless, *Preachers,* both English and American, have not preached to man's nature, as it is.

It is true that in the *applications* of sermons, particularly such as are known in America as Revival Sermons, much knowledge of human nature is shown, and efficient use is made of it. But, in a larger generalization, it may be said that there have been but two schools of Preachers. One may be called the Ecclesiastical school; in which term I include the whole body of men who regard the Church on earth as something to be administered, and themselves as channels, in some sense, of Divine grace, to direct the flow of that Divine institution. Ecclesiastical preachers are those who administer largely and preach incidentally, if one might say so. There is also the Dogmatic school of Preachers, or those who have relied upon a pre-existing system of truth, which has been founded before their day and handed down from generation to generation, and who apparently proceed upon the supposition that their whole duty is discharged when they have made a regular and repetitious statement of all the great points of doctrine from time to time.

Now, the school of the future (if I am a prophet, and I am, of course, satisfied in my own mind that I am!) is what may be called a *Life School.* This style of preaching is to proceed, not so much upon the theory of the sanctity of the Church and its ordinances, or upon a pre-existing system of truth which is in the Church somewhere or somehow, as upon the necessity for all teachers, first, to study the strengths and the weaknesses of human nature minutely; and then to make use of such portions of the truth as are required by the special needs of man, and for the development of the spiritual side of human nature over the animal or lower side—the preparation of man in his higher nature for a nobler existence hereafter. It is a life-school in this respect, that it deals not with the facts of the past, except in so far as they can be made food for the present and factors of the life that now is; but rather studies to understand *men,* and to deal with them, face to face and heart to heart—

yea, even to mold them as an artist molds his clay or carves his statue. And in regard to such a school as that, while there has been much done incidentally, the revised procedure of education yet awaits development and accomplishment; and I think that our profession is in danger, and in great danger, of going under, and of working effectively only among the relatively less informed and intelligent of the community; of being borne with, in a kind of contemptuous charity, or altogether neglected, by the men of culture who have been strongly developed on their moral side—not their moral side as connected with revealed religion, but as connected rather with human knowledge and worldly wisdom. The question, then, comes up, Do men need this intimately practical instruction? and if so, must there be to meet it this life-school of preachers?

But I am asked, "Have we not, in the truth as it has been revealed in Jesus Christ, everything that is needed? If a man take the Gospels, and the life and sayings of the Lord Jesus Christ, and preach these, is he not thoroughly furnished to every good work, and does he need to go outside of the Bible?" Yes, he does, for no man can take the inside of the Bible, if he does not know how to take the outside.

The kingdom of God and of truth, as it is laid down in the New Testament, is a kingdom of seeds. They have been sown abroad, and have been growing and developing in the world; and, whereas, when they were initiated they were but seminal forms, now they have spread like the banyan tree. And shall I go back and talk about acorns after I have learned about oaks? Shall I undertake to say that the Infinite Truth that is in Jesus Christ is, all of it, comprised in the brief and fragmentary histories that are contained in the four Evangelists; that human life has been nothing; that there is no Providence or inspiration in the working of God's truth among mankind; no purposed connection between the history of the world for eighteen hundred years, vitalized by the presence of the Holy Ghost and those truths in the New Testament? All that Christianity has produced is a part of Christianity. All that has been evolved in human existence you may find as germ-forms in the Bible; but you must not shut yourselves up to those germ-forms, with stupid reverence merely for the literal text of the gospel. It is the gospel *alive,* the gospel as it has been made victorious in its actual conflict with man's lower nature, that you are to preach. What Christ is you are to learn, indeed, with all reverence, from the historic delineation of his sacred person and life; but also you are to read him in the suffering human heart, in the soul triumphant over suffering, in the self-sacrifice of the mother for her child, in the heroic father, in every man and woman who has learned from Christ some new development of glorious self-giving for noble purposes. These are the commentaries expounded to you, through which you shall be able to know Christ vitally. All human nature that has been impregnated with a knowledge of Christ is the Bible commentary which you have to read in order to know who Christ is, and to learn that he is not shut up in the Gospels alone.

It is said that ministers ought not to know anything but "Jesus Christ and him crucified," but that is said in a different manner from that of the Apostle. He did not say, "I preach nothing but the historical Christ and him crucified." He said that he put the whole dependence of his ministry upon the force that was generated from Christ and him crucified; and not upon his own personal power, presence, or eloquence. He relied upon the living presence of Almighty God, as revealed in the Lord Jesus Christ. He depended upon moral power; and it is a perversion to say that men are to preach nothing but the literal, textual Christ, or the literal, textual four Gospels, or the literal, textual Epistles; for all of life is open to you. You have a right to preach from everything, from the stars in the zenith to the lowest form of creation upon earth. All things belong to you, for you are Christ's. The earth is the Lord's and the fullness of it. The Lord is our Father, and therefore we are heirs.

It is also said, "Are we wiser than the Apostles were?" I hope so. I should be ashamed if we were not. "Are we better preachers than they were?" Yes, we ought to be better preachers in our time than they would be. They were adapted to their times, admirably; but I think it is as much a misapplication of things to bring down literally the arguments of the Apostles from Jerusalem to our times, as it would have been, were it possible, to carry back all the scientific knowledge, and all the developed political economy which we now have, and preach them in old Jerusalem, within the Temple. We should be barbarians to them, and they would be comparative barbarians to us. *Adaptation to the times in which we live,* is the law of Providence. The Apostles were adapted to their times. We must be similarly adapted—not in a passive, servile way, but in a living, active way, and by taking an interest in the things which men do now. What did the Apostles preach? Did they not preach like Jews to Jews, and Greeks to Greeks? They had liberty, and they took the things they found to be needful in their time, to the people to whom they ministered. The following of the Apostolic example is not to pursue, blindly, their external forms, but to follow the light of their humanity and that of the gospel. This was the example they set: Whatever tended to elevate men from the lower to the higher sphere, the Apostles thought lawful for them to employ in their ministry.

You may ask if they did not understand human nature without all the study that I am recommending. I think that they did understand a great deal of human nature. It does not follow, however, that you should not attempt to understand as much and more than they did; for such an argument as that would really be not only against a more scientific basis of knowledge of human nature for the modern preacher, but against all development of every kind, against all growth, against all culture and all refinement. You must not pattern yourselves on the antique models, altogether, except in principle.

It is said by some, "Has not Christianity been preached by plain men, who did not understand so very much about human nature, in every age of the world?" It has; and what have eighteen hundred years to show for it? Today three fourths of the globe is heathen, or but semi-civilized. After eighteen hundred years of preaching of the faith under the inspiration of the living Spirit of God, how far has Christianity gone in the amelioration of the condition of the race? I think that one of the most humiliating things that can be contemplated, one of the things most savory to the scorner, and which seems the most likely to infuse a sceptical spirit into men, is to look at the pretensions of the men who boast of the progress of their work, and then to look at their performances. I concede that there has been a great deal done, and there has been a great deal of preparation for more; but the torpors, the vast retrocessions, the long lethargic periods, and the wide degeneration of Christianity into a kind of ritualistic mummery and conventional usage, show very plainly that the past history of preaching Christianity is not to be our model. We must find a better mode.

We need to study human nature, in the first place, because it illustrates the Divine nature, which we are to interpret to men. Divine attribute corresponds to our idea of human faculty. The terms are analogous. You cannot interpret the Divine nature except through some knowledge of human nature. There are those who believe that God transcends men, not simply in quality and magnitude, but in kind. Without undertaking to confirm or deny this, I say that the only part of the Divine nature that we can understand is that part which corresponds to ourselves, and that all which lies outside of what we can recognize is something that never can be interpreted by us. It is not within our reach. Whatever it may be, therefore, of God, that by searching we can find out, all that we interpret, and all that we can bring, in its moral influence, to bear upon men, is in its study but a higher form of human mental philosophy.

Now, let us see what government is. It is the science of managing men. What is moral government? It is moral science, or the theory upon which God manages men. What is the management of men, again, but a thing founded upon human nature? So that to understand moral government you are run right back to the same necessity. You must comprehend that on which God's moral government itself stands, which is human nature.

But, again, the fundamental doctrine on which our labors stand is the need of the transformation of man's nature by the Divine Spirit. This is altogether a question of psychology. The old theological way of stating man's sinfulness, namely, "Total Depravity," was so gross and so undiscriminating, and was so full of endless misapprehensions, that it has largely dropped out of use. Men no longer are accustomed, I think, to use that term as once they did. That all men are sinful, is taught; but "what is meant by 'sinful'?" is the question which immediately comes back. Instantly the schools begin to discuss it. Is it a state of the fibre of the substance or the soul? Is it any aberration, any excess, any disproportion of natural elements? Wherein does the fault lie? What is it? The moment you discuss this, you are discussing human nature. It is the mind you are discussing. In order to know what is an aberration, you must know what is normal. In order to know what is in excess, you must know what is the true measure. Who can tell whether a man is selfish, unless he knows what is benevolent? Who can tell whether a man has departed from the correct idea, unless he has some conception of that idea? The very foundation on which you stand today necessitates knowledge of man as its chief basis.

Consider, too, how a minister, teaching the moral government of God, the nature of God, and the condition of man and his necessities, is obliged to approach the human soul. Men are sluggish, or are so occupied and filled with what are to them important interests, that, ordinarily, when a preacher comes into a community, he finds it either slumbering, or averse to his message, or indifferent to it; and, in either case, his business is to stimulate the moral nature. But how shall he know the art of stimulating man's moral nature who has never studied it? You must arouse men and prepare them to be molded. How can you do it if you know nothing about them?

•   •   •

There is another consideration that we cannot blink, and that is, that we are in danger of having the intelligent part of society go past us. The study of human nature is not going to be left in the hands of the church or the ministry. It is going to be a part of every system of liberal education, and will be pursued on a scientific basis. There is being now applied among scientists a greater amount of real, searching, discriminating thought, tentative and experimental, to the whole structure and functions of man and the method of the development of mental force, than ever has been expended upon it in the whole history of the world put together. More men are studying it, and they are coming to results, and these results are starting, directly or indirectly, a certain kind of public thought and feeling. In religion, the psychological school of mental philosophers are not going to run in the old grooves of Christian doctrine; they are not going to hold the same generic ideas respecting men. And if ministers do not make their theological systems conform to facts as they are, if they do not recognize what men are studying, the time will not be far distant when the pulpit will be like the voice crying in the wilderness. And it will not be "Prepare the way of the Lord," either. This work is going to be done. The providence of God is rolling forward a spirit of investigation that Christian ministers must meet and join. There is no class of people upon earth who can less afford to let the development of truth run ahead of them than they. You cannot wrap yourselves in professional mystery, for the glory of the Lord is such that it is preached with power throughout all the length and breadth of the world, by these investigators of his wondrous creation. You cannot go back and become apostles of the dead past, drivelling after ceremonies, and letting the world do the thinking and studying. There must be a new spirit infused into the ministry. Some men are so afraid that, in breaking away from the old systems and original forms and usages, Christianity will get the go-by! Christianity is too vital, too really Divine in its innermost self, to fear any such results. There is no trouble about Christianity. You take care of yourselves and of men, and learn the truth as God shows it to you all the time, and you need not be afraid of Christianity; that will take care of itself. You might as well be afraid that battles would rend the sky, or that something would stop the rising and setting of the sun. The power of Divine love and mercy is not going to be stopped, and will certainly not be stopped by the things that are true.

You cannot afford to shut your eyes to the truths of human nature. Every Christian minister is bound to fairly look at these things. Every scientific man who is studying human nature is bound to open his eyes and ears, and to study all its phenomena. I read that Huxley refused to attend a *séance* of Spiritualists. He said, contemptuously, that it was a waste of time, and gave expression to other sentiments of disdain. I am not an adherent of the spiritual doctrines; I have never seen my way clear to accept them. But phenomena which are wrapping up millions of men and vitally affecting their condition are not to be disdained by scientific men, whose business it is to study phenomenology of all kinds. No scientific man can rightly refuse to examine them. He may say that he has no time to do it, and that some other man must investigate them. That would be right. All men cannot do all things. But to speak of anything of this kind with contempt is not wise. I am not afraid to look at this thing, or anything. I am not afraid that we are going to have the New Testament taken away from us. We must be more industrious in investigation, more honest in deduction, and more willing to take the truth in its new fullness; and we must be imbued with that simplicity in faith and truth which we inculcate in our people.

DISTRUST OF CREEDS

Those involved in the liberal movement tended to look upon creeds as noble, but culturally conditioned and therefore transient, attempts to interpret permanent truths. For Professor Briggs this position implied disapproval not of the Presbyterian standards but of the dogmatists who he thought had hardened and misrepresented them. Few other liberals, however, made a project of defending creeds, and many made it a part of their work to minimize or deprecate them.

The first heresy trial of this period to gain national attention was a test of strength over creeds in general and the Westminster Confession in particular. David Swing, a popular and scholarly Presbyterian minister of Chicago, was brought to trial on twenty-eight charges ranging from his having preached in a Unitarian chapel to his having failed to preach certain Calvinist doctrines anywhere at all. The result was highly significant. Most of the prosecution's factual allegations were irrefutable; yet the Chicago Presbytery refused, by a vote of 48 to 13, to consider Swing a heretic. It was clear that Swing could not fare so well before higher judicatories, and he resigned from Presbyterianism rather than allow the case to be appealed. But Chicago had given early notice, repeatedly confirmed thereafter, that it would be an important base for the new liberalism.

~ 4 ~

A RELIGION OF WORDS
by David Swing

Not every one that saith unto me Lord, Lord, shall enter into the kingdom of heaven, but he that doeth the will of my Father which is in heaven. *Matthew 7:21.*

SOURCES: "A Religion of Words," in *David Swing's Sermons* (Chicago: W. B. Keen, Cooke and Co., 1874), pp. 62–3, 64–5, 67–9; "Declaration in Reply to the Charges of Professor Patton," in *Truths for Today* (2d edn.; Chicago: Jansen, McClurg and Co., 1874), pp. 313–19, 323–5.

46

Spirituality is one of the highest stages of civilization, and therefore comes latest in the course of human development. Material associations are the first, hence man first makes up his language and his pantheon of gods out of the solid substances that surround him. The first man was of the earth, earthy; the second man was the Lord from heaven. That is first which is natural, and afterward that which is spiritual. And as man has borne the image of the earthy, so shall he bear the image of the heavenly. The first Adam was made a living soul; the second Adam a quickening spirit.

In this great transition from the material to the spiritual, years are consumed in the life of the most earnest individual, and in the advance of society in this path a thousand years count only a little. The most sincere heart escapes from materialism so slowly, and so slowly resolves itself and its God into a quickening spirit, that an infinitely long existence would seem to be foreshadowed in this leisurely evolution. To that which grows slowly we attribute long time. The glacier and the accumulating shore of the sea, and the vast oaks of the Pacific slope ask us to allow them long periods in which to have developed their peculiar plan. So the slowness of human unfolding asks us to grant to the individual and to society a vast field called immortality. Instead of drawing only sadness from this tedious march we also find in it an assurance that there are many years beyond.

But our theme for the hour is that a spiritual religion comes last in human experience, and before it comes a religion of things and of words. To offer things to God was earth's first form of being religious. The old temples were full of bows, arrows, shields, helmets and jewels put away from human use by a solemn gift-making to the gods. Horace reveals the fact in one of his poems that the sailor rescued from drowning, hung up in the temple what he wore on his body when the divinity rescued him from the grave. A gift was the only known acknowledgment. Different cities vied with each other in making their gods rich. What gold! what garments, what jewels, what armor in the temple of Juno, and what luxuries there were in the temple of Jupiter!

· · ·

From a religion of gifts the world soon hastened to a Christianity of words. Words were the outward sign and in that the heart paused. There were a few generations of simple piety such as St. John revealed, but the measurement of Christianity was soon found in the propositions to which one was willing to subscribe.

Words are the forerunners only of deeds. They are heralds that announce a coming king, but the king's chariot is slow. Hence when you find in the times of Caesar or Louis XIV, or Calvin, the finest statements about purity and charity, that is no sign that there was any public purity or charity. They had simply been announced, just as a vessel has been signaled when it is yet far out at sea, and perhaps falling back before storms. Words precede actions often by a thousand years. And thus the Sermon on the Mount is not so much man's law as man's prophecy. The world is grand, not when a prophecy is uttered, but when the fulfillment comes.

Millions were finally put to death in the long Christian centuries when they would not repeat the words of the party in power. Honesty of life, religious devotion, prayer, kindness at home, purity of deed and thought, counted nothing if the regular words of the ruling power were not pronounced. The most exemplary men, the tenderest mothers, the most gentle daughters, fathers whose families were dear to them beyond language, were hurried to the flames or rack because they could not say the words fixed upon by the pope or the tyrant in power. It was words, words, words, and death everywhere. No estimate was placed upon the inward life. Myriads died singing or praying to the spiritual God and their lives had been full of purity.

•   •   •

That there are great doctrines, the obedience of which is life, the disobedience of which is death, is very evident. Truth is the food of life, the stuff that life is made of; but these truths are few compared with that assemblage of ideas that can be seen on the bloody field of history. Each aspirant had a discrimination of idea upon which to base hope, not of heaven so much as of earth. Certain ideas stood not for a virtue, but for a party in the church or state. They were not paths of spiritual salvation, but the emblems of authority. Like the secret words of masonry, they were not words that converted a soul, but words that stood for an empire. Morgan was put

to death not because the ideas he uttered were valuable, but because they had been agreed upon and stood for a masonic order.
So heretics were burned, not because what they said interfered with
virtue, but because it interfered with some mitre or crown. A new
idea was treason. This was all done in the name of sincerity for it
was easy for the Deity, who had once been a Deity of gifts, to become one of dogmas. God became a Being to be worshipped with
dogmas. A man not baptized was so offensive to God that hell was
only too good a place for that soul! An infant not baptized died
hopeless, God was so partial to baptism! If this baptism were not
administered by the proper church, it was still worse than no baptism, God was so partial to a particular church! And thus onward,
until the blessed God was wholly occupied in the protection of a
hundred forms of speech, and the human soul was occupied, not
with purity of heart, but with repeating the terms pleasing to the
ideal Deity and the pope. This pope was not always Catholic;
sometimes he was Protestant.

Now salvation is a term whose meaning depends upon that which
is lost. If one has lost property, his salvation will be the recovery
of that property or its equivalent. If one has lost his good name by
false accusation, his salvation will be found in the emblazonment
of the falsehood, and on the return of public good will. This man
does not need much dogma but rather, he needs acquittal and a
better fame. If the soul has lost virtue and piety, then salvation will
be found in a return to piety and purity, and the truths of salvation
will be those that lead him to that one result. This is the destiny
of Christ's mediation. Hence the essence of religion is found in the
one event or phenomenon, a righteous heart. Gifts to the Deity
were the infant creepings of religion, the shadow of a coming reality,
the manifestations of an incipient love that did not know how to
express itself. Not knowing that what God most wished was a pure
heart in His children, they loaded His temples with their jewels
and raiment, and His altars with their lambs.

Then came the days that brought God an offering of words.
Imagining Him to be a God of articles and forms, they repeated
thousands of words and baptized their guilty foreheads in much or
little water as an act of salvation.

And now the world awaits the last transfiguration of human

worship, into a spiritual condition, into a soul lifted above sin, and exulting in a nearness to the image of God. The nations await with tears of past sorrow, a religion that shall indeed baptize men and children, either or both, but counting this as only a beautiful form shall take the souls of men into the atmosphere of Jesus, and into the all-pervading presence of God, and detain them there, until sin shall have become a hated monster, and perfection of spirit the heaven of this life, and that to come. Terms must give place to righteousness and communion with God.

In our day the empire of words still lingers. The churches are still wedded to quantity more than to quality, but wedded by bonds that are growing weaker under the uprising of the "inner life" philosophy. The churches still eagerly keep count of their membership, and publish the members that joined their bodies last year, but keep no record of the number of Christians that lived dishonorable lives in the last decade, quantity rather than quality still being a ruling passion in our half-civilized world. But Jesus Christ was not gifts, nor words, nor quantity, but quality; and surely as the world shall last, mankind, under His leadership shall march nearer and nearer to the world of spirit, where quantity and words shall all be overwhelmed by the sweet music, "Blessed are the pure in heart."

If Christ was anything, He was spiritual perfection. He was not a voice saying "Lord, Lord," but He was a spotless soul. Hence the world coming up to His religion, at last, will find itself in an atmosphere not full of the tenets of Elizabeth, or Mary, or Calvin, but full of that transcendent whiteness that indicates that sin has been washed away and that the righteousness of Heaven has come to the heart, like a joyous morning in paradise.

In this coming era upon whose margin I do feel that the world is standing now, like Florida upon the border of flowery spring, our citizens, our fathers, our brothers, our friends, our children, will move before us, not with conventional words upon their lips, but with faces radiant with the consciousness of a nobler life. The good deeds of yesterday, the good deeds of today, the perfected goodness of the morrow, a deep love for man, a consciousness of the presence of God will fill the whole face with a nobleness and happiness to which earth has thus far been willingly a stranger. This will be a salvation and Christ will be a Saviour.

["DECLARATION IN REPLY TO THE CHARGES OF PROFESSOR PATTON," MAY 4, 1874:]

To the Members of the Chicago Presbytery:

Called upon in the outset of these proceedings to enter my plea to the charges and specifications presented by Francis L. Patton, I beg permission to submit the following: I object to the charges as too vague and as embracing no important offense; yet, not wishing to raise any technical objections, I enter the plea of "not guilty." I admit the extracts from sermons and writings, but I would ask the Presbytery to consider the entire essays or whole discourses from which the extracts are made. I avow myself to be what, before the late union, was styled a New School Presbyterian,[1] and deny myself to have come into conflict with any of the Evangelical Calvinistic doctrines of the denomination with which I am connected, and I beg permission to enter as a part of my plea the following statements: 1. Regarding my relations to the Liberal Churches. 2. Regarding my relation to the Presbyterian Church. Of these I shall speak in their order.

By way of explaining the quantity of the public offense, I will state that of the fifteen lectures delivered in this city for benevolent purposes, all but two were on behalf of the Evangelical churches, and, in all cases but one, remuneration was declined. Hence the spirit that prompted such lectures must have been not any marked partiality for the so-called Liberal societies. This much as to the quantity of the alleged offense. Upon the quality of the conduct I would submit the following observations:

1. There is no valuable theory of life except that of good will toward all men. It is only on the basis of a wide friendship anyone

---

[1] [Old School and New School Presbyterians, estranged for several decades by conflicts over theology and polity, had reunited in the South in 1864, in the North in 1869.—Ed.]

can live well the few years of this existence, and hence to decline to lecture on behalf of a Unitarian chapel would do more harm to the mutual good will upon which society is founded, than it would do good to an orthodox theology, or harm to a Liberal creed.

2.   If the object of the Evangelical pulpit is to promulge its better truth, it can do so only so far as its ministry reveal a deep friend-ship toward all mankind, and so far as they unfurl the banner of their own love, while they are presuming to speak of the impartial love of their Divine Master. There remains no longer any power of authority in the pulpit. The time when the civil police drove a halt-ing sinner into the true church has disappeared, and the modern pulpit must communicate its ideas along the chords of friendship, and he will persuade the most men whose heart can gather up the largest and most diverse multitude into the grasp of its pure affections.

3.   But let us come now to the grandest reason why a Presbyterian may express in many ways a kind regard for these so-called Liberal sects. The sin of the "lecture," as charged, must be based upon the assumption that the Unitarian sects are outcasts from God, having no hope in the life to come. The names of Channing, and Elliott, and Huntington, and Peabody, in the pulpits of that sect and the Christ-lives of thousands in the congregations of that denomination, utterly exclude from my mind and my heart the most remote idea that in showing the brotherhood any kindness, I am offering in-direct approval to persons outside the pale of the Christian religion and hope. The idea that these brethren are doomed to wrath be-yond the tomb I wholly repudiate. It is, indeed, my conviction that they do not hold as correct a version of the Gospel as that an-nounced by the Evangelical Alliance a few years ago, yet I am just as certain that the Blessed Lord does not bestow his forgiveness and grace upon the mind that possesses the most accurate information, but upon the heart that loves and trusts Him. It is possible, that the venerable Dr. Hodge, of Princeton, holds a more truthful view of Jesus than may be held by the distinguished Peabody, who has just lectured from his Unitarian standpoint before the Calvinists in the Union Theological Seminary, but we can point to nothing in the Bible that would indicate that heaven is to be given to only the

one of these two giants who may possess the clearer apprehension of a truth. It may be assumed that God grants the world salvation only on account of the expiatory atonement made by a Redeemer, but that God will grant this salvation to only those who fully apprehend this fact, is an idea not to be entertained for an instant, for this would give heaven only to philosophers, and indeed only to those of this small class who shall have made no intellectual mistake. Looking upon the multitudes who need this salvation, and seeing that they are composed of common men, women, and children who know nothing of the distinctions of formal theology, we cannot but conclude that paradise is not to be a reward of scholarship, but of a loving, obedient faith in Jesus Christ.

When we remember these things, and recall that Dr. Isaac Watts was accused of being a Unitarian, so difficult often is it to perceive the dividing line, we cannot for a moment, place these persons called Unitarians outside the great and generous love of the Savior. I stand ready, therefore, at all times, to express toward these sects a friendship not only human, and wise, and social, but also Christian.

The harmony existing between all these brethren and myself, is not a harmony of views in mind, but a harmony of love in the soul. They each and all know that I differ widely from them, but this they and I know; that only the most gentlemanly treatment in public and private will we all receive always from each other. Much as I love Presbyterianism—a love inherited from all my ancestors—if on account of it, it were necessary for me to abate in the least my good will toward all sects, I should refuse to purchase the Presbyterian name at so dear a price.

The second point to be alluded to was my relations to Presbyterianism. A distinction evidently exists between Presbyterianism as formulated in past times and Presbyterianism *actual*. A creed is only the highest wisdom of a particular time and place. Hence, as in States, there is always a quiet slipping away from old laws without any waiting for a formal repeal, as some of the old statutes of Connecticut are lying dead, not by any legal death, but by long emaciation and final neglect of friend and foe; so in all formulated creeds, Catholic or Protestant, there is a gradual, but constant, decay of some article or word which was once promulged amid great pomp and circumstance. And yet no church is willing to confess its past folly and repeal the injurious or untrue. All, Catholic and Protestant, simply agree to remain silent.

In the Presbyterian Confession of Faith, there are about two hundred formulas of truth, or supposed truth. It is a wonderful argument in favor of this compendium, that not one-tenth of these have been found false to the Bible or false to the welfare of society. To designate these two hundred as Calvinism is a gross injustice, for they are almost all valuable truths, common to all churches, and gathered up from the sacred page.

But from a few statements out of this large number, the *actual* Presbyterian Church has quietly passed away. Conventions cannot be called every few years to amend or repeal some one article. It would entail endless debate and expense, and perhaps promote wide discord, thus to call, from time to time, a new Westminster Assembly. As the Christian world avoids a revision of the translation of the Bible because of the tumult such a new version would probably create among the sects, so each particular church postpones as long as possible any formal modification of its historic statements of doctrine. But meanwhile individual minds cannot be slaves; they cannot suspend the use of their judgment and best common sense. Hence, unable to revoke any dangerous idea by law, the Presbyterian Church permits its clergy to distinguish the [church] *actual* from the church *historic*. To the Presbyterian Church actual I have thus far devoted my life, giving it what I possess of mind and heart.

Chief among the doctrines which our church has passed as being incorrect, or else an overdevelopment of Scriptural ideas, are all those formulas which looked toward a dark fatalism, or which destroy the human will, or indicate the damnation of some infant, or that God, for His own glory, fore-ordained a vast majority of the race to everlasting death. It has been my good or bad fortune to speak in public and in private, to a large number of persons hostile to our church, and in nearly all cases I have found their hostility based upon the doctrines indicated above, and in all ways, I have declared to them that the Presbyterian Church had left behind those doctrines, and that her religion was simply Evangelical, and not *par excellence* the religion of despair. In my peculiar ministry a simple silence has not been sufficient. I have, therefore, at many times, declared our denomination to be simply a church of the common Evangelical doctrines.

* * *

It seems to me the world is now fully ready for an orthodoxy that shall firmly, yet tenderly, preach all of the creed, except its plain errors or dark views of God and man. Not one of you, my brethren, has preached the dark theology of Jonathan Edwards in your whole life. Nothing could induce you to preach it, and yet it is written down in your creed in dreadful plainness. Confess, with me, that our beloved church has slipped away from the religion of despair, and has come unto Mount Sion, into the atmosphere of Jesus, as He was in life and in death, full of love and forgiveness. And yet it is only in the narrow field just pointed out that I have in any way departed from the doctrines of the Presbyterian Church.

One of the most distinguished of our theological teachers in the east has just written:

There is not enough in that indictment to convict one of heresy. All these commotions only point to a time when sectarianism will disappear, and all Christians will meet on the platform of a common faith in one Christ and one Savior, and, fastening all their faith upon Him as a Redeemer, will cast off many of the forms which now perplex them.

Beloved brethren, holding the general creed as rendered by the former New School Theologians, I will, in addition to such a general statement, repeat to you articles of belief, upon which I am willing to meet the educated world, and the skeptical world, and the sinful world, using my words in the Evangelical sense: The inspiration of the Holy Scriptures, the Trinity, the divinity of Christ, the office of Christ as a mediator when grasped by an obedient faith, conversion by God's Spirit, man's natural sinfulness, and the final separation of the righteous and wicked.

I have now read before you an outline of my public method and my Christian creed. It is for you to decide whether there is in me orthodox belief sufficient to retain me in your brotherhood. Having confessed everywhere that the value of a single life does not depend upon sectarian relations, but upon Evangelical or Christian relations, I am perfectly willing to cross a boundary which I have often shown to be narrow; but, going from you, if such be your order at last, it is the Evangelical Gospel I shall still preach, unless my mind should pass through undreamed of changes in the future.

From the prosecutor of this case I would not withhold my conviction that he has acted from a sense of duty; therefore, to him and to you all, brethren, I extend good will, and hope that in a wisdom religious and fraternal, you will be enabled to do what is right in the sight of God.

Yours, with love,
DAVID SWING

BELIEF IN DIVINE IMMANENCE

A. V. G. Allen's *The Continuity of Christian Thought,* published in 1884, provides a striking illustration of the liberals' antipathy to Calvinist orthodoxy, and also of their desire to undermine its tenets by calling upon alternative, suitably ancient, readings of the Christian faith. Allen, church historian at the Episcopal Theological School in Cambridge, blamed the harsher features of the Calvinist conception of God upon a "Latin-Augustinian" tradition that had polluted the stream of Christian thought from the fifth century until the return to theological immanentism—the "true" Christian tradition —in the nineteenth.

~ 5 ~

THE CONTINUITY OF CHRISTIAN THOUGHT

by Alexander V. G. Allen

The traditional conception of God which has come down to us from the Middle Ages through the Latin church is undergoing a profound transformation. The idea that God is transcendent, not only exalted above the world by His moral perfection, but separated from it by the infinite reaches of space, is yielding to the idea of Deity as immanent in His creation. A change so fundamental involves other changes of momentous importance in every department of human thought, and more especially in Christian theology. The epithets applied to God, such as absolute and infinite, have a different significance when applied to Deity indwelling within the universe. When we no longer localize Him as a physical essence in the infinite remoteness, it is easier to regard Him as ethical in His

SOURCE: *The Continuity of Christian Thought: A Study of Modern Theology in the Light of Its History* (Boston: Houghton Mifflin Co., 1884), pp. 1–9, 11–20. Footnotes ómitted.

inmost being; righteousness becomes more readily the primary element in our conception of His essential nature. There is no theological doctrine which does not undergo a change in consequence of the change in our thought about God. Creation and revelation, the relation between God and humanity, the incarnation and the things which concern our final destiny, are lifted into a higher sphere and receive a deeper, a more comprehensive and more spiritual meaning.

The object of the following treatise is to present the outlines of that early Christian theology which was formulated by thinkers in whose minds the divine immanence was the underlying thought in their consciousness of God. The Greek fathers, from the second to the fifth centuries, could not escape, even had they been inclined to do so, from the influence of a philosophy like the Stoic, so entirely in accordance with the well-known tendencies of Hellenic life and culture, and which existed for five hundred years, as the genuine expression of the Greek mind before it was overcome by other forms of theosophical speculation. Although from the second century a retrogressive movement toward Platonism was gaining strength, as seen in Justin and more especially in Origen, yet it was impossible for Christian thinkers, even so late as the age of Constantine, to emancipate their minds from the subtle spell of that philosophy whose distinguishing feature was the belief that God indwelt in the universe and in the life of man. Such an influence was as inevitable as that of scholasticism upon the reformers of the sixteenth century, or of Calvin upon some modern thinkers, who congratulate themselves on having abandoned his system while still adhering to what was fundamental in his method. But the Greek theologians did not stand in an attitude of revolt or alienation from Hellenic philosophy and culture. They knew its value in their own experience, and held it to be a divine gift to the Greek people—a divinely ordered course of preparation for the "fullness of time." From the alliance of Greek philosophy with Christian thought arose the Greek theology, whose characteristics are a genuine catholicity, spiritual depth and freedom, a marked rationality, and a lofty ethical tone by which it is pervaded throughout. For a time its influence was felt and acknowledged in the West, as is seen in the writings of Irenaeus, Hippolytus, Minucius Felix, and to a limited extent even in Tertullian. But the East and West began to grow apart after the time of Constantine, and the first foundations of the later schism between the Greek and Latin churches were already laid, when there arose in the West, under the influence of Augustine, a peculiar theology with which the Greek mind could have no sympathy, whose fundamental tenets it regarded with aversion.

The Augustinian theology rests upon the transcendence of Deity as its controlling principle, and at every point appears as an inferior rendering of the earlier interpretation of the Christian faith. Augustine is the most illustrious representative in history of a process very familiar to our own age, by which men of considerable intellectual activity, wearied with the questionings and skepticisms which they cannot resolve, fall back upon external authority as the only mode of silencing the reason and satisfying the conscience. After the modern fashion, he had swung round the circle of theories and systems in which his age abounded, without finding relief; like Newman, he was painfully impressed with the moral skepticism concealed beneath the superficial appearance of ordinary life; also, like Newman, he possessed an unrivaled skill in dialectic, which he employed in defense of the system which he had chosen to identify with the Christian faith. His conversion took place at Milan, where he was struck by the external power and splendor of the church under its majestic administration by Ambrose; he received, on assent, the Christianity of the time, and included in it the popular notions and tendencies which were current in the church, as part of the divine revelation. After he became Bishop of Hippo, and especially after his entanglement in the Donatist and Pelagian controversies, he stood forth as the type of the ecclesiastic in all later ages: like Newman after his perversion, there was nothing so obnoxious or irrational that he could not make it plausible to the reason; that which seemed to be useful or desirable for maintaining the control and ascendency of the church was stamped to his mind with the signet of the truth. The needs of ecclesiastical policy became the standard by which to test the validity of Christian belief.

The Augustinian theology made possible the rise of the papacy. Leo the Great, in the generation after Augustine, put forth the claim for the authority of the Roman see which was never afterward relaxed, and which saw its realization in the imperial authority over Christendom of Hildebrand and Innocent III. Augustinianism and the papacy owe their appearance to an age when free inquiry and intellectual activity were struck with decline, when the reign of barbarism was about to begin. Under such circumstances we may see in both alike a providential adaptation of Christianity to a lower environment. They did not grow out of the Christian idea as its necessary development, but were rather retrograde forms under which the Christian principle might still be operative, though in greatly diminished degree. One need not speak of the papacy as a usurpation: it was a dispensation divinely appointed for the races of Europe; a schoolmaster, like the Jewish theocracy which it so closely resembled, to bring them to Christ. But the same divine hand which is revealed in its rise and its fortunes is revealed also in the process which led to its overthrow and rejection. The Augustinian theology had subserved a temporary purpose, and began to wane with the papacy when the human mind once more regained its freedom. So far as both yet linger in the modern world, it is an evidence that there are those who still need, or think they need, a religion based upon external authority, or a morality whose sanction is fear of the consequences of sin in the future world.

The motive which lends interest and value to a study of the history of Latin theology in the Middle Ages, or in its later Protestant modifications, is to seek in its varied fortunes for that tendency to revert again to the true interpretation of the Christian faith, from which it was originally a falling away. The transitions of modern thought in regard to the nature of God and His relation to the world are in nowise abrupt or sudden, or the result of a preparation to be found exclusively in our own time. It is of the highest importance to show, if it can be shown, that the preparation for the higher and fuller truth may be traced in the progress of thought during the Middle Ages as well as in the later Protestantism. For all our thought concerning God has its foundation in the consciousness of man—or rather, it is in and through the consciousness that the divine revelation is made—and therefore, among those in every age who have set themselves seriously to find out God, we should expect some testimony, however feeble or overborne by contradictions, to the later and fuller utterance of the consciousness as it speaks in ourselves. There is scarcely a thinker in the whole range of Latin or Protestant theology who has not at moments given expression to a

higher thought of Deity than that which underlies the formal theology, the ecclesiastical institutions, or the current modes of belief
which command his adherence and approval. It is Augustine who,
at a certain stage in his career, could write:

> For God is diffused through all things. He saith Himself by the Prophet,
> "I fill heaven and earth," and it is said unto Him in a certain psalm,
> "Whither shall I go from Thy Spirit, or whither shall I flee from Thy
> presence? If I ascend up to heaven, Thou art there; if I make my bed
> in hell, behold Thou art there;" because God is substantially diffused
> everywhere. God is not thus diffused through all things as though by dif-
> fusion of mass, so as to be half in one half of the world's body and half
> in the other, and thus entire in the whole; but entire in heaven alone, and
> entire in earth alone, and entire in both heaven and earth, and com-
> prehended in no place, but everywhere entire in Himself. He is nowhere
> and everywhere.

And again, speaking of the incarnation, it is Augustine who says:

> And though He is everywhere present to the inner eye when it is sound
> and clear, He condescended to make Himself manifest to the outward eye
> of those whose inward sight is weak and dim. *Not then in the sense of
> traversing space, but because he appeared to mortal men in the form of
> mortal flesh, He is said to have come to us.* For He came to a place where
> He had always been, seeing that He was in the world and the world was
> made by Him.

Even Thomas Aquinas, when the exigencies of reason required it,
could write:

> There have been some, as the Manichees, who said that spiritual and
> incorporeal things are subject to divine power, but visible and corporeal
> things are subject to the power of a contrary principle. Against these we
> must say that God is in all things by His power. There have been others
> again who, though they believed all things subject to divine power, still
> did not extend divine Providence down to the lower parts, concerning
> which it is said in Job, "He walketh upon the hinges of heaven and con-
> sidereth not our concerns." And against these it is necessary to say, that
> God is in all things by His presence. There have been again others, who,
> though they said all things belonged to the Providence of God, still laid
> it down that all things are not created immediately by God, but that He
> immediately created the first, and these created others. And against them
> it is necessary to say that He is in all things by His essence.

Passages like these are gleams of a higher thought, flashing forth
at exceptional moments, when the religious heart speaks out or the

reason forgets its trammels. But the formal theology, the ecclesiastical institutions, which Augustine sanctioned for the ages that followed him, which Calvin renewed for the Protestant churches, are built upon the ruling principle that God is outside the world and not within; that He is absolute Deity in the sense that His being would be complete without the creation or humanity or the Eternal Son.

What is sometimes called "modern infidelity" is mainly, I had almost said exclusively, a protest against the theology based upon such a conception of God. It is not Christianity in itself which is today obnoxious to serious men, but a Latinized Christianity which the thought of the world has outgrown while it is still perpetuated in the formal attitude of the churches. The traditional doctrines concerning the nature and method of the divine revelation, the atonement, and the final destiny of man, are called in question, not because they are irrational in themselves, but because they no longer spring by an inward necessity from that changed conception of God which is consciously or unconsciously postulated by the mind. We often hear of a Catholic faith which is an older reality than any of the theologies which command the popular assent, but those who profess to hold it are too apt to identify the ancient creeds with their Latin interpretation. It is not till we get back into an earlier age, before Christianity was translated into its Latin idioms, that we can discern another interpretation of the Christian faith—the religion of Christ as it appeared to men who were living and thinking under intellectual conditions more similar to our own than any intervening age has since exhibited. The ancient Greek theology, as it was developed from the second to the fourth century under the hand of great masters like Clement and Athanasius, differs at every point from Latin theology as it received its final impress from Augustine in the fifth century.

I have attempted in the following pages to contrast the two theologies, and to trace the genesis of each to its ruling principle. In so doing, I am not presenting any novel view of the history of Christian thought. The distinction between the Greek and Latin theologies has been made by every recent writer of any importance in the field of church history, among whom may be mentioned, as best known, Gieseler, Neander, Dorner, Ritschl, Baur, Pressensé, Renan, Bunsen, Maurice, and Milman.

. . .

A formidable obstacle to the intelligent study of the Greek theology is the lingering hold of Augustine upon the modern mind. The tenets of the Bishop of Hippo have been for so many ages identified with divine revelation, that it requires an intellectual revolution in order to attain the freedom to interpret correctly, not only the early Fathers of the church, but Scripture itself. As there has been a traditional interpretation of Scripture, so there has been a traditional reading of the theologians before Augustine's time, by which they were all made to say about one and the same thing. The idea of a Catholic faith, supported by the unanimous consent of the Fathers, continues to perpetuate the error. A false conception of development has done much to confuse the study of ancient theology, by taking it for granted that because Augustine lived at a later time, he therefore built upon the same foundation with his predecessors and carried their work to a higher stage.

Whatever the source from which it springs, there is one charge so often alleged against the Greek theology that it deserves a moment's notice. It is said that it was deficient in the doctrines of sin and grace.

It is true that the Greek fathers did not accept the doctrine of original sin as propounded by Augustine, with its correlated tenets of total depravity, the loss of the freedom of the will, the guilt of infants, predestination or reprobation by a divine decree, or the endlessness of future punishment. But it does not follow that their conception of sin was on this account wanting in depth or adequacy. If the attitude of Augustine is to be taken as the standard of Christian teaching upon the nature of sin, its origin and its consequences, then other religions, such as Mohammedanism or Buddhism, would seem in these respects to have excelled Christianity. Compared with the few allusions to the future consequences of sin, and these of a somewhat general character, to be found in the New Testament, the Koran invokes on almost every page the horrors of an endless torment in definite language not to be misunderstood. If the nature of man is wholly corrupted by sin, as Augustine taught, Buddhism rises to a clearer declaration of the same principle, when, running counter to life itself, it makes sin exist in all desire. If views like these constitute what some are pleased to call the backbone of theology, then the ancient Greek theology was indeed deficient, for it assigned the chief importance to the belief that man was made in God's image, and relied upon indwelling Deity to lead mankind from sin to righteousness.

In the spirit of this earlier theology sin is regarded as a transgression of the law, not the law which is conceived as an arbitrary appointment of a will external to man, but the law written in his constitution—the life and the truth of God imprinted on the human nature in order that it may become partaker of the divine nature. To this end the incarnation takes place, that man may be delivered from the power of sin, and brought into harmony with that law which constitutes the life of God, in the obedience of which consists the real life of the creature. As obedience is life, so in disobedience is death. The design of God, as revealed in the ages that preceded the coming of Christ, was to teach mankind how sin brought forth death, in order that, in the light of the incarnation, might be discerned the meaning and the value of life. It is said of the late Mr. Maurice, that being asked for the best treatise on the nature of sin, he replied, St. Paul's Epistle to the Ephesians; or, in other words, that method which most clearly presents Christ in his spiritual exaltation is best fitted to reveal the nature, the extent, the enormity of sin. Such might have been the reply of Clement of Alexandria or of Athanasius, such surely was the method of Greek theology in the days of its vigor; and even in its decline, it still remained true, in a formal way, to that which had been its ruling principle. The Greek church, it has been often remarked, had but one dogma, that of the incarnation—a dogma, it should be remembered, resting primarily, not on the authority of a council, but on the reason or the Christian consciousness—and with the evolution of this truth in its relation to God and to humanity, Greek thought and speculation were occupied for over four hundred years. In this truth lay involved all the issues of the Christian faith; in its presence, other questions paled in importance; by its light were to be interpreted all tenets and opinions concerning man and his destiny. Hence the early fathers did not base their theology upon speculations regarding the origin of evil; it was enough to know that the redemption of mankind was an accomplished fact, that humanity had been endowed through Christ in its own right with a recuperative power, which would enable it to struggle successfully against all that was contrary to its true nature. The sense of sin was not regarded as an experience generated in the soul apart from God, for there was a divine presence in the world and in human hearts whose mission it was to convince of sin and righteousness. There was no artificial division in human experience, according to which the sense of sin must first prevail and dominate in the consciousness before a man could receive the Savior; but the knowledge of Christ, and his reception in the heart, became the power by which sin was increasingly revealed, and by which also it was overcome.

It is unnecessary to add that all this was reversed in the Augustinian theology. Another conception of sin and of its remedy dates its rise in the church from his influence, and was maintained by the Latin church through the Middle Ages. The system of the confessional, with its penitential books, its penances, its priestly absolutions, and conveyancing of grace; the distinction between mortal and venial sins, the morbid introspection, may seem to some minds to attach a deeper or more adequate significance to sin, but it is gained by a great sacrifice—for it necessarily involves an inadequate conception of Christ and his redemption.

The objection to the Greek theology, that its view of sin is superficial or defective, is an old and familiar one, and it is suggestive to note how often it turns up in history when any teaching arises which contradicts the traditional methods of dealing with the problem of human evil. To the enemies of Christ, it appeared as though the Savior himself was relaxing the bonds of moral order when He sat down to eat with publicans and sinners, or when He dismissed the woman who had sinned with no reproof, but with the gentle injunction, "Go and sin no more." It seemed to the hostile Judaism tracking the footsteps of St. Paul, as if his doctrine of justification by faith were not only deficient in its estimate of sin, but as if it put a premium upon sin—"Shall we continue in sin that grace may abound?" It seemed to the heathen mind, judging from Celsus' attack upon Christianity, that the doctrine of forgiveness was shallow and immoral; that in order to overcome evil it must be held that forgiveness was impossible, and that every sin must reap its penalty according to irrevocable law. It seemed to the excited mind of Latin Christendom in the sixteenth century, as if the methods of Luther and Calvin, in dealing with sin, were of a nature to undo the sanctions of morality and to promote unbridled libertinism. It is not strange, therefore, that so time-honored an objection, the embodiment of so conservative an instinct, should be alleged against the theology of the Greek fathers.

When it is said that the Greek theology failed, not only in its conception of sin, but in its doctrine of grace, the remark implies a misapprehension of its spirit. The doctrine of grace, as a *specific influence* passing from God to the individual spirit through external channels or in some arbitrary way, a grace applied to the soul from without to recreate or strengthen the will apart from the natural action of the human faculties, a grace which might be forfeited and regained, which on occasions might be and was withdrawn—of such a doctrine, which has played so large a part in the sacramental and Calvinistic theologies, it must be admitted the early Greek theology knew nothing. The place occupied by *grace* in Latin theology is filled by the presence of a divine teacher, whose own eternal life, by contact with human souls, becomes the source of life, of all strength and growth; the infinite indwelling Spirit, whose action is not arbitrary, but uniform as the laws of nature. The doctrine of *grace*, as taught by Augustine, or as it has been held in mediaeval and Protestant theology, was the Latin substitute for that belief in the immanence of God in humanity, which had constituted the principle of Greek theology, and was giving way in the fifth century to another and lower conception of the relations of God to man.

It may be said, that to revert to the theology of a distant age would be a retrogressive movement in religious thought; that we are to seek for some reconstruction in theology by the light of our own reason rather than under the guidance of the Nicene fathers. But such an attitude toward the past carries with it its own condemnation. The ground of hope and progress in this recognition of a theology in the ancient church, higher than that which has

hitherto prevailed in Christendom, is the attestation thus gained for
the human consciousness as the ultimate source of authority in religious truth. Were the present movement in theological thought
emphatically new, had it never found substantial utterance in all
these ages of Christian history, one might well be inclined to suspect
that it had no foundation in the nature of man. That which is
new in theology cannot be true; a proposition of which the converse
holds equally good, that what is true cannot be new. A return to
the theology of the ancient church does not mean the abandonment
of the reason, or the shutting our eyes to the light which God
especially vouchsafes to the later ages of the church. Our task today
is not a mechanical reproduction of past thought, or a literal adherence to the forms in which it was cast. There were elements in
the methods of Greek theology which we cannot accept; there was
much which the early fathers saw imperfectly, or not at all. And
yet, in spite of their defects, and the disadvantages under which they
labored, the Greek theologians may be to us, what Plato and Aristotle
have been to modern philosophical thought—our emancipators from
false conceptions, our guides to a more spiritual, more intellectual,
more comprehensive interpretation of the Christian faith, than the
church has known since the German races passed under the tutelage of
the Roman bishops, and accepted a Latinized Christianity in place of
the original divine revelation. In the words of a recent writer,

We have lost much of that rich splendor, that largehearted fullness of
power, which characterizes the great Greek masters of theology. We have
suffered our faith for so long to accept the pinched and narrow limits of
a most unapostolic divinity, that we can hardly persuade people to recall
how wide was the sweep of Christian thought in the first centuries, how
largely it dealt with these deep problems of spiritual existence and development, which now once more impress upon us the seriousness of the
issues amid which our souls are traveling. We have let people forget all
that our creed has to say about the unity of all creation, or about the
evolution of history, or about the universality of the divine action through
the Word. We have lost the power of wielding the mighty language with
which Athanasius expands the significance of creation and regeneration,
of incarnation and sacrifice, and redemption and salvation and glory.

After all, however, the question is not whether we shall return
or ought to return to what is called the Nicene theology; the fact is,
that the return has already begun. The tendencies of what we call

modern religious thought have been reproducing the outlines of an elder theology, while we have been unconscious even of its existence. There is hardly a point on which there is today a disposition to diverge from the traditional theology, which has not been anticipated by the Greek fathers. None of the individual doctrines or tenets, which have so long been the objects of dislike and animadversion to the modern theological mind, formed any constituent part of Greek theology. The tenets of original sin and total depravity, as expounded by Augustine, and received by the Protestant churches from the Latin church; the guilt of infants, the absolute necessity of baptism in order to salvation, the denial of the freedom of the will, the doctrine of election, the idea of a schism in the divine nature which required a satisfaction to retributive justice before love could grant forgiveness, the atonement as a principle of equivalence by which the sufferings of Christ were weighed in a balance against the endless sufferings of the race, the notion that revelation is confined within the book, guaranteed by the inspiration of the letter or by a line of priestly curators in apostolic descent, the necessity of miracles as the strongest evidences of the truth of a revealed religion, the doctrine of sacramental grace and priestly mediation, the idea of the church as identical with some particular form of ecclesiastical organization—these and other tenets which have formed the gist of modern religious controversy find no place in the Greek theology, and are irreconcilable with its spirit. And, on the other hand, the doctrine of the incarnation, in the fullness and sublimity of its real import—the essence of the Christian faith, from which other beliefs and convictions must spring, and with which they must correspond—this truth is finding in modern times a recognition and appreciation akin to that which it held in the theology of Athanasius.

RELIANCE UPON HISTORICAL PROCESS

The "historicism" that permeated the New Theology, the New Juris-
prudence, and other innovative movements of the late nineteenth
century was a belief, held in varying intensities, that historical process has its own meaning and cannot be considered a mere adjunct
to the Will of God or the Order of Nature. Among religious liberals
this view allied itself with immanentism and a sanguine outlook to
produce the insistence that the Deity, instead of preordaining and
imposing a detailed pattern upon history, works out his ultimate
purposes through wills that retain genuine freedom of decision. The
confidence that men, in spite of perversities, can and do make right
decisions, was a vital middle step in this logic, just as it was in the
thinking of such secular theorists as Lester Ward and John Dewey.

Arthur Cushman McGiffert, a pupil of Harnack at Marburg, was
the ablest of the liberal church historians. His discourse at Lane
Theological Seminary in 1892 (McGiffert moved to Union the
following year) shows how clearly the new liberals had chosen between the two authorities, Nature and History, that the romantic
era had sought to hold in balance. The speech also indicates the
effort liberals were making, their brief for historicism notwithstand-
ing, to warn that ultimate meanings are not fully made clear, nor is
redemption completed, within human history.

~ 6 ~

THE HISTORICAL STUDY
OF CHRISTIANITY
by Arthur Cushman McGiffert

The wide use of the historic method is one of the marked features
of the intellectual life of the present age. In all branches of knowledge its influence has been felt, and a revolution, second only to
that which connects itself with the name of Francis Bacon, has
been accomplished by it in our scientific thinking. The historic

SOURCE: *Bibliotheca Sacra, 50* (January 1893), 150–5, 163–71.

method, in fact, controls all lines of study and investigation. Whether applied to the works of nature or to the works of man, it is the same: in the one case, it gives us the theory of evolution; in the other, human history, which in the modern view is simply the account of an evolution in the sphere of the humanities. Christian thinking, as is always the case, has felt the influence of the spirit of the age, and has become historical. Not that the study of Christian history is a new thing, but that the historical study of Christianity is; for the conception of history and the historic method have undergone a great change since Eusebius wrote his ἱστορία ἐκκλησιαστική* in ten books. To him the history of the church was a drama in which two great opposing forces—God and Satan—were struggling for the mastery. All heresies, schisms, and persecutions were the work of Satan, who by means of them attempted to corrupt and rend and destroy the church of God. With such a transcendental notion of history, no true understanding of the growth and development of Christianity was possible. Indeed, the idea of a development was far from Eusebius' thought. The Christian church was complete and perfect in the beginning, and such it would always be. An evolution or a change of any sort in doctrine or in polity was inconceivable. Heresies and schisms were simply attacks upon Christianity from without, and, having overcome them, the church went on just as before, with perhaps a clearer consciousness of her own position, but otherwise unchanged. This transcendental and dualistic view of Christian history, Eusebius shared with the entire church of the ancient and middle ages. It is the view of the Roman Catholic Church today. That the whole Christian system was complete in the beginning, and has undergone no change, is one of its dicta. John Henry Newman smoothed his own path into the Catholic Church by the elaboration of a quasi theory of development to account for the medieval accretions of the Roman creed. The church, that she might not drive away her new disciple and others like him, preserved a discreet silence in the matter, but she has since given expression to her opinion of the doctrine in terms of unmistakable dissent. To do otherwise were self-stultification. But the Catholic Church has not had a monopoly of the Eusebian con-

* [*Ecclesiastical History*]

ception of Christian history. According to the "Magdeburg Centuriae," the first historical production of the new Protestant spirit of the sixteenth century, the church, perfect and complete in its inception and during the early centuries of its career, had been later corrupted by Satan through the agency of the papacy—the antichrist. No growth or development in Christianity was desirable or even possible. All that was needed, was that the papacy should be destroyed and its corruptions effaced, and Christianity would once more stand forth in its pristine splendor, its form and features unchanged. The conception of the nature of Christian history, it will be seen, is still the Eusebian. The terms are changed, but the essence is the same. To Eusebius, church history is all apologetics; to the Magdeburg writers, all polemics; and the new view is no truer than the old. But during the present century the modern historical spirit has made itself felt, and the modern historical method has been employed in the study of Christianity. The standard works which are now in our hands are all written with the idea, more or less clearly and consistently held, that Christianity has undergone a real development during the eighteen centuries that are past, and that church history is the record of that development.

To study an organism in its antecedents and in its genesis, to trace the course of its growth, to examine it in the varied relations which it has sustained to its environment at successive stages of its career, to search for the forces within and without which have served to make it what it is; to do it all, not with the desire of supporting one's own theory or of undermining the theory of another, but in order to understand the organism more thoroughly, in order to enter more fully into its spirit, in order to gather from its past new light to shed upon its present and its future; to do it all with the humble, docile spirit, and with the eager, inquiring mind of the true student—this is the historic method, and this is the way we study the church today. This is the way the modern scholar studies all the factors of Christianity in all their varied phases.

It is my purpose this evening to discuss some of the results which follow such historical study. These results are manifold and various; for no intelligent student and no department of theological study has failed to feel the influence of the modern spirit and method. But, if I would not unduly transgress the limits of an address, I must be content to confine myself to a narrow section of the subject. Compelled thus to make a selection from the wide range of material, I propose, with your indulgence, to discuss, first, the historic spirit which historical study fosters in the student; and secondly, the influence which the prevalence of the historic spirit and the use of the historic method have exerted in the sphere of Christian doctrine.

The effects of intelligent and judicious historical study upon those who engage in it are of the most beneficent character. That culture of the intellect which opens a man's mind to all that is noblest and highest and best in his own and other ages; that absorption in large interests and lasting forces which liberates him from the bondage of the material and temporal, and raises him above transient trials and discouragements; that chastening of the temper which makes him superior to petty jealousies and quarrels and intrigues; that training, by large and constant exercise, of the critical and judicial faculty which guards him against the allurements of vicious but inviting novelties; that enlargement of the human sympathies which brings him into touch with all humanity, and makes him part and parcel of the human race—one with it in its experiences—his heart beating with the heart throbs of universal man—till he can exclaim in truth, "Humanus sum, humani nihil a me alienum puto"; that cultivation of the spiritual sense which enables a man to discover and to appreciate the spiritual and ideal wherever it exists; that widening of the horizon which engenders true liberality, manly tolerance of others' views and sentiments, and genuine sympathy with the good in every creed and institution; that clarifying of the vision which lets a man through the encircling frame of visible and transient event into communion with invisible and eternal powers and purposes, and gives him a sublime faith in the ultimate victory of the highest and the holiest—all this, and more than this, it *ought* to mean, to study history aright. Alas, that with so many of us in our blindness and our weakness it should mean less than this!

Upon these and other natural and legitimate results of faithful and devoted historical study, I should like to dwell at length, but I must confine myself to one, and as it seems to me the most important, of its effects: the *generation and development of the historic spirit.*

History as we now understand it is the record of a development.

To use the historic method is to study a process of development, and a direct fruit of such study is the *historic spirit*. The true historic spirit, as I understand it, is that spirit which makes for *progress,* not by the *destruction* but by the *fulfilment* of the past, by the conservation of the best that is in it. It is often said that the study of history tends to make a man conservative; and in a sense this is true—in another sense, false. If to be a conservative is to stand still and to repudiate all progress, then the tendency of intelligent historical study is not to make a man conservative. For, coming into touch with the development of Christianity in the past, the student feels the glow of progress and finds himself instinctively moving forward, eager to carry on the grand historic march in his own day and generation. And yet, if he have the genuine historic spirit, he will not be a radical—destroying and overturning the old and re-joicing in its ruin. He will be a true conservative, in that he will realize that genuine progress can come only by the conservation of the past, only by rising upon it to higher heights. The historic spirit gives the student a sense of the continuity of Christian history. Each step he sees to have its place in the development of the whole, and to each he endeavors to do full justice. He stands always upon the confines of two ages, the past and the future, and he faces both ways. He finds the promise of the future in the performance of the past. He finds past growth inseparably linked to future progress. He sees past begetting future day by day, and he knows that they are but undivided portions of one indivisible whole. His life draws nourishment alike from past, from present, and from future.

• • •

I must now turn to the other branch of my subject: the *influence which the prevalence of the historic spirit and the use of the historic method have exerted in the sphere of Christian doctrine.* As the effects of historical study upon those who engage in it are many and momentous, so are its effects upon the Christian system. Our conception of the Bible, for instance, and our knowledge of its teachings, have been modified and greatly enlarged by the use of the historic method in the study of it. Exhibiting the growth and progress in divine revelation of which the Bible is the record; trac-ing the development of theology in successive ages and in the minds of successive writers; bringing out the organic connection of the various books as marking different stages in the evolution of a common race and faith, and thus emphasizing its unity in and through wide variety and diversity; discovering the historic conditions under which those books were written, and revolutionizing our methods of interpretation; showing the Bible in fact all instinct with vitality as the living record of an ever-growing revelation, instead of treating it, as it was far too long treated, as a lifeless code, as a mere *thing* to be twisted and distorted at will—doing all this, the historical study of the Bible which has been pursued for many decades with such unflagging zeal and with an ever larger measure of success has won the lasting gratitude of all Christian students. So our polity, and our ritual, and our general conception of the nature of Christianity and of the Christian life, have felt the beneficent influence of historical study. Upon all of these I should like to dwell, but I must be content again to confine myself to a single line, which I have selected from the many because it seems of peculiar significance, and because in it are exhibited with especial clearness the results of the study which we are discussing. Let us consider, then, the influence which the prevalence of the historic spirit and the use of the historic method have exerted in the sphere of doctrine.

It was only toward the close of the eighteenth century that the history of doctrine came to be regarded as a special discipline. Up to that time it had been treated, when treated at all, as a branch of systematic theology, and as such it consisted in massing patristic and scholastic authorities for or against a particular doctrine, thus being entirely polemic in its aim and method. Even when a more objective treatment began to prevail, the time-honored custom of handling the science theologically, continued, and until quite recent years most works upon the subject did little more than give under each period a catalogue of the beliefs of the leading men of the age upon the various heads of theology in the order in which they occur in the creeds. Though this has been dignified with the name of the "history of doctrine," it cannot be regarded as an historical treatment of doctrine, for it leaves no room for the conception of a growth and development. First, within a few decades has the true historical method been applied to the study of Christian doctrine as it has long been applied to other branches of knowledge, and the results are momentous and far-reaching in their consequences.

In the first place, the historical study of doctrine is clarifying our conception of the nature of doctrine; is emphasizing what has long been known, but too often and too widely forgotten, that our doctrines are not themselves divine truth, but human conceptions and statements of that truth, and that as such they may and have had not an apparent merely but a real growth and development. The Roman Catholic denies such a growth in his own system, and maintains that the creed enlargements which have taken place century by century, mean simply a fuller statement of doctrines held in their entirety from the beginning; and though this view is not ostensibly shared by Protestants, yet the constant tendency even of Protestant theologians has been to look upon the development as a development rather in form than in substance. The application of the true historical method has shown the falseness of this notion. It has shown us that a sharp distinction must be drawn between divine truth and our conceptions of that truth; that, though the former is always and eternally the same, unchanged and unchangeable, in our conceptions of it—in other words in our *doctrines*—there has been as real a development as in our institutions; that out of truths lived and taught by Christ, that out of truths revealed to the apostles and preached by them, we have by the use of our human powers, under divine guidance as we trust, evolved an elaborate system which has been the slow growth of centuries. To deny a real growth in the system were as absurd as to deny a real growth in a plant simply because the germ existed from the beginning. The germ did exist from the beginning in Christ himself and in the truths divinely revealed through him. Out of that germ have come, by a genuine process of development, not our statements merely, but our beliefs as well—not the form only, but the substance, of our theology. We have been too apt, studying theology as a systematic whole, to imagine that all our doctrines were revealed directly by God, and have been too apt to forget that many of them were worked out by the church itself within human limitations and under the play of human forces. Studying them historically, we can trace their origin and growth, and can discover, and to some extent measure, the influences which more or less powerfully affected their rise and their development. We can see more clearly, we believe, than before the hand of God in the process, and can appreciate the power of the divine germ—the revealed truth which lies back of it all and which is working through it all—but we can also estimate more justly the play of other forces, and can analyze more accurately the various factors which have helped to make the product what it is. Such estimate and analysis enable us to appraise existing doctrines more nearly at their true value. The common tendency of the study of theology merely as a system is to lead us to emphasize most those doctrines which are logically essential to the integrity of our system. The best corrective of such a tendency is the study of biblical theology—the study of the Bible, that is—not for the purpose of confirming or defending this or that doctrine, but with the aim of learning not alone the views of Scripture writers, but the true perspective and proportion of their views. But after such a study of the Bible, nothing is so helpful as a thorough investigation of the history of doctrine in the church. If there has been any change or enlargement since the days of the apostles, we shall be able better to understand it and more justly to estimate its worth, when we have learned whence and how the change came, to what extent human agencies had a hand in bringing it about, of what sort those agencies were, and in how far, if at all, the change was the fruit of conditions merely temporary. To be able, with a thorough knowledge of the Bible, studied scientifically and in the light of history, to test existing systems and to form, if need be, our theology for ourselves—this, and only this, is to be a theologian in the true sense, and such theologians the church of God needs in all ages.

Again, the historical study of doctrine guides us in our search for what may be termed the essential truths—those truths, in other words, a knowledge of which is absolutely necessary to the existence of Christianity in the world and to the growth among men of the kingdom of God. These are the truths which it is of the utmost importance for the church to keep constantly in the forefront of her teaching and her preaching. No other truths, however true, should be allowed to obscure them or to crowd them out. Truth out of its true proportion is as false as falsehood. If in the largeness and richness of our revelation the radiance of the great essentials and fundamentals is dimmed by the multicolored glow of lesser truths; if they shine less clearly because of the light that comes from a thousand minor stars, then our spiritual wealth becomes a curse. There is no more fruitful source of discord and of unbelief than the confusion of essential and non-essential truth. So often have the fundamental verities been forgotten or neglected, and the church plunged into the darkness of formalism or of corruption, and its power to electrify and vivify the world been lost!—and that not always through the insidious influence of error, but through the overemphasis of one truth at the expense of another truth more vital, through the failure to preserve truth's due proportion. So often has a distorted picture of Christianity thus been published to the world, and so often have men and nations embraced the caricature only to find it a delusion and a snare, or rejected it in scorn and with it the true original which it belies and hides.

And this failure to distinguish between essential and non-essential truth has led the church into many a needless controversy and bootless war, has begotten most of the quarrels and conflicts which have marred its history, and most of the heresy trials which have disturbed its peace and impeded the onward march of the kingdom of the Christ.

A careful and candid study of history will show us that the real emphasis does not always fall where we might think it would, does not always fall where the logical emphasis does; that many doctrines which stand in the forefront of our systems, and for which we have been all too ready to do battle, have been of very minor significance and influence in times when the church has most fully realized and best fulfilled its mission; that the ignorance or neglect of them has not resulted as disastrously as the ignorance or neglect of other truths of which our systems and our preaching make far less account. Not that history thus proves their falsity—far from it; not that history thus absolves us from the duty of accepting and preaching them— (we would not abuse history as is sometimes done)—but that it advises us which truths and which errors have been proved in practice most pregnant with lasting consequences for good or for evil, and thus confirms and enlarges the knowledge gained by us in our careful and candid study of the Word of God.

Still farther, the historical study of Christian doctrine reminds us that human notions and conceptions change from age to age, that even the categories of thought undergo more or less of a revision, and it thus teaches us, that, if we will be true to the truth as it has been revealed unto us, we must from time to time adjust our statements to the new conditions. The great need of every age is a sound and vital theology adapted to the peculiar wants of the age, and fitted best to mirror to the age the eternal truth of God. To translate divine revelation into the language of today—that is the paramount duty of every theologian, whether in pulpit or in teacher's chair. Not that we would truckle to the wishes of this or of any other generation; not that we would soften the truth that it may not hurt or offend; not that we would prevaricate or palliate our message; not that we would utter fair words to our brethren's undoing; but that we would so speak as most clearly and adequately to present to the minds of our own day and generation the truth which they most need, whether we do it in the speech our fathers used or no. Often indeed our fathers' speech is unintelligible or even misleading if repeated at the present day. A simple illustration of this which will occur at once to you all is found in the doctrine of divine sovereignty. Calvinists of today believe just as sincerely as they ever did in divine sovereignty, but sovereignty does not mean now exactly what it did three hundred years ago. If we shall introduce into the Westminster Confession a statement of the love of God, does it mean that God is less a sovereign to us than he was to our fathers? or does it mean that we are less consistent than they? No! it simply means that in the thinking of the world today there is wrapped up in the idea of sovereignty the responsibility of the sovereign to rule his subjects, in so far as may be, for their good. The idea of arbitrary sovereignty has become obsolete, and if we today define our supreme sovereign, God, in sixteenth or seventeenth century terms, we define to many minds a God other than the God and Father of our Lord and Saviour Jesus Christ. To make God mean to us what he meant to our fathers, we must use terms that our fathers did not use. The language of the nineteenth century is not the language of earlier centuries. We must translate divine revelation into the new tongue, or we shall be teaching the people lies, and not the truth.

A similar change has taken place in the world's conception of the responsibilities and rights of fatherhood, and the alternative faces us—if we will not perpetuate a most vicious misconception and confusion—either to give up the term entirely in speaking of God, or to adjust our other speech about him to the changed conceptions which the term involves. And if history teaches us anything, is it not that these and other changes in our conceptions are the fruit of the Christian spirit working in the souls of men and nations, and that our theology should take account of them just as truly as of any of God's revelations to his people?

To translate divine truth into the language of today: that means creed revision, and to the true historian creed revision, and frequent creed revision—in thought, if not in fact—is a necessity. To accept always and absolutely unchanged, either in form or substance, and in its original sense, the creed of a past age, is to lose touch with the historic progress of the church and fall behind fossilized and forgotten. Even though we were to maintain that the doctrines of our creeds remain ever the same, we should need at times to revise their statements, that the substance might really be preserved intact. Revisionists *may* be more conservative than the adherents of the old creed in its old form. But the historian is not content with such revision. He knows that every age which is not dead or stagnant has had, and that every age must have, its own theology, and that the theology of no other age can fully meet its needs. He knows that an age rich in spiritual life gets new and larger glimpses of divine truth—glimpses which the old words are too feeble to report. He knows that God has been leading his people into ever larger knowledge of himself and of his will, and that in these glorious days of the oncoming twentieth century—when man's earthly vision has been so enlarged and clarified, when revelations of nature are vouchsafed him such as our fathers never dreamed of even in their wildest fancy—there awaits the pure eye of true faith a larger, richer vision of spiritual truth than man has ever known. For "new light shall break forth from the Word of God," and in the pages of history shall be read new lessons, and out of the heavens shall come winged messengers bearing new treasures of wisdom and of knowledge. For to every age is granted light according to the measure of its need and of its worthiness, and this thoughtful, inquiring age needs more light than other ages, and true as it is trying to be, with an earnestness seldom matched, to all the light of the past and present, God grant that it may be found worthy of the larger light it needs.

The historical study of Christianity. All, and more than all, that I have said, it is accomplishing and will yet increasingly accomplish. But, brethren, we have not studied Christianity aright if our study has not taught us that there is more of Christianity than history records—more than history ever can record. For what is Christianity but the perpetual incarnation of God in humanity—the perpetual union of God and man? And if it be this, we have not understood it, and we cannot in any measure interpret it to others, unless we have been led beyond the visible and temporal, which we call historic Christianity, and which is ever changing, into the presence of the invisible and eternal, which we call essential Christianity, and which changes not. However variously, in different places and at different times, it may incarnate itself in objective form, God cometh to the soul of man—whether here or elsewhere, whether now or long ago —in form always and everywhere the same. A history of the visible kingdom of Christ men may write and we may study, but the kingdom which cometh in the hearts of men—that kingdom without which the other were a meaningless and empty show—no man can describe, and only he can know in whose heart it is already come.

PHILOSOPHICAL IDEALISM

Since the 1830's the growth of the liberal movement had run parallel with the widening influence of philosophical Idealism. Theology, under severe attack in the world of sense experience and scientific demonstration, turned for help to philosophies that had always denied the ultimate reality of that sensory world. But much of the resulting Idealism, as it worked its way into academic curricula during the second half of the century, turned out to be too abstract and impersonal to remain in close touch with evangelical Christianity. Academic Idealism became secularized very much in the degree that the universities themselves did.

Thus it was partly because of ability and diligence, and partly by default, that Borden P. Bowne, Professsor of Philosophy at Boston University, gained a leading position as the spokesman for liberal Christian Idealism. The "world of persons" in which Bowne located ultimate reality could contain a more traditional and preachable Deity than that of the other Idealisms. Just as important, it could provide a special place (as did the Pragmatists' correction of Idealism) for the freedom and dynamism of individual personality.

~7~
PERSONALISM
by Borden P. Bowne

The generation just passed had abundant illustration of the practical importance of philosophy. That was a time of great development in the physical sciences and in the commercial application of science to our control of nature. There were great generalizations in physics, such as the conservation of energy, and the correlation of the physical forces; and equally great generalizations in biology. The application of scientific method to historical study, also, and the ever-widening discovery of law, leading to the belief in its uni-

SOURCE: *Personalism* (Boston: Houghton Mifflin Co., 1908), pp. 9–12, 268–78.

versal reign, had great influence. New facts crowded upon us and new interpretations were demanded. The old mental equilibrium was broken up and the new one had not yet been established. The new wine of science and evolution went to the head and produced many woes and more babblings. It was a matter of course that at such time religion should seem to be imperiled. To the passive mind even new truth seems dangerous until it has become familiar. All who had any grudge against religion loudly proclaimed its baselessness, and many who were interested in religion were profoundly disturbed by the new order. Everything seemed to be in solution. The fountains of the great deep were broken up. The elements melted with fervent heat, and some things passed away with a great noise. Naturalism came to the front with a mechanical philosophy, and commercialism tended to fix all eyes on gain as even better than godliness. The latter produced a feeling that we could do just as well without religion as with it, and the former found no place for it. It was proclaimed by many, and feared by more, that the high hopes and dreams of humanity were baseless. The truth about man had been found out, and the truth was that instead of being a child of the Highest he is merely the highest of the animals, having essentially the same history and destiny as they—birth, hunger, labor, weariness, and death. Man was viewed as simply an incident in the condensation of dispersed matter, or the cooling of a fiery gas.

For a time the religious world was in a condition of stampede and panic, but after a while it became clear that the difficulty lay not in the facts themselves but in the philosophy by which they were explained. The great source of the disturbance of that time, apart from the horror of change natural to the passive mind, was the lack of any adequate philosophic equipment. The new facts were interpreted on the basis of a crude sense-realism, and this view has always had a tendency to materialism and atheism. But now that we have a better critical apparatus the difficulties have disappeared. We are now able to live in peace and quietness with the facts once thought so threatening, and we look back on that period of panic only to wonder at the superficiality that caused it. We smile at the naïve dogmatism and the extraordinary logic of the movement. Had we had a generation ago our present philosophical equipment there would have been no flurry over evolution, the transformation of species, the reign of law, and the many other things which were supposed to be fatal to man's higher faiths. The storm we had was part of the price we paid for being philosophically unprepared.

. . .

One great difficulty in bringing popular thought to better philosophical insight lies in its bondage to sense objects. Things that can be seen and handled are preeminently real, and there is always a tendency to think that only such things are real. In this state of mind it is exceedingly difficult for any doctrine of idealistic type even to get a hearing, as it seems so plainly absurd. Some relief from this obsession may be obtained by pointing out how large a proportion of our human life is even now invisible and impalpable. In this way the sense-bound mind may be made more hospitable to the thought of invisible and non-spatial existence in general.

First of all, we ourselves are invisible. The physical organism is only an instrument for expressing and manifesting the inner life, but the living self is never seen. For each person his own self is known in immediate experience and all others are known through their effects. They are not revealed in form or shape, but in deeds, and they are known only in and through deeds. In this respect they are as formless and invisible as God himself, and that not merely in the sense of being out of sight, but also in the sense of not lying within the sphere of visibility in any way. What is the shape of the spirit? or what the length and breadth of the soul? These questions reveal the absurdity of the notion without criticism.

Indeed, the most familiar events of everyday life have their key and meaning only in the invisible. If we observe a number of persons moving along the street, and consider them only under the laws of mechanics, and notice simply what we can see or what the camera could report, the effect is in the highest degree grotesque. A kiss or caress described in anatomical terms of the points of contact and muscles involved would not be worth having in any case, and would be unintelligible to most of us. And all our physical attitudes and movements seem quite ridiculous whenever we consider them in abstraction from their personal meaning or the personal life behind them. What could be more absurd than a prayer described in physical terms of noise and attitude, apart from the religious meaning? Or what could be more opaque than a description of a scientific experiment in terms of bodies and instruments, apart from a knowledge of the problem and of the unseen persons who are trying to solve it? But the grotesqueness in these cases does not exist for us, because we seldom abstract from our knowledge of personality so as to see simply what sense can give. These physical forms we regard as persons who are going somewhere or are doing something. There is a thought behind it all as its meaning and key, and so the matter seems to us entirely familiar. Thus out of the invisible comes the meaning that transforms the curious sets of motions into terms of personality and gives them a human significance. Indeed, our estimate even of the body itself depends largely upon its connection with the hidden life of the spirit. A human form as an object in space, apart from our experience of it as the instrument and expression of personal life, would have little beauty or attraction; and when it is described in anatomical terms there is nothing in it that we should desire it. The secret of its beauty and value lies in the invisible realm.

The same is true of literature. It does not exist in space or time or books or libraries, but solely in the invisible and non-spatial world of ideas and consciousness. A person looking for literature in a book or in a library would hopelessly err and stray from the way, because all that can be found there would be black marks on white paper and collections of these bound together in various forms, which would be all that eyes could see. But this would not be literature, for literature has its existence only in mind and for mind as an expression of mind, and is simply impossible and meaningless in abstraction from mind. Similarly with history. Our human history never existed in space and never could so exist. If some visitor from Mars should come to the earth and look at all that goes on in space in connection with human beings, he would never get any hint of its real significance. He would be confined simply to integrations and dissipations of matter and motion. He could describe the masses and groupings of material things, but in all this he would get no suggestion of the inner life which gives significance to it all. As conceivably a bird might sit on a telegraph instrument and become fully aware of the clicks of the machine without any suspicion of the meaning or existence of the message, or a dog could see all that eyes can see in a book yet without any hint of its meaning, or a savage could gaze at the printed score of an opera without ever suspecting its musical import, so this supposed visitor would be absolutely cut off by an impassable gulf from the real seat and significance of human history. The great drama of life, with its likes and dislikes, its loves and hates, its ambitions and strivings, and manifold ideas, inspirations, and aspirations, is absolutely foreign to space, and could never be in any way discovered in space. So human history has its seat in the invisible.

Similarly with government. The government does not exist in state-houses or halls of Congress. It is a relation of personal wills, as all society is likewise a relation of personal wills, with their background of conscious affection, ideas, and purposes. It is in this hidden realm that we live, and love or hate, obey or disobey, and live in peace or strife. Wars have not existed in space, and real battlefields are in the unseen. They are the conflicts of ideas, of aspirations, of mental tendencies, and all the fighting that ever took place in space was but a symbol and expression of the inner unpicturable strife. And this illustrates what is true of the whole life of man. Love and hate, desire and aspiration, exaltation and depression, the whole contents of human life, in short, are invisible, and the spatial is merely the means of expressing and localizing this unpicturable life; it has only symbolical significance for the deeper life behind it. All this our Martian visitor would miss, that is, he would miss man and his history altogether.

Thus we see to what a large extent human life is now in the invisible realm, and that, as said, not merely in the sense of being out of sight, but as something that does not admit in any way of being pictured. It may use spatial phenomena as a means of expression, but in itself it is strictly unpicturable. And for this great world of reality, if we must have a whereabouts, we must say that not space but consciousness is its seat. These things belong not to a space world, but to the world of consciousness, which is something very different. This is the seat of the great human drama of individual life and of human history. This would be the case on any view of space whatever, but it is self-evidently the case when we view space as subjective, for then the world of consciousness becomes the seat of all worlds, not merely the world of history and personal relations, but also and equally the seat of the world of space appearance and the world of physical science. It will be noted, however, that this view in no way denies the reality of the human world. It merely relocates it. That world remains all that it was before and is just as real as ever. We have simply discovered that it is not to be thought of in phenomenal terms of space and time, but rather in terms of itself, in the incommensurable terms of life and feeling, and love and hate, and aspiration or dejection, and hope and despair, etc. Similarly the space world is not made unreal by this general view. We simply mean that it is not a self-sufficient something by itself, but is rather a means of expression of the underlying personal life which is the deepest and only substantial fact.

The more we dwell upon this view the more mysterious our life becomes for the imagination. We see that our life now actually goes on in the invisible, and that space has only a symbolical function with respect to this hidden life. We impress ourselves upon the spatial system and manifest our thought and purpose in it and through it, but the actors never appear. So far as concerns man, the space world has the ground of many of its determinations in the invisible world of human thought and purpose, and is constantly taking on more and more our human image and superscription. In its relation to man the space world is largely a potentiality, waiting for realization by man himself. There are harvests waiting to grow and flowers waiting to bloom, but it cannot be until man sets his hand to the work. The flora and fauna of the earth are increasingly taking their character from our will and purpose. Even climate itself is not independent of our doings or misdoings. So far as we are concerned, the space world is nothing complete and finished in itself, but is forever becoming that which we will it to be. And when we recognize our own invisibility and the symbolical character of space as only a means of expressing our hidden thought and life, we find a growing hospitality toward the view that there is a great invisible power behind the space and time world as a whole, which is using it for expressing and communicating its purpose.

Unless, then, appearances are unusually deceitful in this case, it is plain that man is no impotent annex to a self-sufficient mechanical system, but is rather a very significant factor in cosmic ongoings, at least in terrestrial regions. He is an inhabitant of the invisible world, and projects his thought and life on the great space and time screen which we call nature. But naturalism, in its sense bondage, misses all this, and seeks for man in the picture world of space images, where, in the nature of the case, he can never be. With this initial blunder, man becomes less and less in the system, first a phenomenon, then an "epiphenomenon," and finally he tends to disappear altogether. Meanwhile matter and motion go on integrating and dissipating as per schedule, and $\frac{1}{2}M V^2$ remains a constant quantity. The whole history of thought contains no more grotesque inversion of reason.

A world of persons with a Supreme Person at the head is the conception to which we come as the result of our critical reflections. The world of space objects which we call nature is no substantial existence by itself, and still less a self-running system apart from intelligence, but only the flowing expression and means of communication of those personal beings.

MODERNISM

The demand for religious adaptation to culture, evident and growing in Protestantism since the 1870's, acquired the name "modernism" (a borrowing from the Catholic progressives) in the early years of the twentieth century. Newman Smyth made use of the term in 1908, and David C. Torrey wrote a volume on *Protestant Modernism* two years later.

Modernism, in the eyes of its major spokesmen, simply revived and made explicit a principle that had been vital to the entire Christian movement. Christ himself, they claimed, had been a modernist in the religious life of his day. If words were used as they should be, the modernist would therefore be recognized as the true "conservative," the conserver of hallowed tradition.

Shailer Mathews, who began teaching at the University of Chicago in 1894 and served as Dean of its Divinity School from 1908 to 1933, summarized in the mid-twenties the consequences of the modernist outlook for Protestant thought, and even, after due acknowledgment of the impossibility of doing so, presented a modernist creed. Within a very few years, Mathews' book, its "credo" in particular, would be the butt of more than one neo-orthodox satire. What struck readers at the time, however, as the *Methodist Review* reported, was that Mathews' portrayal of the much-feared "modernist" was "nothing else than the description of the liberal Christian of today."

~ 8 ~

THE AFFIRMATIONS OF FAITH
by Shailer Mathews

The religious affirmations of the Modernist are not identical with any theology. They represent an attitude rather than doctrine, they involve creative living under the inspiration of Christian connections rather than a new orthodoxy. The Modernist undertakes to

SOURCE: *The Faith of Modernism* (New York: The Macmillan Co., 1924), pp. 171–81.

project, not simply to defend permanent Christian faith. He knows that if it faces its real tasks the church cannot simply reaffirm the past. He sees something more imperative than theological regularity in the expansion of Christianity until it touches all human interest. Yet he would be consistent. If Christians find their impulses and loyalties inspired by a literal acceptance of the inherited doctrinal patterns, he would welcome their cooperation in the Christian service. It would be inconsistent for him to demand that others should accept his theology as a new orthodoxy. He must do unto others as he would have them do to him; namely, recognize the fundamental unity constituted by membership in the Christian group and devotion to the driving and reproductive convictions centering about Christ which it embodies. Let men use and permit others to use such doctrinal patterns as will make these convictions and loyalties effective in human affairs.

Earnest men are subject to temptation born of their strength. The Modernist is no exception to this rule. If the temptation of the dogmatic mind is toward inflexible formula, that of the Modernist is toward indifference to formula. But once aware of this danger he can address himself whole-heartedly to what history and experience show to be the common divisor of Christian groups with the hope that he will thereby be of service to his day.

Tolerance is not indifference to truth that lies below doctrines. The Modernist is loyal to the Christian movement. Just as the patriot would die for his country whose laws he cannot altogether understand, so the Modernist would die for the ongoing Christian movement with its constant ministry to spiritual needs and its Christain organization of human life. He sees the need of loyalty to the Christian church, participation in its common endeavors, the organization of its members for cooperative service, the furtherance of its convictions throughout our social life. He wishes not only to make surveys, but to make converts. The Christian church is not an institution for religious research. It is the agent for ordering life among men in accordance with good will like that of Jesus Christ. However much we may need knowledge, mere intelligence is not Christian living. A man is not necessarily religious because he likes theological discussion. No man is a thorough Christian who holds himself apart from the stream of social endeavor. He should join the Christian group and share in its efforts to help men live. He cannot build himself a house by the side of the road and watch the crowd go by. That is no way to be a friend of man. Friendship means service, helpfulness, sympathy, participation in toil and weariness and anxiety, in ambitions and hopes of others. The way to get together is to work together. *We are Christians when this common effort is controlled by the attitudes and convictions which from the days of its Founder have been the heart of the continuous ongoing Christian community.*

Just because they are loyal to the convictions which have given rise to the Christian movement, Modernists cannot stop with ethics, history, science, sociology and biblical literature. They seek to come themselves and bring others into the very presence of God revealed in Jesus Christ. Only thus can they lay hold upon the God who works in the world of nature and of men. They want men to pray as well as plan, to find the way to spiritual reserves in order that they may get power to resist evil and endure success. The result of their efforts to accomplish these ends is not a philosophy but a religion enabling men and women engrossed in their daily life and social tasks to cooperate with the immanent God of love.

The conviction that such a Christianity is practicable inspires every man who accepts evolution as a mode of God's activity and regards himself as not only the heir of a Christian movement but a part of a social structure which hinders even while it helps Christian ideals.

This is no new discovery. It has always been made when men have had some new and better understanding of themselves, of nature, of human needs, and of their Christian inheritance. So it was in the days of Paul, in those days of renascence when men saw that asceticism was not the Christian ideal, and in those other and more tragic days when men came to feel that humanity had rights which kings and God Himself must recognize. Christian thinkers in each epoch mediated between the continuous convictions of the church and the new spirit of progress. They used analogies drawn from the new conditions. Instead of thinking of Christ as a Jewish Messiah Paul set him forth as Lord and Spirit. Instead of thinking of salvation as made more certain by withdrawal from society, the men of the sixteenth century sought to be Christians in their daily life and in their most humble vocations. Instead of trying to persuade the revolutionists of the eighteenth century that God was an absolute monarch, Wesley taught men to think of Him as fatherly. We must follow the same method. We shall draw the analogies with which the continuous stream of Christian conviction and attitude is to be heralded from the very effort to make faith operative. If we think of God as creating man through the processes of divinely guided evolution, we shall set forth salvation as a continuation of the processes by which humanity from its first days more and more has ever appropriated God's personal influence. If we face social reconstruction we shall think of society as an accomplishment of the evolutionary process by which life builds up a more personal environment to aid it in its personal development. We shall not think of God as a monarch giving laws, or sin as a violation of statutes, or of salvation as a mere bargain between God and man. God will be ever the environing Father revealed by Jesus.

This conviction that God cooperates with efforts to reproduce the way of Jesus may find expression in new patterns drawn from democracy and the various sciences, but it may very likely be that we shall increasingly use explicitly the great Christian convictions and attitudes themselves. We shall defend those convictions by analogies and arguments capable of showing them to be consistent with the world we know, but we shall be less concerned with formulas than with the primary task of showing that the Christian life is legitimate in a world that knows nature as does ours. We shall be less concerned with patterns than with the proper way of adjusting human lives to an increasingly complicated social order, to their own capacities, to cosmic reason and purpose increasingly discoverable by the human mind and incarnate in Jesus. We may be decreasingly interested in the metaphysics of Jesus Christ, but we shall be all the more determined to show that his life and teachings reveal the divine purpose in humanity and therefore it is practicable to organize life upon his revelation of good will. And our way of expressing our basic convictions and attitudes will be more effective for our needs, for it is the outgrowth of action and social experience and is couched in the language of today.

In developing an intellectual apparatus for justifying the Christian life, we shall not feel the need of stressing certain doctrinal patterns which expressed the Christian convictions and attitudes of men in different circumstances and controlled by different social practices. We shall shape new patterns whenever they are needed, from life itself. But we shall not forget they are patterns.

The Modernist will cherish faith in Jesus Christ as the revealer of the saving God, but until he is convinced of the historicity of the infancy sections of Matthew and Luke, and holds different conceptions of generation from those given at present by biology, he will not base that faith upon the virgin birth as the one and only means by which God can enter into human experience.

The Modernist will not insist upon miracles, but he believes that God is active and mysteriously present in the ordered course of nature and social evolution.

Because the Modernist thinks of God as immanent within His world, he counts upon divine help in every struggle for larger freedom and justice. The death of Christ, therefore gets far richer significance for him as a revelation of such participation than is possible from analogies drawn from the sacrifices of the ancient world, the practices of feudal lords, the punishments of an absolute monarch and the demands of a severe creditor.

Because he thus sees the character of Jesus in God, and therefore believes in the possibilities of a life like that of Jesus, the Modernist will practice good will himself and urge it as the only safe and promising motive for social, economic and national life. And he will never doubt that God's good will shall some day reign on earth.

While he believes in the inevitableness of suffering from any violation of the will of God the Modernist cannot think of a literal hell with fire and burning. The ravages of disease are more terrible analogies.

Because he believes in the mystery as well as the reality of the present continued life of Christ, the Modernist will not stake this faith upon untested traditions, but will ground it on literary criticism, history and his own experience, and will therefore hope for a similar advance through death.

In fact, Modernists will very likely have no common theology whatever. They have the same attitudes and convictions as those of the historical Christian community, but they will not codify them in words of authority. They will get uniformity of point of view and expression through a common method of thought. With limitations they may prefer to use the same terms, but they are concerned primarily with Christian attitudes and convictions rather than with doctrinal patterns. They do not believe that it is possible for any body of men to express authoritatively what a group believes, so long as there is a minority of one who differs. The community of interest, the solidarity of undertaking which the Modernist knows the Christian religion involves, he will increasingly find in the activities of the Christian group to which he belongs. In this choice he will feel with certainty that he is reproducing the spirit of him who taught that his friends were those who kept his commandment to love and forgive.

Although it may probably be that the day of new orthodoxies is past among those who are being trained in methods of free investigation and social organizations, new Christian service is inevitable. Modernism is not liberal dogmatism. The underlying evangelical convictions and attitudes which have been carried forward across the centuries by the succession of Christians and Christian institutions, will persevere in more active sacrificial social-mindedness. These convictions the Modernist asserts, not in the interest of theological uniformity but in the interest of a better world, of more Christlike and happier people, of institutions that will make toward justice and fraternity, and of an internationalism which will make towards peace. That such a de-theologizing of the Christian movement will produce other changes is certain. As it becomes more wide spread sectarianism will vanish and cooperation appear. There will be less of ecclesiastical chauvinism and authority, and a more intelligent attempt to put the attitudes and spirit of Jesus into the hearts of men and the operation of institutions. Christianity will grow more moral in its demands.

To what this pragmatic Christianity will tend in the development of the church as an institution remains to be seen. It is hard for me to think that we shall ever be without institutions where youth can be trained in the Christian way of life and in the defence of religion against materialism and pleasure. Nor can I imagine a world in which men and women will fail to associate themselves for

worship and cooperation in the way of Christ. But whether the direction of the Christian group is to be along ecclesiastical lines, or
whether it find increased expression in organizations ministering to
human needs, or in both, is a matter of merely speculative interest.
The community of those who hold to Christian attitudes and convictions will continue.

While by its very nature the Modernist movement will never
have a creed or authoritative confession, it does have its beliefs. And
these beliefs are those attitudes and convictions which gave rise to
the Christian religion and have determined the development of the
centur[ies-]long Christian movement. No formula can altogether express the depths of a man's religious faith or hope to express the general beliefs of a movement in which individuals share. Every man
will shape his own credo. But since he is loyal to the ongoing Christian community with its dominant convictions, a Modernist in his
own words and with his own patterns can make affirmations which
will not be unlike the following:

I believe in God, immanent in the forces and processes of nature,
revealed in Jesus Christ and human history as Love.

I believe in Jesus Christ, who by his teaching, life, death and resurrection, revealed God as Savior.

I believe in the Holy Spirit, the God of love experienced in human life.

I believe in the Bible, when interpreted historically, as the product and
the trustworthy record of the progressive revelation of God through a
developing religious experience.

I believe that humanity without God is incapable of full moral life
and liable to suffering because of its sin and weakness.

I believe in prayer as a means of gaining help from God in every need
and in every intelligent effort to establish and give justice in human
relations.

I believe in freely forgiving those who trespass against me, and in good
will rather than acquisitiveness, coercion, and war as the divinely established law of human relations.

I believe in the need and the reality of God's forgiveness of sins, that is,
the transformation of human lives by fellowship with God from sub-
jection to outgrown goods to the practice of the love exemplified in Jesus
Christ.

I believe in the practicability of the teaching of Jesus in social life.

I believe in the continuance of individual personality beyond death;

and that the future life will be one of growth and joy in proportion to its fellowship with God and its moral likeness to Jesus Christ.

I believe in the church as the community of those who in different conditions and ages loyally further the religion of Jesus Christ.

I believe that all things work together for good to those who love God and in their lives express the sacrificial good will of Jesus Christ.

I believe in the ultimate triumph of love and justice because I believe in the God revealed in Jesus Christ.

III
IMPLICATIONS

CHANGES IN THE MISSIONARY ENTERPRISE

All through the liberal era, champions of orthodoxy contended bitterly that the newer theology would "cut the nerve of missions." Liberals of course denied this; but they conceded that liberal theology did certainly imply new proselytizing methods. The missionary, unless he wished to be laughed out of court by non-Christian peoples, would indeed have to do without certain arguments that conservatives considered especially effective.

The concern, deeply felt on both sides, about the strength and spread of Christianity gave meaning to an otherwise sterile controversy that raged for years over the future state of the heathen. Several professors at Andover Seminary were prosecuted in the 1880's, chiefly for being "wrong" on this point; and many young liberals got past ordaining councils only by a kind of theological one-upmanship. The Scottish immigrant George A. Gordon later recalled his own experience of 1881 with a council in Greenwich, Connecticut:

> Eternal punishment was still a necessary article of belief in the creed of a Congregational minister, and I was obliged to frame my answers on this point with some care. This I did, affirming that I believed in the everlasting punishment of the finally impenitent. When questioned if I believed in the impenitence of any individual person, I replied that on that question I was wholly without knowledge; that the only adequate authority on such a matter was the omniscient God . . . I was installed.

Gordon made his way through further obstructions to the pastorate of Old South Church in Boston, and to a preeminent position among liberal theologians. His writings on missions, even though they retained traces of the traditional condescension toward non-Christian peoples, prefigured the liberalism of the epochal *Laymen's Inquiry* on missions that was to appear in 1932.

～9～
THE GOSPEL FOR HUMANITY
by George A. Gordon

The scholarship of the Christian world, the large and sympathetic study of the religions of mankind, the feelings bred by the honorable international trade of the earth, the steady emergence of a cosmopolitan habit of mind, and the wonderful growth of the idea of humanity, make it impossible longer to live in the traditional theology. It is not big enough, nor is it good enough as theoretic support and inspiration for the best interests and activities of the world today. The vast missionary enterprise of the church must ever demand a larger consecration of wealth, a nobler sacrifice, a wider devotion; but the causal fountain of all this is the character of faith. There is at present no adequate theoretic support and incentive for this magnificent enterprise of the church of our time. The moment that the traditional theology is utilized in developing enthusiasm for foreign missions, that moment the conscience of the best men turns away from the dismal business; and only as the traditionalist abandons theology and betakes himself to Christianity in its New Testament form, and stakes everything upon the prevailing passion of human love as it is born and fired out of the heart of Christ and out of the Fatherhood of God, does he make his appeal effective and overwhelming. The fact that the missionary work of the churches was founded upon the old theology is no reason why it should be continued upon that basis. It was, indeed, founded upon the love of God in Christ for the world, and it must be built again upon that fundamental truth as it is reflected in the larger intelligence of the time. Faith without works is dead, and the best theology that does nothing is worse than a poor theology that agonizes to save the world. Nevertheless, a living faith is the only

SOURCES: *The Christ of Today* (Boston: Houghton Mifflin Co., 1895), pp. 20–21; *The Gospel for Humanity: Annual Sermon before the American Board of Commissioners for Foreign Missions* (Boston: ABCFM, 1895), pp. 7–8, 9–10, 12–19.

permanent source of missionary endeavor, and the faith that is adequate to the world enterprises now on the hands of the church must issue in wider and richer practical results. The missionary enterprise has transcended the conception in which it originated: it has led the church that inaugurated it into a new world; it has been fruitful of ideas and feelings beyond all expectation; and today it is largely a stupendous pedestal in the air, waiting for the new conception of the mission of God in Christ to be put under it as adequate and everlasting support.

We prize our ideas of the gospel, but we must never make the mistake of supposing that our ideas are the gospel. The gospel is the living, loving God, moving with ineffable power in the living, loving Christ, and our thoughts are but poor images of this transcendent reality. Between the picture of the bird and the bird itself on the wing there is an infinite distance. The picture may be great. It may give us the skylark in mid-heaven, with the fires of morning reddening its wings, or it may show us the eagle high over some solitary Alpine height, and the representation may be full of beauty and power. Nothing but thanks should be felt for such a work of art; it renders an essential and noble service. Nevertheless, how incomparable it is to the reality! Its skylark is motionless and songless; its eagle is shorn of the grace and majesty of life. When we ask for life from art we ask too much. The picture cannot give song, it cannot give flight; no more can thought give the final and sovereign touch of God. It cannot ring with the harmonies, nor can it sweep in the forms and rhythms of the ultimate, personal Reality. Conceptions of truth may be great; systems of opinion may be the supreme work of art, the best and highest utterance of the structural power of the mind. They are the mark of rationality, and are inseparable from the whole procedure of man's intellectual life. But they are not the supreme and ultimate manifestation of God. Only life can yield life; only personality can reveal personality, only the perfect personal Christ can utter to mankind the being of the perfect personal God.

• • •

We are not under obligation to export our entire body of belief.

There is no particular call for our church polity, our special theology, or the traditions of our Christian life. These are not wanted; if sent, they would prove unsuitable. Paul's example here is of the greatest moment. He had his faith as a Jew transformed into his faith as a Christian, and he had a hundred convictions and opinions and beliefs that formed the psychological setting to his sense of the sovereign love of God in Christ for the world. He allowed all else to go, good as it was in its own place, essential as it was to the total content of his mind, and reported only the transcendent truth of the living, personal Father revealed through the living Christ. The apostle allowed the Corinthians to manage their churches in their own way; to think widely and freely, if so be that they did not contradict the fundamental facts of the gospel; and he passed no sentence of condemnation upon the wisdom of the world, save as he felt compelled to exhibit its tremendous limitations. Here is the mood for the modern Church. She is to send her God and her Savior and her new life in the Spirit, and she is to leave theological and ecclesiastical forms to the Christian sense of these nations. Varying types of thought differentiate all great peoples. The intellectual traits of the German, the Frenchman, the Englishman, and the American are different. Their philosophies and theologies are different. We look for unity at the present stage of development only in the regions of faith and hope and love, only in the grand objects of our religious devotion and service. Here is the great commission of the foreign missionary today. He is to preach the Eternal Personal Love as attested by the whole career of Christ. This is the test, and the only test, of the spiritual fitness of the man who offers himself as a representative of the church upon the foreign field. Has he a message? Is it that the heart of the universe is Personal Sacrifice, and that revealed and verified by the personal sacrifice of the Lord? Does he carry his message of Jesus Christ and Him crucified in a mind sufficiently enlightened, in a heart adequately deep and tender, in a life profoundly moved by the Spirit of God? If so, he, and he alone, is the foreign missionary of the apostolic type.

·   ·   ·

We have in Paul's gospel to the nations a principle of assimilation. We know that this has been one of the great features of Christianity from the beginning. It first of all absorbed the essential and permanent elements in Hebraism, and then showed that it had besides a distinctive and incomparable life of its own. The Sermon on the Mount takes up into itself the decalogue and at the same time transcends it infinitely. Heaven and earth may pass away, but not a grain of truth stored in the ancient Hebrew world falls to the ground. The whole higher thought of lawgiver and king, prophet and psalmist, is taken up into the mind of Jesus and changed into something universal and final. The same principle is illustrated in the career of Paul. He was born a Jew, and in some respects he remained a Jew to the last; and yet his Judaism was brought to the judgment seat of his Christianity. Whatever in his early belief was of enduring worth as thus judged passed into his new faith; whatever was incapable of being assimilated was allowed to fall away and die. This apostle stood for the uniqueness of Christianity, and also for its power to assimilate the truth found by the preceding ages. He applied his principle in all directions. He found the Greek thought serviceable in his new career, and he made it the servant of his gospel. We all know how this process went on—how Greek philosophy was laid under contribution in working out the Christian conception of God, and how the environment, rich in Roman custom, rite, and institution, was turned to the service of the Church. Christianity attests its divinity by its power to take up into itself all the truth which it meets and by giving to that truth a share in its own life.

This great feature of the gospel has a twofold bearing upon our missionary work. In the first place, the absolute incomparableness of Christianity should leave us free to put a high estimate upon the moral and spiritual achievements of the leading extra-Christian nations. We can afford to do this; we are inflicting injury upon our own incomparable faith when we fail in comprehensive generosity. Whatever of excellence there may be in the feeling of the Japanese, in the morality of the Chinese, or in the thought of the Hindu, Christians can afford to estimate in the most generous ways. There can be no possible competition between the idea of the cross and anything that these natives have to offer. Take the Hindu race. They are spoken of by those who best know them as intellectually one of the most gifted peoples on the globe. I cannot help the feeling that this is a very great exaggeration. The Hindus have no science, and do not even know what the word means. They have achieved no fame in working out a theory of government, and less in the institution of one. Their gift lies in the direction of metaphysics, and this subject they have conceived not as Plato or Aristotle did, nor as Kant and his great successors have done. Their strength has never been in orderly and valid thinking, even when turned upon the great centers of being. But they have a marvelous faculty and fertility of spiritual imagination, and their power of reflecting profound metaphysical truth through the luminous haze of intellectual vision is indeed amazing. Nevertheless, one feels that even here there is a certain cheapness about the product. It is as if there were an illimitable fog bank off our shores, rolling in under a blazing summer sun. It comes in transfigured masses; it is a wonder of beauty, but after all it is thin and cheap and unwholesome. One can hardly resist a . feeling like this in witnessing the exercises of the Hindu mind. It is talk by the mile and the league, and, although pleasant to hear, it lacks the note of reality. It somehow fails of representative worth in respect to the character of the speaker, in respect to the experience of the average sincere man, and, above all, in respect to the order and grandeur of the universe. But whether this is a just criticism or not, one thing is sure, that the Hindu idea of sacrifice and the Christian are wholly unlike. The idea of a sacrifice which, while it wastes individual life for the world, conserves it as an essential part of redeemed society, is foreign to Hindu civilization. When that idea is embodied in Jesus Christ, and taken as a revelation of the heart of the universe, we have a supreme gift to make to all nations. The Christian idea of God, the Christian Savior, the Christian conception of a redeemed society, they do not possess; and they are old, worn out with immeasureable volitional imbecilities, exhausted by an immemorial divorce of the intellect and the will, and corrupted by illimitable clouds of spurious sentiment. They need Christ and His cross as the relevation of the essential nature of God and man.

Still, the other side must not be overlooked. God has not left any of these peoples without witness of Himself, and therefore the work of assimilation must go on. It is in the power of the gospel to enter sympathetically the past of Japan and China and the wonderful reach and richness of Hindu history, and put upon the whole expanse the light of its own divine interpretation. It can, in a way, identify itself with the great traditions of all these peoples; make them live their long histories over again and read their deeper meanings into itself. It can, without in the least endangering its unique character, appear in the light of those empires, and come in the colors which are dear to them; it can put on as dress many of the intellectual habits that are inseparable from their constitution. Until the Jew saw his Judaism transfigured in Christianity he could not abandon the old faith for the new; until the Greek beheld the vision of Plato under grander forms in the vision of Christ he could not forsake the academy for the Church; until the Roman discovered in the sign of the cross a diviner form of the victorious power after which he had thirsted he could not change his allegiance; and until China shall see Confucius idealized and transcended in our Master, and Japan her beggarly elements glorified in the Christian inheritance, and India her sublime names taken out of the region of imagination and in our Lord made the equivalent of the moral order of the universe, we cannot expect them to become His disciples.

It seems to me that our dreams of dominion for our Master must be more and more along this line. He must prove Himself a better ruler to Japan, a nobler Confucius to China, a diviner Gautama to India; the whole sacred past must reappear in Him transfigured and carried utterly beyond itself. He must come, but He must come upon the clouds of heaven, in their morning beauty and in their evening splendor. He must come, but He must come as the consummation of the ideals of every nation under heaven, and as the inapproachable reproduction of their deepest historic life. Dante clung to the vision of the Florentine maiden, whom he met when only a boy of nine, and whose image he found to be unforgettable. He carried in his heart of hearts the sacred picture even after Beatrice had become another's, after it was clear that in this world she never could be his. He was in bondage to the early form until in maturer life and in mystic experience he beheld her in paradise. The new form made him forget the old; the later vision replaced the earlier, the soul in heaven the sensuous life in Florence. But the deep-hearted poet, the passionate and permanent lover, was able to let go the earthly for the heavenly, the human for the divine, because he beheld all that he had loved, the veritable Florentine maiden, the Beatrice of his wondering boyhood, taken up into this new splendor of God. The past could be abandoned because it lived again before him in transcendent form. And this must be the experience of the nations if they are to come into the kingdom of our Lord. They have not been left wholly desolate. They have seen unforgettable faces. They have moved in the power of a venerative love for thousands of generations. From that past, that imperfect, they cannot be torn until under the spell of the missionary's words they behold again what they have revered, and see it in the awful beauty of Jesus Christ. The Christ for the world is the Christ in whom the infinite sanctity of life and all its deepest and divinest dreams reappear, and such a Christ it is our incomparable joy to send to the ends of the earth.

It must further be noticed that this gospel to the nations contains within itself a principle of development. Christian history is a revelation of Christ additional to that contained in the New Testament. It is all from the Divine Life recorded there; but it is a new and more extended and in some respects a mightier exhibition of His character. The Holy Spirit is the supreme gift of Christianity; He is the guide into all truth, the helper of the head and the heart alike, the victorious rational impulse in the attempt to understand the mind of God in nature and in history, the invincible ethical inspiration in the endeavor to conform life to the eternal standard presented in Christ. Christian history is an evolution of the Holy Spirit through the rational and moral consciousness of Christ's disciples, and the evolution must go on until the divine shall prevail in the intelligence and heart of the race. Because there is a Holy Spirit in Christianity there has been spiritual progress and theological development; because our faith rests upon the eternal deeps of the divine wisdom and love, there must be advance in the temper of the soul and in the achievements of the intelligence, on to the end of time. What we are to look out for is that the development shall be real; that it shall be a revelation of its original source; that the historic effect shall conform to and not contradict the transcendent cause; that the movement of the Church shall be a continuous and cumulative exhibition of its founder and Lord.

The great historic theologies are not the New Testament; nor have they an equal authority with it; nor are they true in all their parts. Far from it. Yet are they an expression of the Eternal Spirit laboring with the intelligence of the Church at a completer apprehension of the Lord and His mission to mankind. They are true in their main lines of movement, true in their great affirmatives. The great ideas of Origen and Athanasius and Augustine, Luther and Calvin and Edwards, are valid thoughts for the world. Their systems are in ruins, but the ideal material out of which their systems were made, for the most part remains imperishable. The imperishable in theology is vaster than most people imagine, and that great residuum from the suffering of the centuries is the product of the Holy Spirit.

Now this principle of development is indispensable in any right conception of foreign missions. All that we can hope to carry to the nations is the eternal spirit through the historic Christ. To fill the mind and heart and will with the Divine Life, that must be our supreme aim. All attempts to export systems of theology must fail. They will be tolerated by no people having in them a spark of original genius. Contrasted previous civilizations and the total diverse character of inheritance and environment will forever make impossible the domination of one division of the race by the rigidly formulated mind of another. The moment that a nation, like an individual, attains its majority, intellectual variation, constructive genius, begins to appear. The mind of the boy and youth is the proper subject of domination, and so barbarian Europe is happiest while in bondage to Plato and Aristotle. Manhood means freedom, and freedom means the power of selection and self-movement; and the nations that are good for anything, and to whom Providence has assigned any considerable task in the advance and enrichment of the kingdom of God, come at length to their majority. Then they simply must go their own way; to arrest them or to force them into another way would issue in a measureless sacrifice of power.

The nations are to be left to the control of the Holy Spirit as He enters the life through the presentation of the historic Christ. As from a few living forms the wondrous worlds that science beholds have been evolved, so from the spirit of the living God in a people's heart the development of their Christian faith will come. We are to see to it that the nations have the Lord and giver of life, and then we must trust them to His care. How have the great oak forests grown up all over the world? The acorns have grown upon the few primitive trees, and the winds have shaken them from the boughs and have carried them far and wide and planted them in the living soil. Unconscious ministers of God these winds have been; in a living universe they had but to blow, to bear abroad, to transport life, and behold from their stormy labors forest upon forest appeared. With similar unconcern for consequences, in a depth of trust that looks like that unconsciousness, the foreign missionary is to take and spread the living word of the Lord, to carry from this tree of life the germs of life. In a living humanity filled with the Holy Spirit there need be no concern for the types of thought and ecclesiasticism that shall at length appear. Given the living nations filled with the living God in Christ, and the final growths will be for the good of mankind and the glory of the Lord.

The problem of foreign missions is the reduction of the world under the empire of Christ. We believe that His mind is simply incomparable, and that we are in duty bound to strive to put the whole race under His supremacy. The world that we seek to bring to the Lord is a growing world, and the question will come whether any one historic name can cover humanity's need. This planet of ours had its origin in the sun; it was flung out of the flaming center a mass of liquid fire, and we can think of it as a problem to itself as it went onward, acquiring distinct structure and growing into all the richness and splendor of these later ages. We can think of it asking if the old formula of dependence upon the sun was sufficient for it in its greater estate. And we can hear the answer, that it needs nothing other to account for the highest reaches of its physical history than the simple and everlasting power of the sun. The mighty expansion of our human world starts a similar question. The nations are so various, the great divisions of humanity are so unlike in their history and civilization, in their habits of thought, their ideals, their conceptions of the goodness of life; the mightier peoples are so rich in sacred tradition, in commanding names, and in deep-rooted and widespreading religions; the lower orders of society need something so divine to give them moral hope; and the privileged classes have lived through an experience so varied, wearisome, and barren, and have settled into an apathy so deep and a contempt of life so terrible, that again the Maker of man must become his Redeemer. The grandeur of mankind lies in the depth and awfulness of its need. Nothing but the Highest can fill this deepest in the desolate heart of the race. Is Christ the Master of this world as He was of the smaller world in which our foreign missionary work began? Is He King of the latest as He was of the earliest development? Yes; it is all traceable to Him, in so far as it is good. Because Christ is the source of the whole better life of mankind, He must be the guide and goal of it. This is our faith. We have a Christ for the world because God made man in the image of His Son; we send the gospel of Jesus Christ to the race because He is the fountain of our humanity; we expect to subdue the earth at its greatest to Him because its latest life, no less than its earliest, is out of His eternal love.

A REVISED ETHICS

While a number of theological liberals proved reticent or even vo-
cally conservative on social issues, a majority declared themselves
sympathetic to the "social gospel" proclaimed by Washington
Gladden and others. And most sympathizers confirmed their adherence by working actively for local or national political reform;
or by supporting the labor and peace movements; or by joining in
the Progressive critique of laissez-faire economics.

Here again, as in the case of missions, new theological ideas and
new perceptions of practical need reacted upon each other in complex ways; and several of the liberal theoreticians sought to explore
both sides of this relationship. Walter Rauschenbusch, Professor of
Church History at Rochester Seminary and ultimately the most
venerated of the Social Gospel leaders, proclaimed that "theology
needs periodical rejuvenation," and devoted a major book (*A Theology for the Social Gospel*) to the proposition that social reform demands the re-centering of Christian theology in the doctrine of the
Kingdom. But Rauschenbusch also habitually broadened this formula,
as he does in the early article reproduced here, to show social reform
as both cause and effect of theological revision.

～ 10 ～

THE NEW EVANGELISM
by *Walter Rauschenbusch*

The present interest in the "New Evangelism" is almost wholly an
expression of dissatisfaction with the old evangelism, the waning
power of which is generally conceded. There is as yet no new evangelism before us which we might adopt; we are only wishing that
there might be. Our conceptions of what it ought to be are vague,
as all ideas about the future necessarily are, but that is no cause for
belittling the current inquiry. It is one of the most important topics

SOURCE: "The New Evangelism," *Independent, 56* (May 12, 1904), 1056–
61.

that could be discussed. I shall attempt in the following discussion to apply the same method of historical investigation to this great and threatening fact of contemporary religious history which would be applied to a fact of equal importance in a past era.

The Gospel of Christ is one and immutable; the comprehension and expression of it in history has been of infinite variety. No individual, no Church, no age of history has ever comprehended the full scope of God's saving purposes in Jesus Christ. Neither has any proclaimed it without foreign admixtures that clogged and thwarted it. A fuller and purer expression of the evangel has therefore always been possible and desirable. It is on the face of it unlikely that the Gospel as commonly understood by us is the whole Gospel or a completely pure Gospel. It is a lack of Christian humility to assume that our Gospel and *the Gospel* are identical.

Every individual reconstructs his comprehension of life and duty, of the world and God, as he passes from one period of development to the next. If he fails to do so, his religion will lose its grasp and control. In the same way humanity must reconstruct its moral and religious synthesis whenever it passes from one era to another. When all other departments of life and thought are silently changing it is impossible for religion to remain unaffected. The Gospel, to have power over an age, must be the highest expression of the moral and religious truths held by that age. If it lags behind and presents outgrown conceptions of life and duty, it is no longer in the full sense the Gospel. Christianity itself lifts the minds of men to demand a better expression of Christianity. If the official wardens of the Gospel from selfish motives or from conservative veneration for old statements refuse to let the spirit of Christ flow into the larger vessels of thought and feeling which God himself has prepared for it, they are warned by finding men turn from their message as sapless and powerless. The most familiar instance is that of the Revival of Learning and the repudiation of medieval religion and theology in the fifteenth and sixteenth centuries.

We are today passing through an historical transition as thorough and important as any in history. The last 125 years have swept us through profound changes in every direction. World-wide commerce and the imperialistic policy of the Christian nations have made the problems of international and interracial relations urgent. The

Church responded by a new movement of world-wide missions, but it has failed hitherto to Christianize international politics. The monarchical system, so intimately connected with ancient religion, has crumbled and democracy has taken its place; but the Church has not broadened its ethical teaching to any great extent to meet the new duties of the citizen-kings. It still confines its ethics to the *personal* and *family* life. In industry and commerce there has been a vast increase in the production of wealth and a shifting in its distribution, but the Church has furnished no adequate principles either for the distribution or the consumption of wealth. We are emerging from the era of individualism. The principle of coordination, cooperation and solidarity is being applied in ever widening areas and is gaining remarkable hold on the spirits of men. The Church is applying that principle in its organization, but its message is still chiefly on the basis of individualism.

It is not strange if the message of the Church has failed to keep pace with a movement so rapid. But neither is it strange if humanity, amid the pressure of such new problems, fails to be stirred and guided by statements of truth that were adequate to obsolete conditions. The Church is in the position of a mother talking to her son of seventeen, as if he were still twelve. What she says is good and loving, but it is not what the boy with his new passions and problems needs.

The present paralysis of the churches affects all Western Christendom and only a cause coterminous with modern civlization will explain it. Communities are affected in just the degree in which they are affected by the progress of civilization—the backward countries and rural communities least, the industrial cities most. State churches and free churches alike feel the drag. It is not because the religious spirit has failed. It runs surprisingly strong, but it runs largely outside of the churches. Neither is the trouble due to lack of piety in the ministry, for, on the whole, we are as good as our fathers. We are told that the Gospel has always met with indifference and hostility. But is this today a persecution for righteousness' sake, so that Jesus would call us blessed for enduring it, or is it a case where the salt is trodden under foot of men, because it has lost its saltness? The worst explanation is that which shrugs its shoulders and regards the present alienation of the people from the Church as a mysterious dispensation of Providence against which we are helpless. Effects do not happen without causes, and God's reign is a reign of law. In short, no small or local or passing cause will explain so large a fact as the present condition of the Church.

Now, apply this to evangelism. Evangelism is only the cutting edge of the Church, and it is driven by the weight back of it. The evangelizing power of the Church depends on its moral prestige and spiritual authority. Every evangelist banks on the accumulated moral capital of the Church Universal.

There are two kinds of evangelization. The one proclaims new truth, as Jesus did to his nation, or Paul to the Gentiles, or as a missionary does to the heathen. The other summons men to live and act according to the truth which the Church has previously instilled into their minds and which they have long accepted as true. The latter is, on the whole, the kind which we have to do. To be effective, evangelism must appeal to motives which powerfully seize men, and it must hold up a moral standard so high above their actual lives that it will smite them with conviction of sin. If the motives urged seem untrue or remote, or if the standard of life to which they are summoned is practically that on which they are living, the evangelistic call will have little power. The two questions which every Christian worker should investigate for himself are these: Are the traditional motives still effective? And is the moral standard held up by the Church such as to induce repentance?

The motives urged at any time will vary with the preacher and the audience, and there will always be a large measure of truth and power even in the most defective preaching that touches human nature at all. Yet there is a change in emphasis from age to age. Within our own memory the fear of hell and the desire for bliss in heaven have strangely weakened, even with men who have no doubt of the reality of hell and heaven. On the other hand, the insistence on present holiness and Christian living has strengthened. Good men give less thought to their personal salvation than our fathers, but their sympathy for the sorrows of others is more poignant. Past Christianity has developed in us a love for our fellows and a sense of solidarity so strong that they demand to be considered in every religious appeal. On the other hand, we cannot conceal from ourselves that the old "scheme of salvation" seems mechanical and remote, and its effectiveness as a motive depends largely on the past teaching of it, which is stored in our minds. The sense of great coming changes, begotten by a better knowledge of the plastic possibilities of mankind, is strong upon us. We have a new hope for humanity such as has long existed only where the millennial hope was a vital thing.

Even so brief an enumeration must make us feel that some motives are dropping away, because they were narrow and incompletely Christian, and larger and more truly Christ-like motives are offering themselves. It should be the scientific effort of every Christian worker to observe what motives are today really effective with the young and thoughtful minds who represent the present and future. The fact that some evangelists who are determined in repudiating anything that savors of "modern thought" are so effective in urging the old motives does not invalidate what we have said. In every large city there are many men who belong to the old time and are untouched as yet by the new. They respond joyfully to the ideas in which their Christian life was nurtured and in which their holiest memories are enshrined. But there are other men who come once and then stay away, because they hear nothing to which they can respond. And these men are not counted. Moreover, the strong personality of the evangelist may count for more than anything he says.

What about the moral standard held up by the Church in its teaching and in its collective life? Can she summon men to repentance by it?

The moral teaching of the Church in the past has dealt with private and family life. It has boldly condemned drunkenness, sexual impurity, profanity; it has fostered gentleness and pity, and it has been largely successful in this teaching. It has also drawn the line against Sabbath breaking, dancing, card playing and theater going, but it has not been successful in maintaining that line. In general, the community has risen toward the level of the Church in private and domestic virtue, and the Church has drifted toward the level of the respectable community in regard to amusements. As a result of both movements the gap has lessened. The morality of the Church is not much more than what prudence, respectability and good .breeding also demand. Nor is the morality of church members generally distinguished by the glow of spiritual fervor. There is less family worship and prayerful life than with our fathers. But with this moral outfit can the Church authoritatively say to the world, "Repent and become like me?"

When we pass from private and domestic life to political and business life the matter is worse. About the most pressing questions arising there the Church as a body is dumb. It has nothing to say about the justice of holding land idle in crowded cities, of appropriating the unearned increment in land values, of paying wages fixed by the hunger of the laborers and taking the surplus of their output as "profits," or of cornering the market in the necessaries of life. It feels restless about some glaring evils like child labor, but only moderately so. Individuals in the Church are intelligent and active, but the Church, both as an organized body and as a corporate spiritual force, is inert. The moral guide of humanity is silent where authoritative speech is today most needed. Where it does speak, it is often on the wrong side. When we consider the ideas prevalent in the churches, their personnel, and their sources of income, has the Church a message of repentance and an evangel for this modern world?

One important and growing class in our population is largely alienated from the Church—namely, the industrial wageworkers. The alienation is most complete where the industrial development under the capitalistic system has most completely run its course. In our country that alienation has begun within the last generation, during which this class has become a class, and the process is not yet complete. This constitutes the spiritual barrier to evangelistic efforts as soon as they go beyond the young people of the families already in the churches. Our evangelistic call strikes an invisible wall and comes back in hollow echoes. It is an untrue and cruel charge to say that the Church workers have not done their best to reach the people. The efforts of the churches in the great cities for the last generation have perhaps never been paralleled. And yet they are futile. This is one of the most stunning and heart-rending facts in all our life.

The Church has passed under the spiritual domination of the commercial and professional classes. I do not mean that they alone compose its membership; but they furnish its chief support, do its work, and their ethics and views of life determine the thought of the

Church more than we realize. This is not due to any wrongful attempt to make the Church subservient, but rather to the fact that they are the dominant classes in all industrial nations, in literature and politics, as well as in the Church. Now the stratification of society is becoming more definite in our country, and the people are growing more conscious of it. The industrial conflicts make them realize how their interests diverge from those of the commercial class. As that consciousness increases, it becomes harder for the two classes to meet in the expression of Christian faith and love—in prayer meetings, for instance. When the Christian business man is presented as a model Christian, working people are coming to look with suspicion on these samples of our Christianity. I am not justifying that, but simply stating the fact. They disapprove of the Christianity of the churches, not because it is too good, but because it is not good enough. The working people are now developing the principle and practice of solidarity, which promises to be one of the most potent ethical forces of the future, and which is essentially more Christian than the covetousness and selfishness which we regard as the indispensable basis of commerce. If this is a correct diagnosis of our condition, is it strange that the Church is unable to evangelize a class alienated from it by divergent class interest and class morality?

Let us sum up. The powerlessness of the old evangelism is only the most striking and painful demonstration of the general state of the churches. Its cause is not local nor temporary. It does not lie in lack of hard work or of prayer or of keen anxiety. It lies in the fact that modern life has gone through immense changes and the Church has not kept pace with it in developing the latent moral and spiritual resources of the Gospel which are needed by the new life. It has most slighted that part of the Gospel which our times most need. It lacks an ethical imperative which can induce repentance. In private life its standard differs little from respectability. In commerce and industry, where the unsolved and painful problems lie, it has no clear message, and often claims to be under no obligation to have one. In the State Churches the State has dominated; in the free Churches the capitalist class dominates. Both influences are worldly —in favor of things as they are and against the ideals which animate the common people. The people are becoming daily more sensitive to the class cleavage of society. The Church suffers under the general resentment against the class with which it is largely identified. To this must be added the fact that the spirit of free inquiry engendered by modern science neutralizes the dogmatic authority with which the Church has been accustomed to speak.

The new evangelism which shall overcome these barriers and again exert the full power of the Gospel cannot be made to order nor devised by a single man. It will be the slow product of the fearless thought of many honest men. It will have to retain all that was true and good in the old synthesis, but advance the human conception of salvation one stage closer to the divine conception. It will have to present a conception of God, of life, of duty, of destiny, to which the best religious life of our age will bow. It will have to give an adequate definition of how a Christian man should live under modern conditions, and then summon men to live so.

A compelling evangel for the working class will be wrought out only by men who love that class, share its life, understand the ideals for which it is groping, penetrate those ideals with the religious spirit of Christianity, and then proclaim a message in which the working people will find their highest self. They will never be reached by a middle class gospel preached down at them with the consciousness of superiority.

If we personally are to have a share in working out the new evangel, we shall have to be open to two influences and allow them to form a vital union in our personalities. We must open our minds to the spirit of Jesus in its primitive, uncorrupted and still unexhausted power. That spirit is the fountain of youth for the Church. As a human organization it grows old and decrepit like every other human organism. But again and again it has been rejuvenated by a new baptism in that Spirit. We must also keep our vision clear to the life of our own time. Our age is as sublime as any in the past. It has a right to its own appropriation and understanding of the Gospel. By the decay of the old, God himself is forcing us on to seek the new and higher.

This attempt at a diagnosis of our ills is not offered in a spirit of condemnation, but of personal repentance and heart-searching. We all bear our share of guilt. I have full faith in the future of the Christian Church. A new season of power will come when we have put our sin from us. Our bitter need will drive us to repentance.

The prophetic spirit will awaken among us. The tongue of fire will descend on twentieth century men and give them great faith, joy and boldness, and then we shall hear the new evangel, and it will be the Old Gospel.

PROGRESSIVE RELIGIOUS EDUCATION

Liberalism expressed itself with special vividness in religious education. A revised understanding of heathendom troubled chiefly the gentlemen on mission boards, but a revised estimate of child nature touched almost everyone engaged in the saving of souls. If, as the liberals urged, salvation normally is achieved not through sudden conversion but through the unfolding of inborn capacities for good, then the premises of revivalism were seriously flawed.

Critics in the 1840's, notably Horace Bushnell in Connecticut and John W. Nevin in Pennsylvania, had raised varying objections to the popular theology at this point. Liberals of 1900, consciously indebted to the ideas of Bushnell, worked to combine these insights with the functional psychology and the investigative methods of William James, and with John Dewey's prescriptions for a democratic pedagogy. The leader in this effort, George Albert Coe, taught at Northwestern University and then at Union Seminary and Columbia Teachers College. Joint founder, with Dewey, of the Religious Education Association, Coe was convinced that modern "secularization," far from being an abject capitulation of religion to culture, exhibits God's incarnation in the common life.

~ 11 ~

SALVATION BY EDUCATION
by George A. Coe

If the inner history of the relations between Christianity and education could be written—a history that should not only describe institutions and avowed theories, but also reveal the unspoken assumptions and the inarticulate aspirations underlying the whole—it would be a volume of surpassing interest. It would record many a strange fact, many a quaint idea, many a surprising contradiction. The church would appear now as the leading patron of education,

SOURCE: *The Religion of a Mature Mind* (Chicago: Fleming H. Revell Co., 1902), pp. 293–306, 311–12, 322–6.

117

now as an opponent or reluctant follower of educational reforms. We should find education pressed upon the young in the name of religion at the same time that the spiritual barrenness of all culture is proclaimed from the housetops. We should find the child held up as a type of the kingdom of God, yet declared to be depraved by nature, and needing to be converted before it can see the kingdom. At almost every point evidence would appear of an internal strain, an unreconciled opposition, between two tendencies. On the one hand, divine grace is exalted in opposition to human nature; on the other, the naturalness of the Christian life is insisted upon. In one of its aspects, Christianity offers, not peace, but a sword; in another, it comes, not to destroy, but to fulfill. When the one phase prevails, education is depreciated; when the other comes to the surface, education becomes one of the chief tasks of the church.

All through this history, however, thus much is plain: The Christian religion has an essential affinity for education. Culture may be distrusted, education may be restricted, faith or the sacraments or divine grace may be emphasized in opposition to mere training, yet one thing Christianity can never do, it cannot let education alone. The debate over salvation by works and salvation by faith may seem to exhaust the alternatives, yet there always remains a back-lying assumption that the world's salvation is to be accomplished partly by educating the young.

Is it not strange that salvation by education has never received doctrinal recognition? The churches spend vast sums upon schools and colleges; they maintain Sunday schools at great cost of labor and of gold; they send the schoolmaster side by side with the preacher to heathen lands; yet the principle that governs these things has never been put into words by any official body. We have elaborate theories as to man's part and God's part in other spiritual processes; why not some theory of how God and man cooperate in the education of a soul?

This gap in our theoretical grasp of Christian principles is an index of a serious practical omission. For no one will deny that the weakest point in our campaign for bringing the world to Christ is the relation of the church to the young. Here is our nearest opportunity; here the problems are least complicated, and the difficulties smallest; yet here we are least awake, least aggressive. A hopeful sign of the times, however, is increasing sensitiveness on this point. No sentiment awakens more prompt and universal response throughout the church than the call for reform, or at least improvement, in Christian nurture. Here and there, too, an advance movement has begun, especially in the reorganization of Sunday school instruction, in the formation of boys' and girls' clubs, and in the efforts of a few leaders to bring the young people's societies into line with known laws of mental and spiritual development.

In the main, however, the thought of the church has not gone beyond, if it has even reached, the standpoint of a certain sentimentality which formulates itself into a few propositions that are too broad to be effective. Thus, it is declared to be wasteful to let the young drift away from the church while we are waiting for them to become mature; that they ought to be held to the church from infancy; that the way to save men is to save boys; and much more. But what it means to "save" a child, or to "hold" him to the church, is not as clear as it ought to be. Hazy notions prevail, too, concerning the relation of a young child's soul to its Creator, and concerning the possible influence of training upon that relation. In particular, the possibility that God should be the prime factor in the education of a child as well as in the conversion of an adult, has found scant lodgment in Christian thought, and meager application in Christian practice. The difference between saving a child and saving an adult has not been distinctly worked out in either theory or practice, and for the most part, the official status of children with respect to the church has been altogether overshadowed by that of adults.

The questions here raised concern the point of view rather than the details of work for the young. Discussions of methods, so much indulged in by workers for the young, are often of little use because they lack a fundamentally correct point of view. They are attempts to walk where there is no ground to stand upon. We shall never do justice to the young until we look down through Sunday school methods, young people's societies, junior societies, and every mere device, to the ultimate relation in which the three parties concerned—God, the child or youth, and the adult—stand to one another.

Nor is this all. Religious education has relations to general pedagogy that demand to be recognized and applied. The teacher of religion and the teacher of arithmetic are dealing with the same child. Possibly learning arithmetic has something to do with learning to be religious. In any case, the principles of development in the one sphere cannot be altogether separated from those in the other.

In the last chapter the assertion was made that we are now in the first stages of a great religious revival, which takes the direction of the Christian nurture of the young. Let us now try to see what are some of the influences that contribute to this movement, and whither our expectant eyes and efforts should be directed. Our problem is not the old one of "how to bring up children," but rather that of point of view, of attitude, of pedagogical principle.

The way for such a revival has been prepared by a correction of religious ideals on the one hand, and by a correction of the ideals of general education on the other. The result is that religion and education have moved toward a consciousness of a common goal and a common inner principle.

It is true that a merely casual glance does not reveal any such approximation; for no external mark of modern education is more characteristic than its newly won freedom from ecclesiastical control. Modern education is, in a sense, distinctly secular. It has become an institution of civil government. It is understood to exist for the sake of the life that now is. It is maintained as a bulwark of the state, a necessity for civilization, and a means of "getting on in the world." More and more it becomes practical, relating itself ever more closely to the everyday life and occupations of the people. Scarcely a vestige remains of the other-worldly aspect which the schoolmen gave to it. No longer can we assume that any peculiarly close relation exists between learning and the clerical profession, and if a reason could be found why the teaching of reading and writing should be in the hands of the priest, the teaching of clay modeling, woodworking, cooking, and sewing clearly lie outside the priestly function!

But when we talk of the secularization of the schools, we almost always contrast the school of today with the church of yesterday, the so-called secularism of the present with the monastic ideals of generations that are gone. If, however, we compare the ideals of the new education with those of progressive Christianity, we discover no such gulf as is commonly supposed to exist. On the contrary, we find something more resembling parallel lines of development. The differentiation of function, whereby education and religion seemed to enter divergent paths, is really tending toward a higher unity of the two. This is another instance in which the breaking up of a germ seems at first to be the destruction of it, when in reality it is merely unfolding into a larger, more varied organism. The unity is still there, but it is a higher unity because it includes diversity and wealth of detail.

For Christianity, too, has been outgrowing the shell from which modern education burst. From the spiritual narrowness which was falsely identified with piety, it has come forth into the light of God's wide creation. To some the Church as well as the school has seemed to become secularized; and it would not be strange if some eyes should blink and some feet stumble in the rapid readjustment. But, in general, the secularization that is complained of is of the same kind that Jesus exhibits when, by living a human life, he shows us what God is. More and more we are learning that the Christian life is to be an incarnation, a realization of divine purpose, presence, communion in our everyday occupations. Accordingly, the Christian heart indulges less aspiration to escape the common life, and more to be a whole man, a God-like man, within it. We are not to come down from divine communion to the commonplace, but to raise the commonplace to a sublime level by making it the abode of God.

It follows that the Christian ideal of manhood includes that of "all 'round" development. Every power is to be brought to perfection because every one is a means of incarnating the divine in human life. See, now, how close this Christian view of life is to the ideals of modern education. In both church and school the movement has been toward the recognition of value in the interests and occupations of the common life. In both the one and the other, the ideal of manhood is that of symmetrical development. What religion adds to the modern idea of culture is simply a divine goal and a divine occupation for trained faculties. This is what religion adds, but as far as culture can go in bringing out the powers that belong to a man, the interest of religion is one with that of education.

The bearing of this conclusion upon the general problem of religious pedagogy is exceedingly direct. For education now becomes, not two—religious and secular—but one. There is no ultimate validity in the antithesis that sets religious interests over against secular. There are no religious compartments of the mind divided off from others which are non-religious. There is one personality demanding that all its powers be trained, and there is one sphere of interests in which trained powers are to find use. This sphere of interests, Jesus has taught us to think, is or may be as truly divine as human. The field of the divine life in us is simply our life in its totality.

This thought, like others that have been touched upon in previous chapters, is related to the doctrine of the divine immanence. In whatever our eyes look upon, or our ears listen to, we have to do with God. In all the things that our hands handle, we deal with him. In all our faculties of intellect, of will, of instinct, of conscience, of emotion, we are with and in God. It is as impossible, therefore, to separate religious pedagogy and general pedagogy as it is to expel God from the world which continuously flows from his creative hand.

Education is one, therefore. Some day men will ask what this implies with respect to our so-called secular schools. Already a tide is setting in that is destined to bear us far beyond our present position. Only a few years ago, the public school was assumed to fulfill its function by training and instructing the intellect. But no one who thinks on educational principles at all in this day, has failed to see that the schools must also train their pupils for membership in society. To sharpen the wits without preparing for good citizenship is a foolish undertaking for a state. And so, moral training is now recognized as a necessary part of public education. The schools must aim to make good men and women. Let this movement go a little further, and who knows but that reverence toward God, as well as kindness to animals and good will toward men, will be inculcated in the schools? This might happen, even though church and state remain separate. No doubt any suggestion that religion, in any form, should be taught in the public schools will be looked upon as inopportune, if not wrong in principle. But as surely as the immanent God is the deepest fact of man's mind, progress in the theory of mental development will sooner or later compel recognition of the religious phase as a necessary part of general education.

Until that time comes, the church must make herself a specialist in religious education, and the first condition of her doing so is that she recognize the principles of general pedagogy as being principles, also, of religious nurture. Out of this recognition arises the distinctly modern idea of such nurture. It proposes to utilize, in the interest of religion, the information that general psychology yields concerning the structure of the mind, the information that biology, physiology, and child study can garner with respect to the laws of child development, and all the principles and methods that the history and philosophy of education have stamped with approval. One of the best results of the modern demand that religion be brought out of the mists and close to life is that the religious training of children shows a tendency to become scientific and businesslike. We should not shrink from applying such terms to sacred matters. If God is to be all and in all, why should not scientific and businesslike methods be the rule rather than the exception in religious undertakings?

If it were necessary to give a date to mark the transition to the modern conception of Christian training, we could not do better than to name the year 1847, which saw the first issue of Horace Bushnell's *Christian Nurture.* For though Bushnell did not approach his problem from the standpoint of general pedagogy, he had, nevertheless, the insight and the practical wisdom to put himself, perhaps unconsciously, into the central current of the great educational reform of the nineteenth century.

He announced the thesis of his book in the following words: "What is the true idea of Christian education? I answer in the following proposition, which it will be the aim of my argument to establish, viz., *That the child is to grow up a Christian, and never know himself as being otherwise.*" What is this but an application to religious training of the notion of returning to nature out of which sprung the kindergarten, and in fact, the whole modern movement? It is a declaration of freedom from all those mechanical conceptions which looked upon the child as clay waiting to be molded rather than as a life demanding to grow. Bushnell really grasped the idea that the central fact and aim of education is development of a living organism. He therefore assumed the standpoint of the child-consciousness, as modern pedagogy demands, making it, and not maturity, the standard and the guide.

•   •   •

The way in which Bushnell herein discovered for himself the central ideas of the great educational reform of the nineteenth century is remarkable. This reform centers about the thought that the child is a developing life, whose internal laws of growth prescribe the principles and methods of education. The child is not a miniature adult, but something qualitatively different. To educate him implies, not that we mold him into conformity to the standpoints and methods of the adult mind, but rather that we provide him with abundant food for his mind, so that he may live out his very own life at each stage of growth. Hence the cry of "freedom in education," which has been heard so often from the lips of modern educators. Free self-expression is the recognized means for the training of the mind as well as of the muscles. The popular statement of this principle is that education does not consist in pouring knowledge into the child, but in drawing out his innate powers. This point of view has necessitated direct observation of the child, and the resulting recognition of relatively distinct stages of growth, each with its own peculiar demands. In principle, Bushnell grasped in original fashion this whole circle of ideas. Religious growth was to be a development from within, not an imposition from without; it was to proceed as spontaneous, unreasoned self-expression rather than as deliberate act; it was to be coordinated with the growth of the whole personality.

•   •   •

In spite of the work of men like Bushnell and Hibbard, in spite of the kindergarten movement, in spite of the whole great revival in education, the modern church has never gone at the work of Christian nurture with any such seriousness as the case demands. This work is too commonly regarded as a sort of addendum to church life, and even where it is not so regarded, there is a surprising lack of enterprise in the execution of it. Pedagogical principles cannot even yet secure unequivocal recognition from Sunday school conventions. The methods of the ordinary Sunday school are far behind those of the common school, as far behind as a tallow dip is behind an electric light. In many churches the catechising of children has been largely dropped, and only in a few places has anything taken its place. There is reason to fear that most parents give utterly inadequate attention to religious training within the family. In the minds of many parents, too, there is uncertainty and confusion as to what should be done, or taught, or required, or expected. Meantime, here and there, "children's evangelists" and untrained leaders of children's societies and classes ravage the hearts of the young. It would be easy to make a long catalogue of points at which the ordinary handling of children and youth in the name of religion violates known laws of growth and accepted principles of education. And this is the state of our campaign at precisely the point of greatest strategic importance!

Yet we suffer less from defective methods than from neglect. We are not thoroughly awake, and as a consequence, we are tolerant of ways which the slightest reflection would condemn. We must make up our minds to a task not less strenuous, not less systematic and unremitting, than that undertaken by the schools and colleges. This means more than instructing children in doctrine, more than repressing their immature impulses, more than inducing them to imitate the religious habits of their elders—it means the skillful feeding and nurture of the life of the Spirit. The child is to grow up a Christian in a positive sense. Life must be made to mean to him Christian life. This is as far as could well be from all forcing of religious emotion, all precocity, showing off and morbidness. It implies that children are to be mere children, but it implies, also, that the life of every child is a life in God, and that development of the mind should be growth in the God-consciousness.

What this requires in the way of reformed methods, we need not here attempt to say. When we get the right point of view and are thoroughly awake, we shall discover appropriate methods. But of one thing we may be sure: Any adequate program will require that the religion of us adults become a visible and audible fact, so that children may become aware of its specific presence. Incarnation is the supreme method of Christian nurture. The child must find religion a constant feature of his environment. It must be a perceptible fact in the persons with whom he has to do, and it must enter as a matter of course into his notion of life. You do not have to persuade an American, English, or German boy to have national pride. He acquires it from the unremitting pressure of his environment. Just so, children may be reared under Christian presuppositions so as never to know themselves as being anything but Christian.

We should strive to make this the rule rather than the exception. Christianity must become something other than "a stranger at the door." It must become the presupposition of our family and community life. It must be as pervasive as the atmosphere, as natural as conscience or as love. Only then shall we show the mature and rounded spiritual life that is demanded by the relation of the church to the modern world. Would you have Christian experience come of age? Then give it a childhood and youth.

A NEW CATHOLICITY

Ecumenism, which stresses the essential oneness of Christianity and advocates its institutional reunion, received surprisingly little attention in liberal writings. Liberals did steadily deplore sectarian divisions, whether these were opportunistic or genuinely theological in origin, and they led in promoting practical day-to-day cooperation in numerous areas of endeavor. But with a few outstanding exceptions the liberals left this field to a distinguished line of evangelicals whose greater solicitude for the Church as an institution prescribed a more explicit interest in its unification.

Among the liberals the most striking appeal for Christian unity was Newman Smyth's *Passing Protestantism and Coming Catholicism,* which was published in the same year (1908) as the founding of the Federal Council of Churches. Smyth, pastor of First Church, Congregational, in New Haven, had consistently shown sensitivity to the importance for Protestant theology of movements in secular or non-Protestant thought. In the first years of the twentieth century he discerned in Roman Catholic "modernism" the signs of coming *rapprochement.* Catholics and Protestants, by way of their respective liberal movements, might yet make their way back from the most egregious division marring Christian history.

～12～
PASSING PROTESTANTISM AND COMING CATHOLICISM
by *Newman Smyth*

The world challenges today the hope of Christianity. What is its promise for human life? The question of the scholar may be, What is Christianity? The faith of the people will depend more upon the answer to the question, What can Christianity now do in the world?

SOURCE: *Passing Protestantism and Coming Catholicism* (New York: Charles Scribner's Sons, 1908), pp. 1–14, 139, 169, 202–3.

History, now making before our eyes, has the fascination of swift movement and unknown possibilities. The news of the day may open vast and untraversed social and international problems. Within our churches the thought, often anxious for the morrow, is present— What shall be the religious life of the people?

Thoughout the following inquiry we shall seek to throw a searchlight in one direction only; we shall ask what the prospect seems to be for a reunited Christianity, by which a greater work of faith may be wrought than the world has ever known. It is beyond the scope of this essay to inquire concerning the possibility of a reunion of the Eastern and Western Churches; the signs of that lie as yet beneath our horizon. But all over our Western Christianity there is promise of a dawning day. We shall ask whether with good reason we may discern any signs of our times that the age of Protestantism is passing, and the age of a new Catholicism is coming. We shall acquaint ourselves with Modernism in the Roman Church, which may prove to be a mediating way between the two. We shall then understand better with what reasonable hope we may expect to see again the one "Holy Church throughout all the world," which the first Christian confessors saw, and which Protestantism has lost awhile.

We have no historical justification for regarding these ages of Protestantism as necessarily a final period of Christianity. Our time may prove to be a transitional era, as other periods of Christianity have been before it. No mistake is easier or more fatuous than for those who happen to be living at any hour of history to imagine that the world has come to a full period in their institutions; as, to take but a single instance, it would have been folly if the feudal barons had supposed that their social system was a finality. Indeed, Protestantism in its religious economy bears a striking resemblance to feudalism. Its ecclesiastical confessions remind us of the feudal castles on the Rhine; they are like so many strongly built fortifications, guarded with moat and tower, and many an angle and loophole for shafts of defence in the assaults of theological controversy, provided sometimes with dungeons also for heretics. Each ecclesiastical castle likewise has is surrounding vineyards, and its devoted serfdom over whom it extends its protecting power. But now the castles by the Rhine are in ruins, or at best have been restored into peaceable modern habitations, while by them all the Rhine, as of old, flows on and on. The religious feudalism of armed separations, frequent strifes, and close, fortified ecclesiasticisms, like the economic feudalism, has proved to be by no means a Christian finality.

Already Protestantism is well advanced in a third period of its lifetime. For, so far from its being true that it represents a permanent form of Christian life, it is significant that it has already passed through two periods of growth and activity, which may be compared to the time of early manhood and of middle age. The first of these periods, which are already completed in the history of Protestantism, may be distinguished as the epoch of its protest against the one church then dominating the world—the time long since accomplished of the warfare of Luther and the reformers against the crushing supremacy of Rome. All the conflicts of religious liberty—how the reformers warred and how they reigned, and what they did, are they not written in the book of the chronicles of the kings of our Israel! But Luther's battle hymn, "A mighty fortress is our God," has long since become in our congregations a song of victorious faith, and no more a battle call. We sing it believingly, triumphantly, very much as we might use Deborah's Commemoration Ode in the Old Testament.

The second age of Protestantism was an era of systematic construction. The Reformation was more than a protest. Martin Luther's brave act in nailing his theses on the door of the church at Wittenberg was not all of Martin Luther. Behind the deed was the man; and the spiritual personality of the man became the power of another world age. In his great history of Protestant theology, Professor Dorner has put in the foreground the positive principle of the Reformation, which was embodied in Luther's personality, "the potentialized self of an age"; it gave to Protestantism a vitality and a history such as no mere protest could have achieved. From its beginning the new creative spirit of the Reformation was evident; for a considerable period later it manifested itself in the construction of new churches and the formation of distinctive creeds. By the end of the seventeenth century these were in the main completed. Then the thought of the Reformation having moved into them, for the next hundred years and more it lived in them, defended them, as men will their homes; and it was content with occasionally repairing and refurnishing them, but without desire to tear them down and build new ones. During this period of Protestantism the foundations of our larger denominations were laid, and our chief ecclesiastical enclosures built up. We must turn back to those earlier theological controversies and the definitions of doctrines then current, if we would understand the language of the Protestant creeds which are still retained in many evangelical churches, or if we would comprehend the subconscious ideas which still rule, as ancestral influences, the minds of many orthodox congregations.

It is not indeed true that within these confessions thought has remained imprisoned; the strictest Protestant creeds have in them open windows, and the law of liberty is recognized among them all. Nor is the question here in point, how far these doctrinal statements may be susceptible of modification or interpretation, so that they may still be kept and used, as old houses may be happily occupied when fitted up with modern improvements. The single fact which lies in the present line of our historical logic is, that the character of creed-building and church-making marks distinctively an age of Protestantism which belongs to its past. Some new sects, it is true, have been born in these last days, and others may come to untimely birth; but it is here to our purpose to note that the lines of chief division through the Protestant world were run long ago; that for two hundred years Protestantism has not been much occupied in making new denominations or in devising new formulas of faith. On the other hand, it has of late years been breaking up rather than making creeds. We may therefore justly reason that a movement of religious thought and life, which has already passed through two marked stages of development—the epoch of protest and the era of reconstruction—is a providential preparation for something beyond itself; as our civil war, and the subsequent period of reconstruction, have proved to be only an epoch of transition into a greater nationality. There lies before us in its vaster possibility another Christian age to come. Already we are facing its problems. Shall the Protestant era—its religious warfare accomplished, and its confused years of reconstruction drawing happily to a close—issue in a grander Catholicism? The answer of faith is—the greater Christianity is already at the door.

A first reason for this hope is that in our times there are to be discerned signs of the passing of the Protestant age of history. These are to be seen alike in the success and in the failure of Protestantism.

It were an easy and grateful task to depict the splendid successes of Protestantism. Our free churches have their glory in them. They are the pride of our New England inheritance. They are the ancestral virtues upon which our homes are built. They are the constitutional foundations of our American citizenship. They constitute the historic security of democracy throughout the world. They have opened the door wide for all the sciences to come into our modern civilization; and they have made thought as free as the angel whom the early Christian prophet saw flying through mid-heaven with an everlasting evangel. Protestantism has its triumphal arch, and upon it are depicted the victories of hard-fought fields, and the procession of the mighty oppressors of the nations, led captive by it; and the names of the heroes of its faith remain inscribed in perpetual honor upon it. But it is a completed arch. Its crowning achievement is the victory which it has won forever for the spiritual liberty of the individual man. Henceforth the right of private judgment for every man can never be abolished or destroyed. This keystone has been placed secure for all time in the triumphal arch of Protestantism, and no powers of darkness shall remove it from its place. In the main the distinctive work of Protestants as Protestants has been done. Hereafter there may remain the lesser and decreasing labor of extending civil liberty to remoter regions, or in Christian lands of adding here and there some finishing touches to the Reformation's historic masterpiece of the Emancipation of the Spiritual Man. Henceforth the truth is free which makes us free.

In this fulfilment of its providential mission lies the sign of the passing of the Protestant age. For a work achieved is always the sign of another and a greater work to be accomplished. When one success has been won, a new task invites the spirit that is in man. This is so both in the individual life and in the course of history. Successes of men and of ideas are never ends, but means to further ends. They are not epitaphs, but invitations. They are not dead memories, but living inspirations. This law of progress holds true of the Divine revelation itself, the record of which is preserved in the world's Bible. The law came by Moses; but the age in which the law was given, rendered necessary the age of the prophets. Not to destroy but to fulfil—the ever larger fulfilment of the law and the prophets—is the historic work, still in process of accomplishment, of the Son of man who said, "My Father worketh hitherto, and I work"; it is the unceasing work of Him who sitteth on the throne who said, "Behold I make all things new." This is historically true; in the great tidal movements of human life no wave can remain too long uplifted at its height; one after another the great waves break upon the shores, and God's tide comes flowing in.

We pass then from this assurance that Protestantism has, on the whole, attained the end for which it was sent, to consider what further it is obviously failing to accomplish. For in what a movement fails to do may be given the sign of another service for a new age to fulfil. It is no dirge that we shall have to sing. They are the pessimists who do not see the incompleteness of the forerunner's work, and whose eyes are holden so that they cannot perceive the presence of One greater than he, for whose coming the best past has been preparation. If we point without hesitation to the darkest clouds of the present hour, it is because we see also across them the sweep and the radiance of the bow of promise.

We are not to be understood as asserting a complete inability of Protestantism even where its ineffectualness is most obvious. We are not oblivious of its splendid outspokenness against all unrighteousness. We can see some Christian man or woman pursuing every evil thing under the sun. The missionary spirit is superb; but its means are belittling. The failures of Protestantism are partial; but they are obvious. They may be summed up in a word when we ask, to what extent are the Protestant churches losing control of the forces of life?

Human affairs in the last analysis are problems of forces. Institutions, laws, economics, social conditions, constitute a problem of forces; history is a dynamic, and the study of history, as truly as of physics or biology, is a study of energy. Hence there can be no profound insight into human life, and still less a prophetic discernment of the better conditions that may be obtained, unless one feels the forces which are working beneath and all through the world in which men live and act. We bring our Protestantism, therefore, to a real test and a decisive judgment, if we search it through and through with this question, Is it mastering the controlling forces of life?

Before the Reformation a dominating factor was the authority of the Roman Church. Upon the whole medieval world was set the stamp of the Papacy. Moreover, the authority of the Papacy was an effective authority. It worked. It maintained undisputed control over whole spheres of human life.

This kind of authority has long since been discarded among us; but has Protestantism gained authority of its own? Or by virtue of any power inherent in it, is it keeping a supreme religious control of the modern nations which it has created and made free? Is religion the master passion of Protestant communities? For Christianity must become the mastery of human life, or it is not the final religion. If our existing forms of religion are losing such control, we must look for another coming of the Son of man as one having authority.

. . .

Our discussion of the problems of the union of the churches should start from the fact that the Church *is* Catholic; that, as the primary fact, there is one Catholic Church throughout the world. The real problem given us in our day to work out is, not to create that unity, but to manifest it; not to make it anew out of the destruction of our individual inheritances, but to make it manifest as the one Life through all the forms and organs of it. Our problem, in a word, is the visibility of Church unity. Hence, our logic will revolve in a vain circle, if the first premise of our reasoning be not this primary Church-fact of the actual unity of Christ's society; and our endeavor will be stopped before insurmountable barriers, if it does not begin from this starting point of Christian faith that we all do belong to the one Church of Christ.

. . .

How . . . can a way through the bewilderment of the creeds of Christendom be found? These Modernists are learning an answer for us all. Protestantism may find itself more indebted than we know to those Roman Catholic thinkers and historians for the answer which they have been compelled to discover in order to save the loyalties of their own faith. It is given in their principle of the historical development of the dogmas of the Church. That truth is in

all their thoughts; and it keeps them within their Church, while it
emancipates them from all bondage to its traditions.

· · ·

It has been said that a modernized Pope may be sometime elected;
but that, though possible, does not seem to be an immediate prob-
ability. It is more promising to reflect that the coming power lies
more and more with the people, and that the Pope has good reason
for his apprehension of the part which the laity are destined to play
in the progress of the Church. Sooner or later their insistence on the
limitations of the authority of the Vatican will have to be regarded.
Constitutional government is wrought into the faith of the people.
The Church cannot long survive as an exception. The demand for
"a constitutionalized Papacy" Rome cannot resist and outlive. The
outcry of the Modernists has a double imperativeness; it is an appeal
to history, and a rallying call for an advance. The Roman hierarchy
is a massive fact; but forces are mightier than facts.

Another General Council has been spoken of in some quarters.
When the time for it shall have fully come, the leaven of the modern
learning will have so far pervaded the whole lump that Ultra-
montanism may no longer sift its wholesome working out of the loaf.
A General Council, regaining the voice of reason and conscience,
would prove an immensely reformatory power in Roman Catholicism.

Moreover, if—as Professor Briggs has what may seem the hardy
optimism to suggest—the result of another General Council in which
Modernism has gained influence, should lead as the next logical step
to conference in any direction with representative Protestants, an
unmistakable advance would thereby have been taken toward the
reunion of Christendom.

RELIGIOUS RADICALISM

The liberals, by contrast either with more extreme dissenters or with conservative dogmatists, were men of serene temper. Some, however, found compelling radical implications in the new religious thought, and were seriously torn by the effort to maintain the special claims of Christianity in the face of such implications. The most important thinker of this sort was George Burman Foster, who taught philosophy of religion and theology at the University of Chicago from 1895 to 1918.

Foster was impressed by the accumulating evidence for the functional explanation of religious phenomena, the view that man's religions arise as responses to the successive and varying challenges of his environment. Such an interpretation helps one understand why men at each stage of evolution adopt the particular ideas or religious forms they do adopt. For Foster, however, it also raised the disturbing question whether any sort of objective reality lies behind the forms and symbols thus evolved. Ancient men required a Yahweh, and came to believe in one. But was Yahweh "there" or not?

Although Foster went through periods of skepticism about the objective reality of God, his first and last position was the one expressed in *The Finality of the Christian Religion* (1906) and in the article below. Modern man, he held, can give up the "Biblical-ecclesiastical God-idea" without giving up the "God-content." Though Yahweh departs, the real God is still there. The subjective or functional origin of a symbol, said Foster, cannot stand as proof that there is no reality behind the symbol; for nothing human can be valid "if the validity of our ideas is jeopardized by the subjectivity of their origin."

A vital portion of subsequent liberal religious thought consists, in effect, of a discussion between those who could accept the uneasy Idealism of this solution and certain humanists and philosophical Realists who could not accept it.

~ 13 ~
THE FUNCTION OF RELIGION
by George B. Foster

The old forms of *authoritatively* or *speculatively* vindicating the right of religious faith have become unusable, hearkening to a sacred tradition, many of the thoughts and commandments of which are in harsh contradiction to our science and our morality, and can no longer stand before the judgment seat of the scientific and the moral conscience. Can we now understand that religion is not a kind of reality that can be demonstrated by proofs which compel the assent of the intellect? As a matter of fact, the question of the "truth of religion," as former generations used the word truth, has died out of the consciousness of the modern man. The man of today must think of religion as a necessary creation of human nature and evaluate it from that point of view, or else be excused from further interest in the problems of God and freedom and immortality.

We raise a new question in our day. Does religion contribute to the rich and deep unfolding of the life of the human spirit? Does it render and has it ever rendered some functional service on account of which it has the same right to be that language, or art, or morality has? If so, why should there be a different mode of validation of the right of religion to a place in experience, from that of the right of these other servants of the higher life of man? Is not religion simply one of the modes by which the human effects inner and outer equilibration in its situation? Is not religion the psychological phenomenon of the soul's superior adaptation to the evil consequences of anticipatory forethought, and the warding off of those evils in the use of the means at its disposal? And has not man created and adored the gods who served him in those interests for which otherwise he found that he was unequal on account of his ignorance and his weakness? Take an illustration. One of the lowest

SOURCE: "The Function of Religion in Man's Struggle of Existence [*sic*]," *University of California Chronicle, 11* (1908), 69–81.

tribes in Ceylon knows no agriculture and uses no fire. At times its members seek the deepest forests and thickets where they dance their wild nocturnal dance around a huge arrow stuck in the ground. With rhythmic supplications and thanksgiving, finally with ecstasy, the dance goes on. There is no spirit, no god, in the arrow, but the arrow is the center of their existence, the cardinal means of their preservation. Around the arrow their whole meaning revolves. In every important hour, in sickness and in need, the arrow is worshiped. A power irradiates from the arrow in those nocturnal excitements which reconstructs their whole world. The arrow helps and will help. It triumphs over hostile nature. The very world exists in order to serve that arrow which man needs and by which all opposition is overcome. Now, there is a direct line of ascent throughout the long human story, from the ecstasy of those feathered folk and wild who have attained no real belief in spirits as yet, to the religion in spirit and in truth on the part of the noblest modern church. The arrow-thought and the God-thought fulfill the same function of equilibration, the unification of triumph and satisfaction and peace. To be sure, the kind of thing that satisfied human life there at the bottom, and that satisfies human life here at the top, is very different. The man of Ceylon adored his arrow because it brought him his dinner; the man of higher culture adores his God because his God brings him moral harmony and spiritual blessedness. At the bottom, religion was the conviction of the achievability through the arrow of satisfactions of a lower kind; but at the top religion is the conviction of the achievability through a cosmic God of universally valid satisfactions of the human personality. But each in its own way, each instigated by motives of human need, arrived at the notion of a reality through which it receives its satisfying portion. There are many interesting stages in this pilgrimage from the lower to the higher, and I must ask you to think for a moment of a crucial point or two. Generally the primitive man used not something like the arrow, but something like the human soul which he thought was in things as his god. And like men, these god-spirits were of two kinds: one kind was hostile, tricky, malicious; the other was friendly, helpful, kind; but because he knew from experience how to deal with men he was sure that he knew how to deal with his gods, whom he thought were like men. Hence he importuned his gods, or flattered them, or threatened them, or promised gifts or honor to them, prayer, vows, sacrifices—ever according to the circumstances are the means to be employed in accomplishing his end. Furthermore, it was noticeable that some persons were more skillful in securing the services of the gods than others. On this account, it would seem advisable to avail oneself of the good offices of such superior men. Such men of course became priests, through whose ability to predict, ignorance was dispelled; and through whose power of magic, weakness was made strength. The prophecy and the prayer of higher religion came about through a long development of prediction and magic from such humble beginnings. But the maintenance of faith in the gods required agreement with the experiences of the devotees. Did the prediction of the future agree with the course of things? Was the danger which menaced neutralized by the magic of which the priest was master? Then one had the clearest proof of the help of God, of the power of God, of the truth of faith. But perhaps the result of the prayer and of the offering disappointed expectations. What then? It was a bitter moment. Agony of doubt, a sense of ignorance from which there was no illumination, of a weakness for which there was no defense, must have terrorized the soul. And yet religion, like everything else, puts off dying as the last thing it will do. Adjustment and readjustment will be undertaken in the interests of self-preservation on this side of life as well as on all others. Perhaps the prayer was not importunate enough, perhaps the sacrifice was not offered in the right way, or at the right place. Jerusalem is the place where men ought to pray. Or it may be that the supplicant had offended God; then he will say to himself that he deserved the punishment of the Divine silence, for does God ever judge unrighteous judgment? Or, if the saint believes that in his integrity he can stand before God, even though God knows his most secret thoughts, perhaps he thinks that his God means to try him, to see whether his faith is firm and his piety strict. So his God withholds from him health and goods. Or, if there is no other way of adjustment, the saint learns to say that the ways of God are unsearchable and his judgments past finding out. Who has known the mind of the Lord? My God acts according to his own wisdom, he says, and it is my place to humble myself before him. Now and then the saint looks about him and sees that the godless and blasphemous are prosperous, while he himself is in adversity. This too is a grievous moment, and the adjustment of his religion thereto is one of the most difficult problems of his life; but faith finds a solution. The saint must suffer, not for his own sins, but for the sins of others. If he be bruised, it is for the iniquity of others, and with his stripes others are healed. Besides, what is the present life but a preparation for the afterlife? There must be an immortality, and there the saint will be rewarded for what he suffered here, and the wicked will be punished. If equilibration can not be effected here, let him not despair. Things will be evened up on the other side, even if it takes eternal life for the one, and eternal death for the other, to square accounts.

So the religious man keeps his religion amid prayers which are not answered and hopes that are not realized; amid the promises that are not fulfilled. It is a part of the pathos and the tragedy, of the pain and the disappointment of which life is so full. The desperate lengths to which the man of religion goes in effecting adjustments that his religion may live, is a greater evidence of the essential and inalienable humanness of religion than can possibly be found in an external authority or in a scientific demonstration.

There are two epochs of the adjustment of religion, necessary to the growth of religion, of which I must ask you to think quite specially. I have already said it was ever the habit of man to think that his god was like himself. So long as man cared primarily for the things that satisfied the body, he thought of his god from the same point of view. If the end of life among men was wine, women and song, the end of life among the gods was the same thing; but through the course of history a higher moral consciousness developed in stress and storm, in the fate of the human. Moral requirements which were infratribal came to be extended beyond tribal limits. Last of all, conduct came to be evaluated according to the disposition of the agent. But when men developed moral ideals in the human world they transferred these ideals to the god world also. Thus the moralization of the gods went on. Morals were first achieved by the human, then they were carried over into the divine. Just as there would have been no god of thunder had there been no experience of thunder, so there would have been no god of holiness, love, and faithfulness, had there been no man of holiness, love, and faithfulness. A deepening and inwardizing of the human was followed by the deepening and inwardizing of the Divine. A unifying of peoples resulted in a unifying of gods. Monohumanism must precede monotheism. If a man concludes that the ideal life is the real life, he will begin to appease the gods, not by meat offerings and lip-service, but by a pure heart, clean hands, and just behavior. It a man concludes that his supreme freedom is evinced and his supreme power exhibited in triumphing over his enemy by forgiving his enemy, he will arrive at the thought of a God who sends his rain upon the evil and the good and whose mercy endureth forever. If fatherliness becomes so great in the world of the human, it can not but be that God will be thought of as "our Father which art in Heaven." To be sure, while thus all our values are first human achievements and then transferred to the world of the divine, it is also true that the values once lodged there will react into the human in a way that will greatly aid in the idealizing and transfiguring of the human. Human fatherliness is transferred to the world of the gods, but on that account it reacts into the experience of our fatherhood here for its ennoblement and beauty.

But you observe that in all these processes, necessary to the growth of religion in its function of the preservation of man—the man growing larger and finer—there is at the same time that self-effectuation of religion, on account of which it is inadequate and unworthy to speak of it as that experience which is a mere means to other experiences. It is of the utmost importance to add that it is an experience which has a right to be on its own account as a part of the completion of the human organism. You remember that I said that what arises in the organism in the interests of its self-preservation, becomes itself necessary to the organism's self-completion and self-harmony. What is thus true, for example, of the eye in the body, or of judgment in the mind, is true of religion. Means though it is to the ends of the whole, it is itself an end to which the whole contributes, by which the whole is consummated. So I trust that you will not think that I am going out of my way when I add this word in my evaluation of the functional importance of religion. I do not wish to be guilty of the degradation of religion as one would be guilty of the degradation of anything by treating it as mere means to an end. We must think of this phenomenon as non-ancillary,

as autonomous, as self-glorious, just as we do of the beautiful form
and face of a woman, the penetration of the human intellect, the
moral discernment of the human conscience, or the heroic spirit of
the martyr—this religious feeling of the unfathomable deep of the
world, of the ideal-achieving capacity of existence, of the depend-
ableness and helpfulness of the order of which we are made so constantly aware. All this is to be taken into account as a part of the
human which is worth while for its own sake, and not as an instrument, simply, which will serve other ends.

Were not this true, our deepest need—the need of a fidelity in
things which we may trust, of a glory that we may adore, of an all
beautiful and all fair that may charm—would not be satisfied. So
you see that the very satisfactions which are achieved by the functions of religion can become our possession only in case that religion
be not means alone but end as well.

But in the formation of our religion, both as to its structure and
as to its function, the enlargement and change of our knowledge
has played a most serious part. The time was when the behavior of
things, inwardly and outwardly, was entirely dependent upon their
guidance by manlike beings on the outside. This was true for
reality, individually and collectively. But man gradually observed
that things were very far from being subjected to caprice and ar-
bitrariness. The observations of his own conduct pointed in a different direction. In an ever-widening region he came to know of
fixed rules which things obey, and through his knowledge of these
rules his own control of things was facilitated. By and by bold
pioneers of thought arose who declared that what was thus true in
the small region of experience was true without exception—true
not only for material processes, but for spiritual processes as well.
Once the character of the behavior of reality was thought to be
determined from without; now it is seen to be determined from
within. Once the law was supplied to reality from an alien source;
now it is a self-legislation of reality at which reflection has arrived.
Once changes, especially world-historical changes, were due to the
encroachments of an alien will; now reality is self-changing, self-
directing, and its order is punctured at no point with a view to
the correction or improvement of which new emergencies were in
need. Moreover, the force by which things were moved, was once

looked upon as external; now it is held to be internal. Again, to a former mode of thought, present existence was empty of value. It was a vale of tears, down which we walked that we might reach the bridge of sunset over into a better world and a better day. Time was vain and valueless; eternity alone was the home of the worthful. But a great change has taken place; values are here, whether they are hereafter or not; and they are here, not as a donation, from miraculous supernaturalism, but as an achievement of the human as we toil life's thorny fields. And eternity is not duration before time or after time or concurrent with time. Eternity is the persistence of our values amid the mutations and illusions of the temporal and changing. Like anything else that is true, our values have come to be; indeed, the only thing that has not come to be is coming-to-be itself, and the only thing that does not change is change—unless there was thought to be at the outset a fixed and finished and perfect plan of all that has taken place or shall take place. Now it is becoming increasingly clear that there has been not simply an evolution of reality in its content, but that there has also been an evolution of the plan of reality as well. As our human experiences are not perfect at the beginning of the human, so the plan of the whole, if there be a plan of the whole, was not perfect at the outset, but grows with the growth of those agencies by which it is realized. Meaning of fact and fact are not temporal sequences, so that one must be before the other. The most that we can claim is the logical priority of plan; and this plan, as I say, is not supplied from alien agencies to the processes and products of what is. It is rather immanent and constant and developing. In a word, the cosmos is self-originating, self-lawgiving, self-directing, self-judging, and, if it have an end, self-end. This is the modern view of the world. Now, is the ground cut from under religion by this view? Must we conclude that if Deity cannot arbitrarily encroach into things and into the hearts of men it cannot help them? Does it follow that if the insight be sustained that the formula God plus world is tantamount to the formula God plus God, we shall have to assume a cosmos, which, if unitary, is vain and valueless? I do not think so. Religion which in the past has been capable of so many adjustments, is now in process of readapting itself in the interests of its harmony with the new and larger knowledge. The values for which it cared may be in-

wardly achieved instead of outwardly donated. The structure and
function of the universe may be such that we can do on that account what was formerly supposed to have been done for us by a
particular God on the outside of the universe. After all what is our
theism but a sort of polytheism, but with the number of gods
reduced to but one? Would we cease to pray? Again, what right
have we to pray that events should transpire if at the same time
we are unwilling to assume the consequences which would follow
those events to the end of time. For what consequences of prayer
would we be willing to be responsible save our petitions for an
inner world of truth and beauty and goodness, for the holy and
eternal, for ourselves and for our kind? But such an inner world,
in the nature of the case, cannot be ours save as an achievement of
our own efficiency.

So the only prayer we have a moral right to pray is precisely the
prayer which after all we ourselves must help to answer. The function of prayer comes to be the filling of us with hope and confidence
and courage, so that we may do in our own strength what once men
so often idly entrusted to the gifts or to the activities of some god-
spirit apart from life. Again, there are the predictions of a past
religion. In our new world all that must be relegated to the
clairvoyant, astrologer, the card reader, perhaps the spiritualist; and
the real predictions on which life can depend become the task of
the man of science, but in a different sense than formerly. And as
to the magic of the old religion by which the forces of nature and
human nature were controlled and utilized, it is now clear that
modern techinque must take its place. By science and technique
men are conquering the powers that be and making them minis-
trant to the comfort and culture and career of the human. Magic
still survives in the sacraments of religion; but a growing science is
purging human consciousness; and as fast as this is done the moral
miracle of regeneration and sanctification which was once supposed to be effected by the sacraments will be compassed by the
slower and saner processes of growth and maturity—under the influence of the life of the family, of the school, and of society. The
power now supposed to be lodged in supernatural materialism will
be found in the inner development of the individual and of the
race; and the god of the old religion, whom modern science at first

expelled completely from the universe, allowing him no other function than the inactive contemplation of how it goes, has now been drawn completely within the universe, not as a free will, active and interactive within the cosmos, but as the meaning and value side of that whole whose fact side it is the business of science to understand. Now man is transferring the values for which he lives and for which he is willing to die—those values which it is the human vocation as such to achieve—not into an external deity to be static and stagnant there, but into the cosmic whole of which he himself is so small a part. He is not transferring those values as ready made and finished into the cosmic whole, even; he is finding out that he must be content and that he may be content with the conviction that the cosmic whole is such that these values are by him achievable.

Religion, as I say, from this point of view, is the conviction that the cosmic existence is such that man on that account is in essence an ideal-achieving being, and that the achievement of his ideals is possible. Is existence as a whole interpretable in terms of the human? Is the concern of the whole centrally and permanently the production of those kinds of values that satisfy the human? We do not know. There does not seem to be any way by which we can find out. We have no way of knowing whether existence is such as to achieve value save from the fact that values, as we count values, have been achieved. The race of man would never have known that water would quench thirst had not thirst been quenched by water as a fact of experience. What is water? Two parts hydrogen, one part oxygen, we say. But what is hydrogen and what is oxygen? So I push you back very quickly to a point where you do not know what water is; much less do you know what the cosmos in its allness is. We are shut up to ontological agnosticism. But religion can adjust itself to values; for what man needs most of all, is not a science of the essence of things, but a system of the values of things. The former he can never have; and the latter is a requirement of human personality, and for that requirement religion is still in position to furnish the basic satisfaction. Our world view is a world view, not of the unity of ontological essences, but of the harmony of values. There is the value of the connection system created by science. There is the beauty value, the morality value, the pleasure value.

Each has its right to be on its own account; but in our experience
they are in conflict one with another. It is only as each and all are
jointed into the larger unity of the holy and the eternal that man is
at rest. This basic unity of the satisfactions of the human will it
is the function of religion to achieve; and, so long as this is the
case, gods may come and gods may go, but religion will abide
forever. There were Martin Luther and Spinoza. Think of the religion of Luther, who threw his meal bag at the door and said to his
Lord God, "There it is; you know it is empty; you set me to running the Reformation, and you will have to attend to the meal
bags";—Martin Luther, who said to his Lord God that Melancthon
was sick, and it looked as if he was going to die, and that the
Reformation could not be run without Melancthon, and that if the
Lord God ever wanted his servant, Martin Luther, to pin his faith to
him again, he had better get Melancthon well;—Martin Luther, who
berated the devil in the Billingsgate of the peasants of his time, who
even threw his inkstand at the devil and hit, not the devil, but the
wall at the other side;—Martin Luther, who thought his individual
God apart from things! And think of Spinoza, who contemplated
the locked-up and legal and even purposeless system of things, and
did so with intellectual love resulting in inner repose! In his own
way each sought and found the same thing—that which is common to all religion—protection from the mysterious unknown and
from the menace of the overpowering. Each found rest for the restless heart. Each found that equilibration of the elements within and
of the powers without, which is at once the soul's supreme need and
achievement, because not simply are the values a creation of the
human, but the very unity of values is also such a creation, and costs
us toil no less than does science or art, or industry. Has religion,
then, an intellectual function? Yes; for the world view, of which I
have been speaking, while not a product of science but a conviction
of faith, is in part a fruit of the intellect. Has religion an emotional
function? Yes. It purifies and tempers the feelings, and the values
in which we are interested will be all the finer on this account.
Finally, has religion a volitional function? Still yes. For the world
of satisfactions, which the human personality requires, is no easy
gift to us, but must be earned by us. In sum, religion is the conviction of the achievability of universally valid satisfactions of the hu-

man personality. And the intellect must conceive the world to be such that the task is practicable; the feelings must report whether the human organism is healthfully at its work; and the will must ever press toward the mark of the prize of its high calling.

IV
COMPLICATIONS

THE "GREAT WAR" AND LIBERAL THEISM

The First World War came as a severe shock to religious thinkers who up to that time had been too complacent or too young to doubt the growing and proliferating liberal faith. "When the war started," Reinhold Niebuhr wrote later, "I was a young man trying to be an optimist without falling into sentimentality. When it ended and the full tragedy of its fratricides had been revealed, I had become a realist trying to save myself from cynicism."

But for many others the war was not this kind of watershed. Liberals who had practiced as well as preached receptivity to secular culture had been aware, well before 1914, of the questions about "moral evolution" raised by such impressive figures as Thomas Huxley. The philosophically-minded had found their monistic theism seriously challenged by the assaults of the Pragmatists.

For Dean W. W. Fenn of Harvard Divinity School, a prominent prewar spokesman of this self-critical liberalism, the shocks of 1914–1918 merely intensified long-standing doubts; and his Lowell Lecture of March 1918 placed the experience of war in this perspective. The lecture also spoke for most liberals in accepting the need for American participation in the conflict even as it emphasized the common burden of guilt for the war's occurrence.

∼ 14 ∼

WAR AND THE THOUGHT OF GOD
by William W. Fenn

In the course of an address made last June at the fiftieth anniversary of the Episcopal Theological School, it was suggested that perhaps the three divinity schools in Cambridge, working together, might signalize their present affiliation by contributing something towards the formulation of the changed thought of God which the present war seems to require. It was added that as a map of the heavens is not made by a single observatory but by many in conjunction, so the thought of Him who created these things, equally and indeed much more, demands the labor of many thinkers, each observing at his own angle and under his own limitations.

To these suggestions the present course of lectures is due. But it may be asked whether the presupposition is sound. Has the war made necessary any modification of our thought of God? And if so, why?

A few weeks ago, a clergyman settled hereabouts, when publicly asked whether the war called for any alteration in our idea of God, replied flippantly: "No more than the bumble bee's sting." It was too superficial an answer for so searching an inquiry; and the implied comparison between the vast suffering which the war has caused and the pain of a bumble bee's sting was, to say the least, infelicitous. Yet his meaning is plain. It was only a clever, rather sophomoric, way of saying that the war is but part of the great problem of evil which has always attended theism since it became unitary and moral. That indeed is true.

In the days of polytheism, there was no problem of evil. If misfortune befell a man, it was either because he had in some way offended a particular deity, by transgressing his will or withholding his due, or because the man was being used as a pawn in a battle

SOURCE: "War and the Thought of God," Lowell Institute Lecture, 1918, edited by Dan Huntington Fenn and W. R. Hutchison from typescript and notes in the W. W. Fenn Papers, Harvard University Archives.

royal among the heavenly kings. He might feel himself unjustly treated and reproach the god whose victim he was; but he did not therefore dream of denying that god's existence, for injustice was not then regarded as necessarily incompatible with deity.

But when an advance was made from polytheism to monotheism, and particularly when the one God was declared to be true and righteous altogether, then indeed evil became a problem. If God is an active factor in human affairs and is at once all good and all powerful, why does He permit injustice and cruelty? If He loves and cares for men, why does He not protect them from harm? If He is a kind and gracious Father, why does He allow His children to suffer? If, being righteous Himself, He is on the side of righteousness, why does wrong triumph even temporarily on the earth? Nay, why should it be here at all? So with every advance in the thought of God in the direction of unity and goodness the problem of evil becomes darker and more urgent.

Since such questions are no novelty in human thought, is it not ridiculous to suppose that this war presents peculiar difficulties, as if it were a wholly unprecedented fact? Why, the pages of human history are bloodstained from the beginning even until now! Yes, and even before man appeared nature was a scene of cruel conflict and pain, bitter both in itself and as focusing the grave problems of evil. No strange thing has happened unto us of this generation.

Quite true. Yet war as an actual attention-compelling fact has never until now been brought home to the minds of this generation. There have been wars—in South Africa, the Balkans and elsewhere —but they were so remote from our active interests as not to challenge sharply our religious beliefs. Nor have previous wars confronted precisely the thought of God which has been widely held during the past half-century, especially here in New England and especially among those who have felt most deeply the influence of Emerson.

This new thought of God, which arises out of idealistic philosophy, has been the subject of much and increasing rejoicing; it is supposed to be widely different from that previously held, and infinitely superior to it as well as far more satisfying. Well, it is just this new thought of God which now meets the old fact of war—

old indeed, but novel to the present generation—and we are compelled to recognize that between the idea of God which has been
theologically fashionable, and facts which the war has thrust upon
our horrified attention, there is an incompatibility which calls for
our most serious consideration.

What then was that thought of God, held by many of us, which
the war has made to appear almost ghastly in its unreality? Briefly
put, it was this: God is immanent in the evolving world, the very
life of its being; and history is the record of His progressive manifestation in determined forms of ever increasing worth. By virtue
of His indwelling presence, as creative principle, there has been increasing growth toward the production, maintenance and increase
of the highest human values, which in turn represent the central
inevitable urge of the universe. Hence the future is deemed perfectly secure, for God is at the heart of all, a gradually but uninter-
ruptedly and inevitably unfolding principle of truth, goodness, and
beauty. This is viewed as a divine universe wherein all parts are
perfect, each at its stage and in its season partaking in the perfection of the whole. So we were taught, and so many of us believed.

Many of us, not all: for there were some to whom such a thought
of God was far from convincing. When our religious teachers
boasted, not without reason, of this new, this larger thought of God,
there were grave misgivings. Of course it was not wholly new, for
the Stoics, not to mention others, had taught immanence. It was
certainly "larger." But sometimes it seemed too large. For certain
natural phenomena gave us pause. If God is literally and actively in
all, then He is in earthquake and flood as well as in smiling land-
scapes and waving trees; in the roar of the lion and the snarl of
the tiger, as well as in the song of the birds and in sweet human
voices. Was a bigger God also a better God? Was there not danger
of a demoralized God, when He was deemed present and active in
all the events of life?

There was also an uneasy feeling that under this new and poetic
God the Calvinism whose demise we were triumphantly chanting was
still with us in disguise. The voice was the voice of Emerson but the
hand the hand of John Calvin. To change the figure, we sometimes
suspected that the sweet strain so charming to our ears was a siren
song luring us into dangerous ways. And the suspicion was strength-

ened by the palpable fact that in addition to natural evil there was also moral evil; the disorders of human nature were even more disconcerting than earthquakes and volcanoes. Yet did not the new thought of God literally make light of human sin? By its advocates this was sometimes openly acknowledged and defended.

It was often confidently asserted that there had been quite too much talk about sin; that the word might advantageously disappear from our religious vocabulary, and "ignorance" or "disease" be substituted in its place. On one occasion a noble advocate of this way of thinking was asked, "Do you never do anything which, at the time, you know to be wrong?" To which inquiry, both pertinent and impertinent, the reply was, "Certainly not. Who does? How could any man be so foolish as to set himself against the vast movement of this universe?"

The answer was given with entire sincerity and, I am disposed to believe, with perfect truthfulness so far as the speaker himself was concerned. Knowing him rather well, I am quite prepared to believe that *he* never *does* do anything which at the time he believes to be wrong; but I know another man more intimately than I do him, and of that other man I can say with a certainty of personal knowledge, that he often falls short in this matter. Sin is truly in evidence in this world, and is not to be complacently dismissed as a necessary incident in the divine evolution. Our mortal nature protests, in one or another instance of sin's actual occurrence, that it is not "necessary"; nor can we permit any physical or moral determinism to obscure that fact of personal conviction. Furthermore, we simply cannot admit that men are mere functions of an all-moving will animating a perfect and all-embracing unity. We feel compelled to acknowledge individual initiative as well as responsibility, the two being different aspects of the same reality. God cannot be all in all: we feel that somehow we too are involved, as agents and not merely as automata.

There were many, therefore, to whom the Transcendental faith seemed fit for comfortable folk living in happy times. Before merely individual suffering and loss, it might maintain itself by a sort of social pressure, but if calamities multiplied they were sure to turn upon this faith with penetrating criticism. So long as the suffering individual was but a member of a social group living in fortunate circumstances, the group's faith might encourage his and enable him to conquer his doubts; but should the many be in grief, this support would fail and the doubts of the many would confirm the doubts of each. Precisely that is the present situation.

Now it must be confessed that here, as so often in the history of human thought, philosophy proved more sensitive to approaching changes than theology, which indeed by its very nature is more conservative in character. Some twenty-five years ago a new philosophical tendency appeared which took to itself the name of Pragmatism in this country, although in England the title Humanism was preferred. Among its representatives, here and abroad, there was considerable diversity as to positive doctrine; but all were at one in attacking the thought of the world which was the philosophical counterpart of the unitary idea of God. Against the block universe, the tight and trim unity of which had been preached by philosophy and theology and supported by "the indubitable results of science," James in America and Schiller in England brilliantly fulminated.

In my judgment their bolts found their mark and shattered it completely. Monistic absolutism got its philosophical *coup de grace*. There was a vigorous assertion of the rights of man, of the individual man, which again was in harmony with the spirit of democratic principles in politics and industry. You and I were not mere pieces in the cosmic game, phases and functions of a unified whole. We were, or at any rate we could be and ought to be, players in the game and not mere lookers-on. The progress of mankind was a living adventure, not a dead sure thing. We were charged with solemn responsibility as possessors of individual initiative and effectiveness. Every man of us was in duty bound to bear his part in the great conflict of the ages between good and evil. Philosophy took heed of the man in the street, endorsing his natural beliefs and standing up stoutly for his powers and prerogatives. Philosophy was democratized. If scientific tendencies seemed to favor a monistic absolutism, social movements were aligned with this pragmatic humanism.

In theological circles, the same tendency began to show itself in many indirect ways, particularly in a pressing of the ancient dilemma between the omnipotence and the benevolence of God. The fact of evil was again brought into the focus of attention. It is significant that in theological literature after the publication of Müller's *Doctrine of Sin* [1839] there was no thoroughgoing treatise on the subject until F. R. Tennant began to write, early in this century. Doubtless the revival of interest in the subject was due in some degree to a reaction against the rise and progress of Christian Science. But from whatever cause arising or by whatever influences aided, the fact is that there was a growing disposition to emphasize the reality of evil and in consequence to think of God in terms of becoming rather than of being. We began to employ dynamic instead of static categories, to hold that God Himself was making the best of things and of men, and to believe that it was up to man to join issue with God in the glorious enterprise. Things were not best as they were: God and man must labor together to make the best of them. God could not make Stradivarius' violins, much less the rich music from them, without Stradivarius and Paganini.

Accompanying this was a denial of the omnipotence of God as traditionally accepted. It was hinted that we must think of His power as limited: first, by His own wisdom and love; secondly, by the wills of independent human beings; and thirdly, although this point was less often made, by the material conditions in which His activity is exercised. Thus it was that both philosophy and theology, as if premonitory of what was coming, prepared the minds of thoughtful folk for the great change which the war has brought.

What was the cause of the war? Was God ultimately responsible for it, or to put it otherwise, was it the necessary and inevitable outcome of an existing situation? Was it His reply, as some have foolishly suggested, to the doctrine of evolution, or to the teachings of German theologians with respect to Biblical criticism? Of course that is arrant nonsense. But perhaps, others have urged, the war was inevitable in the circumstances. That is, given the intellectual development and political theories of Germany, it may be that the war simply had to come.

Theories doubtless played an important part by providing a congenial milieu. But even so it must be observed that they were theories accompanied and nourished by ambitions for world dominion, pride, power and greed of gain—all of which were reciprocally nourished by theories of nationalism. So we are carried back into the human mind with its folly, into the human mind with its sin. And more immediately, the world seems to be virtually agreed that direct responsibility for the war lies with men who willed and planned that it should be, and who craftily intrigued to carry out their infamous purpose. These men, bred to the trade of war, meditating continually upon its problems and confident of its methods, were eager to test their theories and try their weapons on actual battlefields. To be sure, no sooner had the war begun than other and deeper ideals came into conflict—cruelty against mercy, *Schrecklichkeit* against pity, honor against dishonor, and right against might and the like. But it must be said that in its origin and continuance the war has thrown into hideous relief the sin of man— sin not in its technical and theological sense but in its human significance and horror. So we have become keenly conscious of human sin as an act of the human will. The war has compelled us to a thought of God different from the one which blinked this awful and actual fact.

Just at this point, therefore, we must rephrase our thought of God. Put it how you will—as a function of the imperfection of man, or of his unwillingness to yield to the upward push of the universe, or in any way you please—the fact remains that man is responsible for the war. And when theology recognizes this, it puts itself in line with current philosophical tendencies. The notion of an unbroken unity of the universe, of its gradual but necessary evolution by an immanent principle of goodness, is inconsistent with the fact of a shattered, backward, staggering world. Man is a factor in human affairs.

Granted that there is in the world a deep undercurrent flowing steadily towards the highest human values, and that tradewinds blow in the same direction, we human beings are not chips on the surface, nor even sailing vessels. A modern steamship can make its way against wind and tide; and man, who is not inferior to that which he has made, can resist the urge of the universe. Temporarily at least, he can move against the current. In our thought of God, then, we must find room for the full recognition of man as an active participant in the evolutionary process, having power through his will to further or retard.

It must not be forgotten, however, that there are also verifiable facts to which the idealist's thought of God did appeal, and which are totally unaffected by the tragedy of war. Granted that the facts of evil have been forced into the forefront of our thinking and that upon them our minds are now focused, yet for that very reason the danger is that we shall now consider these as disproportionately as we have been wont to consider the opposite class of facts. Accurate perception, or at any rate true perspective, depends upon binocular vision. If we realize keenly the folly and sin of man which the war reveals, let us realize equally the superb exhibition which it is making of his noblest possibilities. Human ideals shine out more splendidly against the somber background. Of all the young men we know who are in this war, how many are in it for love of adventure or for any reason save a sense of obligation? Their easygoing, happy, comfortable lives have heard the silent whisper of duty—"Thou must"—and the response has been sad but unhesitating. If forced to confess that some men are worse than we had supposed, we also acknowledge proudly that others are nobler than we surmised. The apparent dead level of humanity is broken up, the valleys run deeper, the peaks rise higher than we had suspected.

We must remind ourselves, moreover, that other momentous facts which supported the prevailing idea of God remain unshaken. This is still a world of natural order. Not a single natural law has suspended operation because of the war. Laws established in quiet laboratories work also on the battlefield. Shells obey the mathematical laws of projectiles—else cannons could not be successfully aimed. Gases employed in Flanders act like the same gases in chemical laboratories—else they could not be used or guarded against. Nothing has occurred to affect the confidence with which we affirm that this is a world of natural law, transparent to the mind of man. On the contrary, this is even more firmly established than ever. Five years ago we were interested in anti-intellectualism as a tendency of thought. The war has made way against it. For the worth of the intellect has been confirmed by a war in which science has been invoked to an unprecedented degree and has vindicated itself by its achievements.

But, by the same token, the intellect has proved its inability, alone, to secure the well-being of man. In a Sunday school hymn written perhaps thirty years ago occurs the line, "Fair science will banish our doubts and our fears." How nonsensical that sounds today! Science employed by an evil will, knowledge controlled by malign purpose, only increases the misery of life. Human control of the forces of nature has enormously increased, but whether this vaster power shall be used for good or evil depends upon the character of the man who wields it. The world is indubitably a world of natural law, but whether it is also a world of moral law is a more difficult question.

To that question many would reply unhesitatingly in the negative. Nevertheless, there is a moral law in the world which it was the greatness of Jesus clearly to discern and effectively to teach—that love is life and hate is death—and this law the war has confirmed beyond a peradventure. It sounds in the roar of cannon and the rattle of musketry, in the yells of maddened men and the shrieks and groans of the wounded. This is a world in which there has been a process of evolution, according to the law and by means of resident forces, in the course of which the human has grown out of the animal, the civilized out of the savage. Sympathy, tenderness, self-sacrifice, love—all the higher human values—have emerged out of their precise and frightful opposites. That fact the war leaves precisely where it was. Indeed, as has just been said, these values are more conspicuous and commanding now in the drumming days of war than in the piping days of peace. When we permit our minds to dwell upon such facts as these, we feel even more irresistibly than before that they must be the manifestation of intelligent order. The world is not a scene of chaos. It is the residence of order. In some sense it is a world of unity.

In some sense, but in what sense? This takes us to the very crux of the problem. It seems to have been taken for granted by monism that any unity in which we can believe must be marked by the absence of contradictions. That is indeed the form unity assumes in the realm of thought. But life is deeper than thought, and it may well be that there is a unity of life more fundamental than the unity of logic. Perhaps, indeed, this was the powerful lesson which anti-intellectualism had to teach us. If ideas are secondary and the interests which they serve, the purposes which they embody, are primary, unity in terms of purpose is deeper than unity in terms of logic. And unity of purpose is, in fact, the sort of unity which we know most intimately and honor most highly. How often we are guilty of inconsistencies in conduct which actually are all consistent with some purpose which we have made the regent of our lives. Furthermore, this is a world of process, and plainly process has its unity in purpose.

Within unity of purpose contradictions are not excluded. On the contrary, the very concept of purpose implies the presence of contradictions, since if there were not something which is not now as we would have it, purpose would have absolutely no meaning or sphere of operations. Unity of purpose then, unlike unity of logic, finds room for contradictions. The result which purpose seeks to gain, moreover, must exist even now as a possibility in the world that actually is—else purpose would have no field of operations, no promise of result.

But purpose, unifying these contradictions and possibilities, can work effectively only in a world of law. Otherwise activity would be mere fumbling amid uncertainties, with no way of knowing, save empirically, whether one or another action would advance or retard the fulfillment of our aims.

·   ·   ·

When we consider from what unpromising beginnings the human qualities have grown, we cannot fail to be impressed with the might of the purpose lying behind this growth; and we can hardly resist the conviction that a power which has already done so much is capable of final fulfillment. We may tumble back towards the slime, but we cannot reach a point lower than that from which the purpose has brought us; and the power which has lifted us once is surely sufficient to do it again. Is not here a sufficient basis for religious faith and hope and endeavor?

As has previously been said, and let us repeat it more explicitly and emphatically, the new thought of God will be one in which the assertion of human freedom will be definitely and emphatically made. There is the gist of the whole matter. Not that there are unlimited possibilities present in any moment of decision. Experience testifies that such is not the case. So far as conscious recognition goes, the possibilities before us are not numerous; but the contention is that among the possibilities actually perceived there is freedom of determination. Into the philosophical difficulties involved in such an affirmation I cannot enter here, beyond saying that they do not seem to me sufficient to force a denial of the unequivocal testimony of conscious experience. This is a world of real purpose, and of real possibilities contained within the limits of that purpose and hence provided for within it. When moral alternatives appear, the choice of one will further, the choice of the other will retard the fulfillment of the purpose. Retard but not defeat it, for harmoniously with us or victoriously over us that purpose will move to its triumphant end.

DOUBTS ABOUT THE LIBERAL VIEW OF HUMAN NATURE

Though Fenn's concern for the "thought of God" and Foster's doubts about the objective existence of divine things would continue to represent leading issues, the complementary question of human goodness or perversity had the real future in American theological discussions. It was also the argument with a real past; for Americans, unlike Europeans, had always tended to find the center of theological discussion in the doctrine of man.

Willard L. Sperry, a Boston Congregational minister who was to become Fenn's successor at Harvard, wrote forcefully in 1921 of the need for "A Modern Doctrine of Original Sin." To the complaint of Fenn and others that liberals were not so squarely in the philosophical vanguard as they liked to think, Sperry added the awkward suggestion that perhaps the doctors of divinity were no longer the men best equipped to diagnose the human condition.

～ 15 ～

A MODERN DOCTRINE OF
ORIGINAL SIN
by Willard L. Sperry

As I walked through the wilderness of this world, I lighted on a certain place, where was a Den, and I laid me down in *that* place to sleep. And as I slept, I dreamed a Dream. I dreamed and behold *I saw a Man cloathed with rags, standing in a certain place, with his face from his own house, a Book in his hand, and a great Burden upon his back.* I looked and saw him open the Book and read therein; and as he read, he wept and trembled; and not being able longer to continue, he brake out with a lamentable cry, saying, *What shall I do. . . . I am undone by reason of a Burden that lieth hard upon me. . . . I care not what I meet if so be I can also meet deliverance from this Burden.*

SOURCE: *The Disciplines of Liberty: The Faith and Conduct of the Christian Freeman* (New Haven: Yale University Press, 1921), pp. 59–60, 66–73, 77–80.

159

There is no point at which modern liberal Protestantism stands in sharper contrast to historic Christianity as a whole than in its indifference to this initial mood of Christian experience. It does not matter where we turn, in what past century or to what type of record, the Christian life uniformly began, in the generations gone, as an effort to roll away the heavy burden of sin and guilt from the bowed shoulders of the human conscience.

The preaching ministry of Jesus opened with an unqualified command to repent. Jesus did not seek to create the sense of sin or even to explain it, he presupposed it. Christianity came to Paul as a great deliverance from the moral horror of a body of spiritual death to which he had been chained. It released him from his ghastly comradeship with ethical corruption. The classical world into which Christianity entered and in which its early conquests were made, was bowed down by the sense of sin. Neoplatonism and the mystery religions, the only significant extra-Christian movements of the first three centuries of our era, both appealed to the troubled conscience of paganism. Christianity competed with them and prevailed because it proffered a sounder healing for the hurt at the heart of the ancient world.

The mystics, of whom Saint Martin says, "They all come from the same country and speak the same language," are at one in their account of the rungs in the ladder of perfection. The first of these steps, following hard after the moment of the soul's conscious awakening, is that of purgation, self-discipline, the effort of the ardent conscience to roll from off its shoulders its heavy and weary weight of guilt.

For eighteen hundred years the dominant theology of all creeds and churches had, as its point of departure, its sting "that bids nor sit nor stand but go," this universal consciousness of inherent and original sin. However Paul, Augustine, Calvin and Edwards may have differed in theological detail they are all agreed in appealing primarily to the *malaise* of the human conscience. The comparative study of all religions, indeed, bears out William James's familiar statement that "The completest religions seem to be those in which the pessimistic elements are best developed. Buddhism, of course, and Christianity are the best known to us of these. They are essentially religions of deliverance." Tyrrell puts it in another way when he says that the Christian view of the world is an ultimate optimism, but that this optimism rests on a provisional pessimism. A religion which makes its initial appeal to the consciousness of original goodness, to moral self-complacency, would not have been recognized before 1850 as the Christian religion.

"The modern man," says Sir Oliver Lodge, "is not bothering about his sins. If he is good for anything he is up and doing." The conceiver of that premature birth which was known as the "New Theology" began his Pilgrim's Progess with a very different statement from that of John Bunyan's. He tells us that, although the average Christian still kneels in church and confesses Sunday by Sunday that he is a miserable sinner, he really does not mean it. If someone were to stop him on the street Monday morning and charge him with actually being a miserable sinner, he certainly would be very angry, would demand that the libelous critic specify in detail and then would probably institute legal proceedings for defamation of character!

•   •   •

The problem which faces the modern preacher who still has a message of salvation and redemption to preach to the world is to find the equivalent forms of the agonized conscience of Calvinism in the thought of our own time. Once we define the doctrine of original sin as an early and inadequate effort to express the sense of personal participation in the corporate moral liabilities of humanity as a whole, we begin to see our way ahead. We may candidly leave the items of private vice and virtue to one side altogether. They have nothing to do with the major problem, save as they are interesting casual manifestations of the moral situation as a whole.

The true successors to the Calvinist with his agonized conscience and his initial dogma of original sin are to be found today among the biologists, the psychologists, the novelists and the dramatists. It is very seldom that one hears in the modern pulpit any note approximating to that of the elder theology voicing its burden of human guilt. But one does not have to seek far in these other quarters before one realizes that one is still in the presence of the agonized human conscience and that although it now speaks a new dialect, its central consciousness is qualitatively unchanged.

Perhaps the most important and epoch-making utterance in the realm of biological science since Darwin's *Origin of Species* was Huxley's Romanes Lecture on *Evolution and Ethics,* given at Oxford in 1893. That is a full generation ago. But Huxley, as he well enough knew, in delivering that address, was before his time and he raised then what has since become the really important problem in connection with the whole biological reading of man's life in nature and society.

In that address Huxley turned state's evidence against the whole overhopeful ethical deductions drawn by Spencer and John Fiske and Henry Drummond from the theory of natural selection. Huxley came in that maturest moment of his thinking to the conclusion that the struggle for existence was immoral, or at the best nonmoral in its methods. His argument need not be reproduced in detail. Suffice to say that he took his stand as an ethical teacher against all the neopaganism of our day which would seek salvation by abandoning ourselves to the instincts which drive the cosmic process. The ape and the tiger served their part in the hot youth of the race. They have ceased to be an asset and have now become a liability. "The practice of what is ethically best—what we call goodness or virtue—involves a course of conduct which, in all respects, is opposed to that which leads to success in the cosmic struggle. It repudiates the gladiatorial theory of existence. Let us understand, once for all, that the ethical progress of society depends, not on imitating the cosmic struggle, still less in running away from it, but in combating it."

The significance of the Romanes Lecture for the religious thinker lies in the fact that it aligned Huxley with Calvinism, and that he knew it and was content to stand there. He himself caricatured his own lecture as "a very orthodox sermon on 'Satan the Prince of this World.' " In other words, he felt that the science of biology had revealed in some new and terrible way the moral liability of every child of man, a liability reaching back of the mythical Garden of Eden to the jungle where the saber-toothed tiger roamed at large, and where red ravin went its lawless way. And he felt the stirrings of the tiger in his own blood to be more real and ominous than any spell cast by Adam over the race.

"It is," he writes to a friend, "the superiority of the best theological teachers to the majority of their opponents that they substantially recognize the reality of things, however strange the forms in which they clothe their conceptions. The doctrines, of predestination, original sin, of the innate depravity of man and the evil fate of the greater part of the race, of the primacy of Satan in this world, of the essential vileness of matter, appear to me vastly nearer the truth than the liberal popular illusion that babies are all born good, that it is given to everybody to realize his ethical ideal if he will only try, that all partial evil is universal good and other optimistic figments which bid us believe that everything will come right at the last." Huxley's moral consciousness, as a biologist, was agonized, and his initial outlook on life was a provisional pessimism. He stands in the straight line of ethical succession from Edwards, Calvin, Augustine and Paul. He proffers no facile gospel of social salvation—he did not conceive that to be his task. His task was rather to find the facts and make men face the facts, and these facts he held to be such as compel in some form or other a doctrine of original sin. With the moral problem which he stated, modern science is still wrestling. But there is little or no tendency among sober scientists today to question the ethical presupposition which Huxley laid down.

Mr. Wells has more than once popularized the Romanes Lecture in his novels and semi-theological tracts. And he tells us quite candidly that this life force in the struggle for existence may not be deified—that it is in substance a sinister and ominous thing. "The forms in which this being clothes itself bear thorns and fangs and claws, are soaked with poison and bright with threats or allurements, prey slyly or openly on one another, hold their own for a little while, breed savagely and resentfully, and pass. . . ." So far have we come from John Fiske. And this advance of modern thought is nothing but a circling back to the old haunting obsession of a fundamental human liability, a burden of corporate racial guilt. Huxley and Wells and all such preach this old somber gospel of man's sinful nature with a conviction and terrible earnestness unsurpassed by any of the fathers. The language they use is the language of our own time, but their central message to our time is that of the elders to the earlier time, man is by nature a sinner and needs salvation.

The modern psychologist in his study of human instincts is also reverting to Calvinism. The best that he can say for our instincts is that they are the nonmoral sources of power in human nature. Of themselves they are no more good or bad than any other form of energy. Left to themselves uncontrolled and uncoordinated, they set up a civil warfare in our natures, disrupting and destroying the house of flesh and spirit they ought to energize. There is always potential moral evil in instincts not wrought into some central harmony by a good will. And it needs but a little remitting of the strong hand of the will to make this potential moral evil a present actuality.

One of our own American philosophers has just written of *Human Nature and Its Remaking*. The very title implies an initial unfavorable verdict upon human nature in the raw. For there is no moral necessity to remake that which is inherently and inevitably good in itself. Every idealism, says the writer, has its origin in some deprecatory judgment upon the primitive human stuff out of which character is to be fashioned. There is no escape for any idealist from his initial dictum that there is in this welter of human instinct some maladjustment, some chaos that needs saving and solving. The names which we give to the facts and to the remaking process he regards as irrelevant. But he insists that upon the facts themselves we shall agree. He will not suffer us to put away the doctrine of original sin as a childish theological nightmare. He even doubts whether this somber judgment upon the nature of man is primarily a product of theological speculation. He shrewdly suspects it to be an inevitable deduction from the life of humanity as a whole and insists that it has "a strong support in common experience." The modern psychologist is essentially a Calvinist when he surveys the chaos of human instinct.

But there marches beside this modern biological and psychological restatement of the doctrine of original sin a further expression of this same conviction which makes an even more direct and deeper appeal to the mind of today. That is the conception of man, not so much a sinner in nature, as a sinner through society. It is through the voice of the social conscience that Calvinism finds its most adequate expression in this present time.

The social conscience is by no means a discovery of the nineteenth and twentieth centuries. It is a fair question whether it has

ever been absent from simple Christian piety at its best. The rank
individualism of the Anglo-Saxon temperament, and of the ultra-
Protestant attitude suppressed it for generations in our English-
speaking world. But exact and entirely adequate statements of its
central position can be found all through Christian history. *Piers
Plowman* is nothing but a tract on the social conscience, written,
indeed, over six hundred years ago, but essentially true to the modern form. Behind the institution of voluntary poverty which inspired
most of the lay brotherhood movements of the two centuries before
the Reformation lay a sensitive social conscience. John Woolman's
Journal is nothing but a study in the agonized conscience of a single
sensitive individual following the social implications of his life to
their sources and their consequences. The thing is not new.

But the social conscience has come into a prominence in our own
time never so widely and deeply felt before, and its importance for
theology lies in the fact that it must now do major duty as the ve-
hicle for that strange sense of original sin which men seem always
to have felt in some form or other. What did the fathers mean, at
bottom, by their doctrine of original sin? Let Mr. Wells answer in
the person of Mr. Britling, who, learning to drive his new automobile, had all but killed a hapless cyclist, and thus soliloquizes:

This last folly was surely the worst. To charge through this patient
world with—how much did the car weigh? A ton certainly and perhaps
more—reckless of every risk. Not only to himself but to others. Once more
he saw the bent back of the endangered cyclist, and then through a long
instant he drove helplessly at the wall. . . .
Hell perhaps is only one such incident, indefinitely prolonged. . . .
Anything might have been there in front of him.
"Good God!" he cried, "if I had hit a child! I might have hit a
child." . . .
But this was not fair! He had hurt no child! . . .
It wasn't his merit that the child hadn't been there.
The child might have been there!
Mere luck.
If he had not crushed a child other people had. Such things happened.
Vicariously at any rate he had crushed many children. . . .
Why are children ever crushed?
And suddenly all the pain and destruction and remorse of all the ac-
cidents in the world descended upon Mr. Britling.
He became Man on the automobile of civilization crushing his thousands
daily in his headlong yet aimless career. . . .

This was a trick of Mr. Britling's mind. It had this tendency to spread outward from himself to generalised issues. Many minds are like that nowadays. He was not so completely individualized as people are supposed to be individualised—in our law, in our stories, in our moral judgments. He had a vicarious factor. He could slip from concentrated reproaches to the liveliest remorse for himself as the Automobilist in General, or for himself as England, or for himself as Man. From remorse for smashing his guest and his automobile he could pass, by what was for him the most imperceptible of transitions, to remorse for every accident that has ever happened through the error of an automobilist since automobiles began. All that long succession of blunderers became Mr. Britling. Or rather Mr. Britling became all that vast succession of blunderers.

It would be difficult to find in modern literature, theological or otherwise, a more entirely adequate account of what the sense of original sin actually is when stated in the terms of the moral consciousness of the twentieth century. Mr. Britling did prevent the night watches with these sober reflections. Sir Oliver Lodge to the contrary, he lay awake worrying about his Sin, not the concrete actuality, but the potentiality new with each day he took the wheel of his car, and wide as his vicarious sense of being the Automobilist-at-Large. That he missed the cyclist was a minor happy accident which in no way mitigated his daily social burden of "original sin."

If the modern novel strikes this penitential note of the agonized conscience, the modern drama strikes it even more effectively. No one who has ever read or seen Galsworthy's *Justice,* for example, is left without a sense of social guilt. Josiah Royce once said that when he met a wooden mind he felt "bitterly ashamed" that he lived in a world where truth could be made so dull and uninteresting. One closes the cover or leaves the theater after the last act of *Justice* bitterly ashamed that one lives in a world where such cruel injustices prevail. Galsworthy is essentially a Calvinist in the stuff of his agonized social conscience, and he preaches to the present age the doctrine of corporate social sin with tremendous effectiveness.

But in many ways the most effective modern spokesman for the elder theology is George Bernard Shaw. The play-going, play-reading world is divided into three parts. One part insists upon treating Shaw as a buffoon. Another part regards him as the high priest of a new religion. While a third part is always irritated and angered by Shaw. Neither of the first two reactions are what Shaw himself seeks for his work. He wishes to be taken seriously, indeed, but not solemnly. The laugh is always there and Shaw is too adroit a humorist to wish us to miss it. But what he is really trying to do is to wound the vanity and self-complacency of our modern world.

Bishop Creighton used to say that after we have gotten rid of the ape and the tiger we shall have to dispose of the donkey, "a much more intractable animal." Shaw is willing to leave the problem of the ape and the tiger to the keepers of the ethical zoo. His mission is to run down the donkey-at-large in us all. This stupid domestic brute is quite as much a moral problem as his companions of the jungle. Indeed, as modern society is organized, he is a good deal more of a problem.

．　　．　　．

If the Christian preacher fails to discern the reappearance of the old, persistent, agonized conscience of the human race, not in the now antiquated terms of the Pauline theology, but in these contemporary voices of modern science, fiction, drama and verse, he misses one of his signal opportunities to preach the central Christian doctrine of salvation.

The deeper ministry of the religions of salvation looks not so much to the deliverance of the individual sinner from his specific dilemmas as to the redemption of his whole human status. That is why Christianity never can subscribe to the monastic solution of the problem of evil. A religion which proffers me salvation but leaves my world unsaved can be no true religion for me today. I can only be saved in so far as I am saved in and with my race and age as a whole. And if it comes to the choice there are many passionately earnest men in the world today who would choose to go to hell with the majority rather than to heaven with the minority, simply because the sense of participation for better or for worse in the major lot of the race is our deepest source of spiritual satisfaction. In other words, the habitat of a moral minority cannot be heaven for us.

Meanwhile our religion which looks to nothing short of the redemption of the sinner's total human status in nature and in society can well afford to take up the intimations of "original sin" to be found in all these extra-ecclesiastical sources and carry them on to their fulfillment in the sincerely penitential spirit.

Shaw is a moral diagnostician, he is not a moral penitent in any characterically religious sense of the word. It is in John Woolman, in Tolstoi, that one finds the profoundly penitential note. The Psalmist and the Hebrew prophet are needed to make spiritually urgent the facts discovered by the biologist and the dramatist.

We have invoked in the past few years the prophetic ideal of righteousness as the granite foundation of human society. We have preached the Old Testament gospel of justice because it has been so hard to preach the New Testament gospel of love. Each of us in his own way has profited by the tonic of Hebraism. What the mind of Christ may have to say to the more bloodthirsty preaching from the vast majority of Christian pulpits over these latter years only time can tell. One is reminded of Hardy's remark that a century ago the churches of England substituted hatred of Napoleon for the love of God!

But even if we rest the case for the modern church during the War and postwar troubles primarily upon the Old rather than the New Covenant, it is still perfectly clear that we have fallen short of the total moral message of the Hebrew lawgiver and prophet. We have been willing to play Amos in our denunciation of the sins of the nations round. We have been very loath to follow Amos to an equally clear confession of our own sins. The immediate aims of the temporal kingdoms are not always best served by the penitential mood. That mood does not strengthen the hands of the men of war, or of big business, or of anarchic purpose. One still looks in vain, as one has looked through all these recent years, for any appreciable spirit of repentance. There has been international recrimination without stint, there has been mutual criticism between the classes. The truculent and abusive voice has gained its followers by the thousands while the profoundly prophetic summons to repentance has gathered only its handful. After all, Huxley, Tolstoi, Galsworthy, Shaw, are at the best voices crying in a moral wilderness. And though an increasing number of men admit the truth of their ethical indictment of the status of the average man, our age is still too inert and comfortable to let these known facts sting us into any moral action.

It is very hard to find on the present horizon any signs which indicate that the Kingdom of the Heavens is to dawn tomorrow.

Once more the apocalyptic hope of the imminent Kingdom is dispelled. Again Christ's Kingdom is as a man journeying into a far country. But if this Kingdom tarries, its tarrying is somehow bound up with the untroubled self-righteousness of the crowd. The voices of the politician, the class agitator, the maker of platforms and treaties are still strident with Pharisaism. There has not been over the past six years and there is not now a single official voice in Christendom which has begun to rise to the moral level that Lincoln reached in the Second Inaugural. That address is fitly called the greatest state paper of the nineteenth century. The twentieth century has produced nothing as yet, even out of the agony and bloody sweat of a Gethsemane fiercer than the Civil War, which approximates to the spiritual austerity of Lincoln's major utterances. That nobility of his rested, not so much upon his brief for the justice of God in history, as upon his appeal to the penitential temper in his own race and nation.

We need in the Christian pulpit today a full and candid use of all that modern science and modern literature have done to restate the doctrine of original sin in intelligible and credible terms, that we may press home to men their lost and needy state, their opportunity for repentance and their prospect of forgiveness and salvation. In no other way is there the slightest hope that the years immediately before us are to be in any real way more truly the days of the Son of Man than the years immediately behind us.

> The tumult and the shouting dies,
>   The captains and the kings depart.
> Still stands thine ancient sacrifice,
>   An humble and a contrite heart.

CONSERVATIVE COUNTERATTACK

Liberals quite naturally achieved greater visibility through external combat than through torturous self-questioning; the confrontations of the 1920's between Fundamentalists and Modernists are therefore the most widely-known episodes of the Liberal Era. On the Modernist side attention became fixed upon Harry Emerson Fosdick, a Baptist serving a New York Presbyterian congregation. Fosdick was by no means the most extreme of the liberals. But he was the most eloquent and probably the most widely known. Since 1915, moreover, as Jessup Professor of Practical Theology, he had been helping to infect the innocents at Union Seminary. The fact that he displayed an old-time evangelical spirit, and also indulged in public criticism of the liberal movement, simply confirmed, for the Fundamentalists, that the Devil could quote Scripture. All in all this man was an admirable target.

Fosdick intended his famous sermon, "Shall the Fundamentalists Win?" (1922) as "a plea for good will." But the plea was fashioned in Fosdick's usual direct language, and its national distribution led to a serious controversy that ended, nearly three years later, with Fosdick's resignation of his Presbyterian charge. "If ever a sermon failed to achieve its object," he wrote later, "mine did."

Though it perhaps missed the mark as a "plea for good will," the sermon, and the struggle that followed, had enormous effects in nerving the liberal defense. Fosdick's message and demeanor encouraged countless younger men whose adherence to Christianity depended, as it did for Fosdick himself, on the availability of a liberal option.

~ 16 ~

SHALL THE FUNDAMENTALISTS WIN?
by Harry Emerson Fosdick

This morning we are to think of the Fundamentalist controversy which threatens to divide the American churches, as though already they were not sufficiently split and riven. A scene, suggestive for our

SOURCE: *The Christian Work, 112* (June 10, 1922), 716–22.

thought, is depicted in the fifth chapter of the Book of the Acts, where the Jewish leaders hale before them Peter and other of the apostles because they had been preaching Jesus as the Messiah. Moreover, the Jewish leaders propose to slay them, when in opposition Gamaliel speaks: "Refrain from these men, and let them alone; for if this counsel or this work be of men, it will be overthrown; but if it is of God ye will not be able to overthrow them; lest haply ye be found even to be fighting against God."

One could easily let his imagination play over this scene and could wonder how history would have come out if Gamaliel's wise tolerance could have controlled the situation. For though the Jewish leaders seemed superficially to concur in Gamaliel's judgment, they nevertheless kept up their bitter antagonism and shut the Christians from the Synagogue. We know now that they were mistaken. Christianity, starting within Judaism, was not an innovation to be dreaded; it was the finest flowering out that Judaism ever had. When the Master looked back across his racial heritage and said, "I came not to destroy, but to fulfil," He perfectly described the situation. The Christian ideas of God, the Christian principles of life, the Christian hopes for the future, were all rooted in the Old Testament and grew out of it, and the Master himself, who called the Jewish temple his Father's house, rejoiced in the glorious heritage of His people's prophets. Only, He did believe in a living God. He did not think that God was dead, having finished His words and works with Malachi. He had not simply an historic, but a contemporary God, speaking now, working now, leading his people now from partial into fuller truth. Jesus believed in the progressiveness of revelation, and these Jewish leaders did not understand that. Was this new Gospel a real development which they might welcome or was it an enemy to be cast out? And they called it an enemy and excluded it. One does wonder what might have happened had Gamaliel's wise tolerance been in control.

We, however, face today a situation too similar and too urgent and too much in need of Gamaliel's attitude to spend any time making guesses at supposititious history. Already all of us must have heard about the people who call themselves the Fundamentalists. Their apparent intention is to drive out of the evangelical churches men and women of liberal opinions. I speak of them the more freely because there are no two denominations more affected by them than the Baptist and the Presbyterian. We should not identify the Fundamentalists with the conservatives. All Fundamentalists are conservatives, but not all conservatives are Fundamentalists. The best conservatives can often give lessons to the liberals in true liberality of spirit, but the Fundamentalist program is essentially illiberal and intolerant. The Fundamentalists see, and they see truly, that in this last generation there have been strange new movements in Christian thought. A great mass of new knowledge has come into man's possession: new knowledge about the physical universe, its origin, its forces, its laws; new knowledge about human history and in particular about the ways in which the ancient peoples used to think in matters of religion and the methods by which they phrased and explained their spiritual experiences; and new knowledge, also, about other religions and the strangely similar ways in which men's faiths and religious practices have developed everywhere. Now, there are multitudes of reverent Christians who have been unable to keep this new knowledge in one compartment of their minds and the Christian faith in another. They have been sure that all truth comes from the one God and is his revelation. Not, therefore, from irreverence or caprice or destructive zeal, but for the sake of intellectual and spiritual integrity, that they might really love their Lord their God, not only with all their heart and soul and strength, but with all their mind, they have been trying to see this new knowledge in terms of the Christian faith and to see the Christian faith in terms of this new knowledge. Doubtless they have made many mistakes. Doubtless there have been among them reckless radicals gifted with intellectual ingenuity but lacking spiritual depth. Yet the enterprise itself seems to them indispensable to the Christian Church. The new knowledge and the old faith cannot be left antagonistic or even disparate, as though a man on Saturday could use one set of regulative ideas for his life and on Sunday could change gear to another altogether. We must be able to think our modern life clear through in Christian terms, and to do that we also must be able to think our Christian faith clear through in modern terms.

There is nothing new about the situation. It has happened again and again in history, as, for example, when the stationary earth suddenly began to move and the universe that had been centered in this planet was centered in the sun around which the planets whirled. Whenever such a situation has arisen, there has been only one way out: the new knowledge and the old faith had to be blended in a new combination. Now, the people in this generation who are trying to do this are the liberals, and the Fundamentalists are out on a campaign to shut against them the doors of the Christian fellowship. Shall they be allowed to succeed?

It is interesting to note where the Fundamentalists are driving in their stakes to mark out the deadline of doctrine around the Church, across which no one is to pass except on terms of agreement. They insist that we must all believe in the historicity of certain special miracles, preeminently the virgin birth of our Lord; that we must believe in a special theory of inspiration—that the original documents of the Scripture, which of course we no longer possess, were inerrantly dictated to men a good deal as a man might dictate to a stenographer; that we must believe in a special theory of the atonement—that the blood of our Lord, shed in a substitutionary death, placates an alienated Deity and makes possible welcome for the returning sinner; and that we must believe in the second coming of our Lord upon the clouds of heaven to set up a millennium here, as the only way in which God can bring history to a worthy denouement. Such are some of the stakes which are being driven to mark a deadline of doctrine around the Church.

If a man is a genuine liberal, his primary protest is not against holding these opinions, although he may well protest against their being considered the fundamentals of Christianity. This is a free country and anybody has a right to hold these opinions or any others, if he is sincerely convinced of them. The question is, Has anybody a right to deny the Christian name to those who differ with him on such points and to shut against them the doors of the Christian fellowship? The Fundamentalists say that this must be done. In this country and on the foreign field they are trying to do it. They have actually endeavored to put on the statute books of a whole State binding laws against teaching modern biology. If they had their way, within the Church, they would set up in Protestantism a doctrinal tribunal more rigid than the Pope's. In such an hour, delicate and dangerous, when feelings are bound to run high, I plead this morning the cause of magnanimity and liberality and tolerance of spirit.

I would, if I could reach their ears, say to the Fundamentalists about the liberals what Gamaliel said to the Jews, "Refrain from these men, and let them alone: for if this counsel or this work be of men, it will be overthrown; but if it is of God ye will not be able to overthrow them; lest haply ye be found even to be fighting against God."

That we may be entirely candid and concrete and may not lose ourselves in any fog of generalities, let us this morning take two or three of these Fundamentalist items and see with reference to them what the situation is in the Christian churches. Too often we preachers have failed to talk frankly enough about the differences of opinion which exist among evangelical Christians, although everybody knows that they are there. Let us face this morning some of the differences of opinion with which somehow we must deal.

We may well begin with the vexed and mooted question of the virgin birth of our Lord. I know people in the Christian churches, ministers, missionaries, laymen, devoted lovers of the Lord and servants of the Gospel, who, alike as they are in their personal devotion to the Master, hold quite different points of view about a matter like the virgin birth. Here, for example, is one point of view: that the virgin birth is to be accepted as historical fact; it actually happened; there was no other way for a personality like the Master to come into this world except by a special biological miracle. That is one point of view, and many are the gracious and beautiful souls who hold it. But, side by side with them in the evangelical churches is a group of equally loyal and reverent people who would say that the virgin birth is not to be accepted as an historic fact. To believe in virgin birth as an explanation of great personality is one of the familiar ways in which the ancient world was accustomed to account for unusual superiority. Many people suppose that only once in history do we run across a record of supernatural birth. Upon the contrary, stories of miraculous generation are among the commonest traditions of antiquity. Especially is this true about the founders of great religions. According to the records of their faiths, Buddha and Zoroaster and Lao-Tsze and Mahavira were all supernaturally born. Moses, Confucius and Mohammed are the only great founders of religions in history to whom miraculous birth is not attributed. That is to say, when a personality arose so high that men adored him, the ancient world attributed his superiority to some special divine influence in his generation, and they commonly phrased their faith in terms of miraculous birth. So Pythagoras was called virgin born, and Plato, and Augustus Caesar, and many more. Knowing this, there are within the evangelical churches large groups of people whose opinion about our Lord's coming would run as follows: those first disciples adored Jesus—as we do; when they thought about his coming they were sure that he came specially from God—as we are; this adoration and conviction they associated with God's special influence and intention in His birth—as we do; but they phrased it in terms of a biological miracle that our modern minds cannot use. So far from thinking that they have given up anything vital in the New Testament's attitude toward Jesus, these Christians remember that the two men who contributed most to the Church's thought of the divine meaning of the Christ were Paul and John, who never even distantly allude to the virgin birth.

Here in the Christian churches are these two groups of people and the question which the Fundamentalists raise is this, Shall one of them throw the other out? Has intolerance any contribution to make to this situation? Will it persuade anybody of anything? Is not the Christian Church large enough to hold within her hospitable fellowship people who differ on points like this and agree to differ until the fuller truth be manifested? The Fundamentalists say not. They say that the liberals must go. Well, if the Fundamentalists should succeed, then out of the Christian Church would go some of the best Christian life and consecration of this generation— multitudes of men and women, devout and reverent Christians, who need the Church and whom the Church needs.

Consider another matter on which there is a sincere difference of opinion between evangelical Christians: the inspiration of the Bible. One point of view is that the original documents of the Scripture were inerrantly dictated by God to men. Whether we deal with the story of creation or the list of the dukes of Edom or the narratives of Solomon's reign or the Sermon on the Mount or the thirteenth chapter of First Corinthians, they all came in the same way, and they all came as no other book ever came. They were inerrantly dictated; everything there—scientific opinions, medical theories, historical judgments, as well as spiritual insight—is infallible. That is one idea of the Bible's inspiration. But side by side with those who hold it, lovers of the Book as much as they, are multitudes of people who never think about the Bible so. Indeed, that static and mechanical theory of inspiration seems to them a positive peril to the spiritual life. The Koran similarly has been regarded by Mohammedans as having been infallibly written in heaven before it came to earth. But the Koran enshrines the theological and ethical ideas of Arabia at the time when it was written. God an Oriental monarch, fatalistic submission to his will as man's chief duty, the use of force on unbelievers, polygamy, slavery—they are all in the Koran. The Koran was ahead of the day when it was written, but, petrified by an artificial idea of inspiration, it has become a millstone about the neck of Mohammedanism. When one turns from the Koran to the Bible, he finds this interesting situation. All of these ideas, which we dislike in the Koran, are somewhere in the Bible. Conceptions from which we now send missionaries to convert Mohammedans are to be found in the Book. There one can find God thought of as an Oriental monarch; there, too, are patriarchal polygamy and slave systems, and the use of force on unbelievers. Only in the Bible these elements are not final; they are always being superseded; revelation is progressive. The thought of God moves out from Oriental kingship to compassionate fatherhood; treatment of unbelievers moves out from the use of force to the appeals of love; polygamy gives way to monogamy; slavery, never explicitly condemned before the New Testament closes, is nevertheless being undermined by ideas that in the end, like dynamite, will blast its foundations to pieces. Repeatedly one runs on verses like this: "It was said to them of old time . . . but I say unto you;" "God, having of old time spoken unto the fathers in the prophets by divers portions and in divers manners, hath at the end of these days spoken unto us in His Son;" "The times of ignorance therefore God overlooked; but now He commandeth men that they should all everywhere repent;" and over the doorway of the New Testament into the Christian world stand the words of Jesus: "When He, the Spirit of Truth, is come, He shall guide you into all the truth." That is to say, finality in the Koran is behind; finality in the Bible is ahead. We have not reached it. We cannot yet compass all of it. God is leading us out toward it. There are multitudes of Christians, then, who think, and rejoice as they think, of the Bible as the record of the progressive unfolding of the character of God to His people from early primitive days until the great unveiling in Christ; to them the Book is more inspired and more inspiring than ever it was before; and to go back to a mechanical and static theory of inspiration would mean to them the loss of some of the most vital elements in their spiritual experience and in their appreciation of the Book.

Here in the Christian Church today are these two groups, and the question which the Fundamentalists have raised is this, Shall one of them drive the other out? Do we think the cause of Jesus Christ will be furthered by that? If He should walk through the ranks of this congregation this morning, can we imagine Him claiming as His own those who hold one idea of inspiration and sending from Him into outer darkness those who hold another? You cannot fit the Lord Christ into that Fundamentalist mold. The Church would better judge His judgment. For in the Middle West the Fundamentalists have had their way in some communities and a Christian minister tells us the consequences. He says that the educated people are looking for their religion outside the churches.

Consider another matter upon which there is a serious and sincere difference of opinion between evangelical Christians: the second coming of our Lord. The second coming was the early Christian phrasing of hope. No one in the ancient world had ever thought, as we do, of development, progress, gradual change, as God's way of working out His will in human life and institutions. They thought of human history as a series of ages succeeding one another with abrupt suddenness. The Greco-Roman world gave the names of metals to the ages—gold, silver, bronze, iron. The Hebrews had their ages, too—the original Paradise in which man began, the cursed world in which man now lives, the blessed Messianic Kingdom some day suddenly to appear on the clouds of heaven. It was the Hebrew way of expressing hope for the victory of God and righteousness. When the Christians came they took over that phrasing of expectancy and the New Testament is aglow with it. The preaching of the apostles thrills with the glad announcement, "Christ is coming!"

In the evangelical churches today there are differing views of this matter. One view is that Christ is literally coming, externally, on the clouds of heaven, to set up His Kingdom here. I never heard that teaching in my youth at all. It has always had a new resurrection when desperate circumstances came and man's only hope seemed to lie in divine intervention. It is not strange, then, that during these chaotic, catastrophic years there has been a fresh rebirth of this old phrasing of expectancy. "Christ is coming!" seems to many Christians the central message of the Gospel. In the strength of it some of them are doing great service for the world. But, unhappily, many so overemphasize it that they outdo anything the ancient Hebrews or the ancient Christians ever did. They sit still and do nothing and expect the world to grow worse and worse until He comes.

Side by side with these to whom the second coming is a literal expectation, another group exists in the evangelical churches. They, too, say, "Christ is coming!" They say it with all their hearts; but they are not thinking of an external arrival on the clouds. They have assimilated as part of the divine revelation the exhilarating insight which these recent generations have given to us, that development is God's way of working out His will. They see that the most desirable elements in human life have come through the method of development. Man's music has developed from the rythmic noise of beaten sticks until we have in melody and harmony possibilities once undreamed. Man's painting has developed from the crude outlines of the cavemen until in line and color we have achieved unforeseen results and possess latent beauty yet unfolded. Man's architecture has developed from the crude huts of primitive men until our cathedrals and business buildings reveal alike an incalculable advance and an unimaginable future. Development does seem to be the way in which God works. And these Christians, when they say that Christ is coming, mean that, slowly it may be, but surely, His will and principles will be worked out by God's grace in human life and institutions, until "He shall see of the travail of His soul and shall be satisfied."

These two groups exist in the Christian churches and the question raised by the Fundamentalists is, Shall one of them drive the other out? Will that get us anywhere? Multitudes of young men and women at this season of the year are graduating from our schools of learning, thousands of them Christians who may make us older ones ashamed by the sincerity of their devotion to God's will on earth. They are not thinking in ancient terms that leave ideas of progress out. They cannot think in those terms. There could be no greater tragedy than that the Fundamentalists should shut the door of the Christian fellowship against such.

I do not believe for one moment that the Fundamentalists are going to succeed. Nobody's intolerance can contribute anything to the solution of the situation which we have described. If, then, the Fundamentalists have no solution of the problem, where may we expect to find it? In two concluding comments let us consider our reply to that inquiry.

The first element that is necessary is a spirit of tolerance and Christian liberty. When will the world learn that intolerance solves no problems? This is not a lesson which the Fundamentalists alone need to learn; the liberals also need to learn it. Speaking, as I do, from the viewpoint of liberal opinions, let me say that if some young, fresh mind here this morning is holding new ideas, has fought his way through, it may be by intellectual and spiritual struggle, to novel positions, and is tempted to be intolerant about old opinions, offensively to condescend to those who hold them and to be harsh in judgment on them, he may well remember that people who held those old opinions have given the world some of the noblest character and the most rememberable service that it ever has been blessed with, and that we of the younger generation will prove our case best, not by controversial intolerance, but by producing, with our new opinions, something of the depth and strength, nobility and beauty of character that in other times were associated with other thoughts. It was a wise liberal, the most adventurous man of his day—Paul the Apostle—who said, "Knowledge puffeth up, but love buildeth up."

Nevertheless, it is true that just now the Fundamentalists are giving us one of the worst exhibitions of bitter intolerance that the churches of this country have ever seen. As one watches them and listens to them he remembers the remark of General Armstrong of Hampton Institute, "Cantankerousness is worse than heterodoxy." There are many opinions in the field of modern controversy concerning which I am not sure whether they are right or wrong, but there is one thing I am sure of: courtesy and kindliness and tolerance and humility and fairness are right. Opinions may be mistaken; love never is.

As I plead thus for an intellectually hospitable, tolerant, liberty-loving Church, I am, of course, thinking primarily about this new generation. We have boys and girls growing up in our homes and schools, and because we love them we may well wonder about the Church which will be waiting to receive them. Now, the worst kind of Church that can possibly be offered to the allegiance of the new generation is an intolerant Church. Ministers often bewail the fact that young people turn from religion to science for the regulative ideas of their lives. But this is easily explicable. Science treats a young man's mind as though it were really important. A scientist says to a young man, "Here is the universe challenging our investigation. Here are the truths which we have seen, so far. Come, study with us! See what we already have seen and then look further to see more, for science is an intellectual adventure for the truth." Can you imagine any man who is worth while turning from that call to the Church, if the Church seems to him to say, "Come, and we will feed you opinions from a spoon. No thinking is allowed here except such as brings you to certain specified, predetermined conclusions. These prescribed opinions we will give you in advance of your thinking; now think, but only so as to reach these results." My friends, nothing in all the world is so much worth thinking of as God, Christ, the Bible, sin and salvation, the divine purposes for humankind, life everlasting. But you cannot challenge the dedicated thinking of this generation to these sublime themes upon any such terms as are laid down by an intolerant Church.

The second element which is needed, if we are to reach a happy solution of this problem, is a clear insight into the main issues of modern Christianity and a sense of penitent shame that the Christian Church should be quarreling over little matters when the world is dying of great needs. If, during the war, when the nations were wrestling upon the very brink of hell and at times all seemed lost, you chanced to hear two men in an altercation about some minor matter of sectarian denominationalism, could you restrain your indignation? You said, "What can you do with folks like this who, in the face of colossal issues, play with the tiddledy-winks and peccadillos of religion?" So, now, when from the terrific questions of this generation one is called away by the noise of this Fundamentalist controversy, he thinks it almost unforgivable that men should tithe mint and anise and cummin, and quarrel over them, when the world is perishing for the lack of the weightier matters of the law, justice, and mercy, and faith. These last weeks, in the minister's confessional, I have heard stories from the depths of human lives where men and women were wrestling with the elemental problems of misery and sin—stories that put upon a man's heart a burden of vicarious sorrow, even though he does but listen to them. Here was real human need crying out after the living God revealed in Christ. Consider all the multitudes of men who so need God, and then think of Christian churches making of themselves a cockpit of controversy when there is not a single thing at stake in the controversy on which depends the salvation of human souls. That is the trouble with this whole business. So much of it does not matter! And there is one thing that does matter—more than anything else in all the world—that men in their personal lives and in their social relationships should know Jesus Christ.

Just a week ago I received a letter from a friend in Asia Minor. He says that they are killing the Armenians yet; that the Turkish deportations still are going on; that lately they crowded Christian men, women and children into a conventicle of worship and burned them together in the house where they had prayed to their Father and to ours. During the war, when it was good propaganda to stir up our bitter hatred against the enemy we heard of such atrocities, but not now! Two weeks ago Great Britain, shocked and stirred by what is going on in Armenia, did ask the Government of the United States to join her in investigating the atrocities and trying to help. Our government said that it was not any of our business at all. The present world situation smells to heaven! And now, in the presence of colossal problems, which must be solved in Christ's name and for Christ's sake, the Fundamentalists propose to drive out from the Christian churches all the consecrated souls who do not agree with their theory of inspiration. What immeasurable folly!

Well, they are not going to do it; certainly not in this vicinity. I do not even know in this congregation whether anybody has been tempted to be a Fundamentalist. Never in this church have I caught one accent of intolerance. God keep us always so and ever increasing areas of the Christian fellowship; intellectually hospitable, open-minded, liberty-loving, fair, tolerant, not with the tolerance of indifference, as though we did not care about the faith, but because always our major emphasis is upon the weightier matters of the law.

THE REALIST REVISION

The twenties brought constructive advance within liberalism as well as self-criticism and defense. The most creative, if not the most cheerful, revisions of the liberal outlook proclaimed what came to be called "religious realism." Realists extended the inquiries of George B. Foster and others whose work had cast doubt upon the philosophy undergirding liberalism. But unlike their humanist colleagues of the twenties, for many of whom the decay of Idealism implied radical skepticism, these men asserted almost fiercely that God is indeed real: God is the supreme Fact in a world of facts open to empirical investigation. While the exact sciences could never in themselves achieve the totality of vision needed for solving human problems, still, the realists claimed, scientific method could be used to test the ultimate propositions of religious knowledge.

Douglas C. Macintosh of Yale, who had chided his mentor Foster for continuing to wander "in the strange land of a subjective idealism," set the direction of the new realism, a year after Foster's death, with a volume on *Theology as an Empirical Science* (1919). Of equal or greater eventual importance to the movement was Henry Nelson Wieman, who had studied under Whitehead at Harvard and who taught at Chicago from 1929 to 1947. Wieman's empirical theism, setting forth a God who is "superhuman but not supernatural," was a gospel for the tough-minded, and it was the tough-minded, men heavily indebted to Wieman if not bound to his conclusions, who were shortly to inherit the theological kingdom.

~ 17 ~
RELIGION AND ILLUSION
by Henry N. Wieman

If religion has any peculiar way of salvation to offer it can be only because it brings to light certain facts of vital importance which would otherwise be ignored, or because it suggests better adaptation

SOURCE: *The Wrestle of Religion with Truth* (New York: The Macmillan Co., 1927), pp. 1–7. Footnotes omitted.

183

to facts. We believe that religion at its rare best does both of these and hence does offer a peculiar way of salvation; and that without it men are lost.

But for the most part religion has not done either of these two things. Most religion most of the time, both within Christendom and without, has blinded men to facts, has magnified illusion, and has hindered men from making adaptation to things as they are. We believe that nothing has so persistently and effectively blocked the way to salvation as religion, because nothing has done so much to confuse and darken the discernment of cold, hard facts. Next to religion, in this evil work, is art. And yet the concrete facts of most vital importance can never be discerned except by means of religion and art. Nothing can ruin human life so completely as that upon which it must depend for its greatest good. For this reason we pronounce religion the most horrible of all evils, and next to it art and science. But the hope of the race lies in religion. And art and science must be the indispensable collaborators of any saving religion.

Religion is cherished chiefly for the illusions it provides; and such religion is a deadly poison. When a man is in trouble he wants to think that things are not as they seem; and this religion of illusion provides him with a fairy realm where all is beautiful and happy. When he discerns the fact of his contemptible inferiority he wants to think that somehow, somewhere, by some supreme standard he is just as excellent as other men. He clings to the religion that enables him to cherish this illusion. When some method of procedure brings disaster because it is not adapted to the facts, it is easier to dream that God will bring all good things to pass in his wisdom and providence than to modify one's behavior in adaptation to the facts. Much popular religion consists of such a dream.

The popular way of depicting God runs something like this: We couldn't believe in a God who wasn't this and that. Then we proceed to portray God as an ideal being—ideal in the sense that he satisfies most completely the cherished dreams of the speaker. Manifestly this is mere myth-making. The actual God is a fact like a stone wall or a toothache. I can stand before a stone wall and say I refuse to believe in any stone wall unless it obediently opens up and lets me pass when I desire. But if I act on that belief I shall swiftly come to trouble. My dreams of what is most delightful and pleasing have no more to do with the making of God than they have to do with the making of the stone wall. The chances are that God in fact is very far from pleasing. There is too much in me of evil to find God very pleasing; I am not sufficiently divine myself. I may refuse to believe in such an unpleasing God; but God and the stone wall stand just the same.

The religion of illusion, this religion of sugar and spice and all things nice, must be fought as we fight the White Plague and the Black Death. It may serve to draw people into the church as the ice cream counter draws them into the drug store. But they will not stay to get the truth any more than the consumer of a "Lovers' Delight" will stay to buy castor oil. Insofar as the writer engages in any fight at all it is not against either fundamentalism or modernism as such, but it is against all religion of illusion wherever it may be found.

There is such a thing as a religion which seeks for fact at all costs. It cultivates doubt in order that beliefs may be questioned and corrected and thus the facts more clearly discerned. It does not doubt that there is fact. No one can doubt that. But everyone can and should doubt that we know precisely and completely what the fact is. It insists that facts are far more important than any cherished mistaken beliefs, no matter how unpleasant the facts and how delightful the beliefs. It insists that this is not a nice world and God is not a nice God. God is too awful and terrible, too destructive to our foolish little plans, to be nice. But God is a fact and this world is made up of facts; and if we are ever to live securely and magnificently in this world (or any other) it can only be through adaptation to these facts.

Religion is man's endeavor to adapt himself to the facts of existence. It differs from other such endeavors in that it seeks adaptation of the whole of life to ultimate facts. Professor Whitehead has made two very significant statements on this point. He has said: "Religion is the art and the theory of the internal life of man, so far as it depends on the man himself and on what is permanent in the nature of things. . . . It is the transition from God the void to God the enemy, and from God the enemy to God the companion." If we may be permitted to translate these two statements into our own thought we find them most illuminating of the method of religion.

As a person goes about he undergoes first this experience and then that, here something joyous, there something sad; one view of things comes to him here, another and different view possesses him there. Here someone he loves treats him cruelly and causes him bitter pain; there new friendship springs up, here an old hope dies and leaves an aching void. These diverse, confused and conflicting experiences constitute his reactions to many different situations. But all these conflicting reactions cannot dwell together peacefully in a single personality. And all these diverse situations, thus treated, cannot be put together into a total situation to which one can adapt his life.

One must pull himself together. These conflicting and confused reactions must be brought into some kind of unity. One must find some way of fitting these diverse situations together into a world to which it is possible to adapt oneself. One must get the hang of things. One must find some way of getting along. We do not refer primarily to the need of getting an intellectual grasp of things or to achieving a unified philosophic view. We refer to something much deeper. It is often more emotional than it is intellectual. It is the problem of how to organize one's reactions in such a way as to live without internal anguish or external disaster.

Anyone with a fair degree of sensitivity, anyone who has not become so callous and mechanical that he no longer feels the slings and darts of outrageous fortune and the seemingly impossible, because conflicting, demands which life makes upon him, any such person must occasionally feel the need of practicing "the art and theory of the internal life of man." That is to say, he feels the need of organizing his responses in such a way as to carry on. But to do that he must be able to detect some character underlying these diverse situations and conflicting demands and through adapting himself to it find some way of dealing with what is otherwise a baffling confusion.

When a man first experiences this sense of need, this sense of being wounded and buffeted in spirit, this sense of maladaptation and futility, God is the "void," to use Whitehead's phrase. He has not found that underlying character of events to which he can make adaptation and so achieve mastery. Some people, of course, may never experience this sense of need and of void, either because they live like the animals on so superficial a plane, or because they are so stupid and insensitive that they are quite blithely unaware of the maladaptations which characterize their conduct. They never detect the outrageous blunders they make and so have no sense of need. Others bear old wounds that never heal because they have not found the method of religion which cures such ill. Others go crazed and tortured to their graves, like Edgar Allan Poe.

The second stage, again to use Whitehead's phrase, is to find God the "enemy." When one begins to discover that underlying character, that hang of things, that deeper fact, to which he must adapt himself and in relation to which he must organize all his experiences, he must subject himself to discipline. It is more pleasant to dream than to adapt oneself to facts. At this initial stage facts appear like enemies. Here is the point where the ways part in matters of religion. Here is where some break away and cling to their illusions rather than face the facts. To those who cherish the religion of illusion, God is never the enemy; but to those who identify God with the ultimate factual character of events to which adaptation must be made, God may well appear as the enemy. He is that ultimate fact with which human life must struggle and to which it must adapt itself if it is to survive and flourish. He is that ultimate character of events with which the prophets have all struggled until they have found how to adapt themselves to it.

This brings us to the third stage, God the "companion." When a man has achieved the required adaptation to the ultimately determining character of events, this fact becomes the source of mastery and joy. He has solved the problem of how to live. He has discovered how to organize his reactions in such a way as to catch the lifting power of this determining character which underlies the events of life. The character of God now becomes a source of unfailing strength, a friend and companion. It gives him assurance for the future and mastery for the present. He has learned how to make adaptation to the most important and permanent facts. Other facts can be treated as they arise or even ignored if need be. One can let the waves crash over him if he has caught the drift of the ocean current.

This method of religion is like the method found in any problem-solving. There is first the sense of need and the void, because the essential facts have not been discovered. Then there is the discovery of these facts and the consequent necessity of casting away one's illusions, giving up what has been mistakenly prized as precious and accepting what may have been mistakenly esteemed as hateful. Finally there is the achieved reconstruction of habits and valuations in adaptation to these facts.

Religion differs from other problem-solving in that it has to do with the ultimate character of events, rather than with the more superficial facts which engage the mind in other walks of life; and it requires the organization of all one's experiences, the reconstruction of that totality of reactions, which makes up the whole personality, rather than some department of the personality.

It should be made very plain that the exact sciences are quite helpless when it comes to these more complex and profound problems of human adjustment. He who depends upon the sciences, taken severally or collectively, to guide him in the conduct of his life is suffering from a very sad illusion. What science will enable me to catch the deep meaning and the need of my friend as he stands there inarticulate and miserable, hoping against hope that I shall understand him and make the required adaptation? Friends do sometimes understand one another in such moments, but it is not science which informs them. We call it insight. As a matter of fact it is that ability to discern the subtle and complex needs of a human personality because of much association with humankind and with that personality in particular. But such association can give one insight only when one has constantly made experimental adjustments to others with constant sensitive observation to detect the consequences of his adjustments, and thus has gradually acquired the ability to "read human personality." But this is only one example of those many complex and profound problems of human living wherein science is of no avail. Religion is the name we give to problem-solving when it undertakes these most profound and complex problems of human life, not merely as intellectual problems (that is philosophy), but as vital problems in which the experiments by which solution is sought are experiments in living and the solution is a way of life that is actually lived.

THE NEO-ORTHODOX ATTACK

The editor of the *Christian Century*, reminiscing years later about shocks to his own liberalism, asserted that "Wieman was my Barth." Others remembered having their complacency shaken in the twenties by Miguel de Unamuno, or by the Baron von Hügel, or by William Inge, the "Gloomy Dean" of Canterbury. But the most common attitude of those who became "neo-orthodox" in the 1930's was that these earlier forays had been mere preludes to the great assault. After Phony War had come *Blitzkrieg*.

For a few, Barth was their Barth. The rest imbibed the so-called Crisis Theology from Emil Brunner, Paul Tillich, and such American interpreters as the brothers Niebuhr. Influences and forms of expression were so varied that many have questioned whether unifying terms such as "neo-orthodoxy" are appropriate. But the views held in common by the revisionists—moral realism, emphasis upon Divine transcendence, reliance upon Biblical revelation, the conviction that liberal theology was superannuated—did certainly add up to a movement. And this movement, in its return to important elements of orthodox supernaturalism, went well beyond what Wieman's realism could approve.

Walter Marshall Horton, a young liberal theologian at Union Seminary who later settled at Oberlin, had been recharting his own course in the 1920's in the direction of religious realism. When Crisis Theology made its entrance, Horton was able to convey the magnitude and excitement of the event and yet maintain his composure in dealing with it.

~ 18 ~

THE DECLINE OF LIBERALISM
by *Walter Marshall Horton*

No one who has kept in touch with the recent trend of religious thought and discussion can fail to be aware that something calam-

SOURCE: *Realistic Theology* (New York: Harper and Bros., 1934), pp. 1–10. Footnotes abridged.

itous has been happening to the type of theology known as "liberalism."

Fifteen years ago, at the close of the World War, liberalism was still self-confident and aggressive. Strong in the faith that all truth and all value belonged to a single harmonious system, of which the religious insights of the Bible and the guiding conceptions of modern science and philosophy were mutually consistent parts, liberal theologians were convinced that the great task of Christian thought was that of "restating" the Christian Gospel in terms "acceptable to the modern mind." When the fundamentalists took fright at some of the consequences of this attempt to reconcile Christ and Culture, the liberals denounced them as "obscurantists," clinging to "outmoded thought forms"; and when they were in turn denounced as "modernists," many of them accepted the terms of opprobrium as a badge of honor, correctly describing their conviction that it was possible to be at once thoroughly modern and thoroughly Christian.

Today, the self-assurance of the liberals seems to have melted away. Instead of pursuing the retreating hosts of "obscurantism," in the name of light and truth, they now stand beating their own breasts and lamenting their errors. Instead of repelling the harsh criticisms of the fundamentalists, they are now criticizing themselves, just as severely and ten times as destructively. A teacher in a well-known liberal seminary said to me recently that hardly a sermon had been preached or a lecture delivered within its walls for a year which did not at some point go out of its way to take a crack at liberalism—and that in spite of the fact that most of these sermons and lectures were thoroughly liberal in all their presuppositions! Professor John Bennett is right, I believe, when he says that "The most important fact about contemporary American theology is the disintegration of Liberalism." Disintegration is not too strong a word. The defeat of the liberals is becoming a rout. Harried by the fundamentalists on the right flank and the humanists on the left, their position has long been a difficult one; but it could be maintained as long as their own morale remained unimpaired. Now their morale has cracked, rebellion and desertion are rife within their ranks, and the greater part of their forces are ready to "flee when no man pursueth."

What has happened to destroy the self-confidence of the liberals?

That is not altogether easy to determine. Doubtless a part of the explanation is to be seen—as has just been suggested—in the difficult position into which they have fallen, between the conservative defenders of Christian tradition and the radical proponents of complete "experimentalism" in religion. So long as the liberals were permitted to make their own interpretation of the Christian Gospel —as, for example, in Harnack's famous lectures on "What is Christianity?"—and so long as they were permitted to draw their own conclusions from their "modern" methods and principles, they found little difficulty in harmonizing the two. When the more scholarly fundamentalists, such as Professor Machen, pointed out the real divergencies between the liberal Gospel and the New Testament Gospel, it was still possible to profess allegiance to the "abiding experiences" which underlay the outmoded "categories" of early Christianity, and rethink these experiences in modern terms. But when the humanists appeared upon the scene, with their Gospel of salvation by scientific research and cooperative effort, the dilemma of liberalism became acute. The humanists professed to be the real moderns, and it must be admitted that their position represented, in some respects, a logically consequent outworking of principles to which the liberals themselves had appealed in their critique of fundamentalism. If now they refused to carry out these principles to the bitter end, what reasons could they give for their refusal? Had they not sworn to "follow the truth, if it led them over Niagara"? Was it honorable or courageous of them to desert the truth and make for the shore, as soon as they felt the pull of the current and the roar of the Falls? Was there in fact any shore to which they could return, now that they had cut loose from churchly tradition and infallible revelation, and committed themselves to the outcome of free inquiry, whatever it might be?

These are embarrassing questions, and they are not imaginary ones. More than once, in recent years, I have had just such indignant questions put to me by earnest religious thinkers of the younger generation, whose hopes of a great new age for religion had been kindled by the prophetic trumpet blasts which came from the liberal camp a dozen years ago, but who now felt personally betrayed and cheated when the liberal movement refused to march on into the Promised Land of humanism. Dr. Fosdick—who for some reason is always selected to serve as sin-bearer for liberalism—appears to these young humanists as Wordsworth appeared to young Browning and Shelley after his defection from the principles of the French Revolution: as a "Lost Leader," deserting "to the rear and the slaves," from sheer failure of nerve, just when his blade was thought to be uplifted to strike the decisive blow for freedom.[1]

It is not hard to understand the disappointment and indignation of such impetuous minds when they see their erstwhile leaders beginning to draw back; and yet I venture to suggest that their bitter emotion springs from a superficial diagnosis of the reasons for the liberal recoil from humanism. Fear of the unknown may have influenced the rank and file, but what brought the liberal leaders to a halt before the spectacle of humanism was something more than fear. It was a sudden doubt as to the validity of some of their own guiding principles, which seemed to be finding in humanism a sort of systematic *reductio ad absurdum;* and this doubt was rooted in a sudden perception of the historical relativity of their whole undertaking. They now began to see that in their endeavor to "modernize" and "liberalize" Christianity they had brought it into a compromising alliance with the peculiar presuppositions, prejudices and illusions of a particular type of civilization (Western industrialism) and even of a particular section of society (the middle class). Since this particular type of civilization has begun to suffer a decline, and since this particular section of society has passed its apogee, the liberal theology has now fallen beneath the same sentence of doom which it so often pronounced upon older systems of theology: O irony of ironies, its "thought-forms" have become "outmoded"! The thoroughness with which liberalism did its work has been its own undoing; having completely assimilated the characteristic ideas of a particular era in history, it was foredoomed to perish with the passing of the era.

[1] As a matter of fact, Dr. Fosdick has been for years a severe critic of the liberal theology. It used to be his habit to prescribe to his homiletics class the writing of a sermon on "The Perils of Liberalism." In *Christianity and Progress,* he subjects the favorite liberal dogma, of progress, to a drastic overhauling; while in his recently published volume of sermons, *The Hope of the World* (1933), he exhibits what I should call distinctly "realistic" tendencies. See especially the Christmas sermon on "Beautiful Ideals and Brutal Facts," pp. 214–21.

It is no longer possible to doubt, in this year of our Lord 1934, that we are really standing, in the arresting phrase of Karl Barth, *"Zwischen den Zeiten"*—"between eras." So long as the postwar debauch of individualism and self-expression lasted, it was natural to hope that when we sobered down after our petulant fling, we might take up the tasks of civilization again at the point where the war interrupted us. Now that five years of economic stagnation and social distress have cleared our heads and sharpened our vision, we see plainly enough that we can never return, in any sense, to prewar "normalcy." We are sure now that neither the war, nor the emotional storm that followed it, nor the great economic depression that resulted from it was a mere episode. They were the first tremendous indications of a great turn in the stream of history, the beginnings of a new era to which as yet we have no chart or compass. The "First World War," as Laurence Stallings calls it, was only the curtain-raiser in this new drama. The Jazz Decade, with its fantastic mood of bitter bravado, was only a "Strange Interlude" with which our minds were temporarily distracted while the stage carpenters were hammering away, setting the scenery for the main performance which has just begun, and whose plot so far is hard to unravel.

If it is impossible to describe the new era in advance, it is at least possible to describe the era which is now at an end, and note the direction in which the line of change seems to be tending. It was an era of mounting faith in man's ability to control his own destiny through creative intelligence, and to make a heaven on earth with the aid of science and machinery. The material basis for this faith may be discerned in the steadily mounting prosperity of the Western industrial nations—unequally distributed, to be sure, and resting upon imperialistic exploitation of less fortunate peoples, but sufficiently widespread to give a kindly and hopeful outlook upon life to the great mass of the population in America and in Western Europe. If this "era of good feeling" was not so evidently a happy one for the dispossessed American Indians or King Leopold's black subjects in the Belgian Congo, or even for the "Hunkies" who worked in the steel mills of Pittsburgh, it was nevertheless obvious to the members of the great middle class, from which Protestant Christianity has been mainly recruited, that they lived in a highly rational and moral universe, where virtue and industry were sure to find their reward. In so far as they were conscious of any lack of equity in the distribution of privileges, they were sincerely desirous—up to a certain point—of doing something to redress the balance; and they gave out of their comfortable superfluity to an astonishing variety of charitable, humanitarian and missionary causes. Through education and the growth of "understanding" between nations, classes and races; through the extension of modern science, sanitation, and machinery to the backward peoples; through the gradual, peaceful, pervasive influence of the spirit of universal good will which they so honestly felt, they were sure that the benefits of Christian civilization could be communicated to all the world, within a measurable length of time, and without serious setbacks.

It was inevitable that the theology of this era, like its political credo, should be hopeful, idealistic, easy-going, world-affirming. In a time when "modern science" and "modern civilization" seemed to be going on from strength to strength, and from triumph to triumph, it was most natural that theology should address to the "modern mind" a plea for reconciliation and partnership; natural that it should find its chief task in keeping up with the rapid intellectual expansion of the era, and believe that all apparent incompatibilities between Christ and Culture should be resolved by the magic formula, "both . . . and." It is ungrateful to speak disparagingly about this type of religious thought, for we still talk and think, in the very act of condemning it, in words and phrases borrowed from the liberal dictionary. Liberal concepts are indeed, for many of us, our whole theological stock-in-trade, and we should be unwise to consign them to the dump-heap until we can get better ones. Yet it is very plain already that they are dead concepts—as dead as the shibboleths of the Gnostics and the Arians, though they have only just died and their flesh is still warm. They have not died as a result of any concerted, effective attack upon their validity, but simply as the result of a general change in the intellectual climate. Their truth and their value will outlive them, of course, as has occurred in the past with other outgrown theological ideas; but it must now be announced, as an accomplished fact, regrettable but duly certified, that their vital sap has departed from them.

The death of liberalism means that multitudes of sincere Christian men, clergy and laity alike, are plunged into a crisis of uncertainty. Liberalism was for many ministers, as Professor Bennett points out, a "coherent pattern of theological assumptions"—a "new orthodoxy," which gave self-confidence to their preaching, and without which they are left with a "feeling of theological homelessness." How some of these ministers now feel, may be inferred from a letter which I received in 1933 from a denominational secretary who had been devoting much of his time to conducting seminar discussions on the Christian preacher's message for today:

> Many of our men are at sea; [he writes] so much so in fact that too frequently the note of earnestness and conviction, not to say enthusiasm, is missing in pulpit utterances. For instance, one of the . . . men called me aside after one of the seminars and said that for the last two years he had repeatedly been impelled to call his people together after church and say to them that they were at liberty to get any good out of what he had been saying that they found it possible to receive, but that in honesty he wanted to tell them that he didn't believe it himself. This man was evidently sincere; he represents an extreme type, it is true, but I think our preachers do need, possibly above everything else, to get their feet on the ground theologically, or to leave the figure, to find a new sense of reality in the things they are preaching, or want to preach.

I venture to suggest that Christian preachers will not "get their feet on the ground" nor "find a new sense of reality in the things they are preaching" unless they can squarely face and clearly come to terms with the religious requirements of the new era which is upon us. So long as they attempt to address the men of today in the language of yesterday, their words will ring hollow, and they will not even believe their own message, much less inspire faith in their hearers. It therefore becomes the imperative present business of Christian thinkers to turn from the quiet of the library to survey the turbulent spectacle of contemporary affairs; to desert their scholarly preoccupations for the perilous role of prophecy; to seek somehow to unravel the plot of the new era in advance, as one deduces the outcome of a mystery story from the—often misleading—clues and hints thrown out in the first chapter.

V

RECONSTRUCTION

PARTLY-SOBER SECOND THOUGHTS

In 1939, the *Christian Century* asked thirty-five leading American churchmen to describe "How My Mind Has Changed in This Decade." The resulting series was a remarkable, if almost monotonous, testimony to the incursions of neo-orthodoxy among men who for the most part had been nurtured in liberalism. But a significant number characterized themselves, in Robert L. Calhoun's phrase, as "bandaged but unbowed." Halford Luccock of Yale, who admitted the weaknesses of liberalism, applied his characteristic mix of wit and critical high seriousness to the new theological consensus. Crisis Theology, he contended, was no answer as doctrine, and something worse than no answer when applied to social action.

~ 19 ~

WITH NO APOLOGIES TO BARTH
by *Halford E. Luccock*

The ghost of Mother Hubbard disturbs me deeply as I undertake to write on the pretentious subject of "How my mind has changed in ten years." I cannot forget the tragic anticlimax: "When she got there the cupboard was bare." When I take the alleged mind out of its ivory box and try to look at it objectively I discover

SOURCE: "With No Apologies to Barth," *The Christian Century*, 56 (August 9, 1939), 971–4.

that there has not been so much change as ten years ought to show. That is a humiliating confession to make under the fierce light that beats about a page of *The Christian Century.*

The report, in brief, must be that outside of sharing genuinely in what has been the major religious trend of the decade, the recovered emphasis on a God-centered faith, my central convictions concerning the social compulsions of the Christian faith are substantially the same as in 1929, but deepened and intensified by ten years of history. This leaves me out on a limb as an unrepentant liberal, a position badly exposed to the strong winds of crisis theology and apocalypticism. But up to date I am still hanging on.

Inevitably through all the discussions on this topic of ten years' change in thinking there must be one great similarity. The best which those writers whose papers are published toward the end of the series can aspire to is a sort of "variations on a theme." It involves no risk to say that in all the papers there will be a recording of sensitiveness to what amounts to a rediscovery of God in the theological thought of ten years. There has been a shift from a faith which was largely an appendage to the culture of its time, intellectual and economic, to a faith more solidly on its own feet, standing to confront the world with revelation. The typical Christian outlook of the 1920's shared, to a degree which can only be realized in retrospect, in the secularism of its day and environment, leaving out almost all but mundane factors.

The theme song of the 1920's, expertly harmonized with the dominant notes of the time, was, "At length there dawns a glorious day." When the mood was hortatory, the hymn was "Work for the night is coming." Preaching was marked by range rather than depth, by vigor rather than intensity, by color rather than light, by outside sheen rather than apostolic content. The prayer was rarely, "O God our help in ages past." Ten years of thought and experience have made for the recovery of a more definitely Christian faith. In the most thoughtful minds in the churches the dark eclipse of God by man is passing. The weird and distorting shadows which such an eclipse cast over the face of faith are lifting. In some degree at least, old words have become freshly meaningful: "I saw the Lord, high and lifted up."

The movement of religious thought in ten years might be expressed in two lines of a great hymn:

> When other helpers fail and comforts flee,
> O Thou who changest not, abide with me.

From the collapse of other reliances to which man has looked for salvation, but which he now knows to be houses built on sand, there has emerged into clearer visibility the essential reliance of the Christian religion, God. Indeed, allowing our imagination to gallop a bit, we may say that since 1929 we have been watching throughout the world a sort of secular Tenebrae service, of the kind held on Thursday of Holy Week. The service begins in light but gradually the lights on the altar and in the body of the church are dimmed, and the service ends in total darkness.

The world illumination in 1929 was not dazzling; but impressive candles of hope were burning. One by one they sputtered out. To many, the Munich pact was the snuffing of the last candle. Christian theology and the church are deeply indebted to all the various forces which have acted in bringing about the shift to a God-centered faith—to the disillusionment with contemporary civilization, to fear, to Barth and the whole range of continental theology. In looking over the ten years we can no more miss the impact of these forces on Christian thought than a historian can miss the Great War in the decade 1910–20, or than one traveling through Switzerland can miss the Alps.

It is not too much to say that at the beginning of the decade Protestant Christian theology was somewhat generally diluted to an ethic which was supposed to be in the process of realization with the same march time as the general march of progress. There was much talk about God, of course, and about sin, but it was not sharp enough to disturb the orderly parade to Zion. The emphasis on a God of judgment which is a theological commonplace today would have been complacently dismissed in many quarters ten years ago as an inevitable, but temporary, survival of fundamentalism. For ten years ago the slide to Avernus was just beginning. On October 29, 1929,

> The king was in his counting house
> Counting out his money.
> The queen was in the parlor
> Eating bread and honey.

Then the paper boy delivered the evening paper telling about a momentous stock slump. And they lived miserably ever after.

The foregoing three sentences contain a compressed history of the United States, and of a large part of the world, for the last ten years. Already in retrospect writers are searching for a descriptive adjective for the decade of the 1930's; the choice at present seems to lie between "the dismal decade" and "the doleful decade." The latter has its points, for it was the decade of the "dole." The jazz party of the 20's, paralleled by the optimistic trust in automatic progress, broke up; the sound of revelry by night was interrupted by the subterranean rumble of an earthquake. The elevator loaded with humanity, due to shoot upwards to some sixty-fifth story of a skyscraper of man's own construction, jammed at about the tenth floor and then dropped. In that drop it was not only General Motors and A. T. & T. and other similar hopes of salvation that were deflated, but faiths as well.

All this is a commonplace, and was one powerful force in bringing about the changed outlook in Christian thinking in which we all share. Indeed, there may be data here for some future Marxian philosopher to use in a thesis demonstrating the economic determination of theology. The economic system, following a war, is stalled; the flow of dividends is dammed; consequently theology follows the advice of Paul and turns "from these vain things to the living God." But the history is too deep and wide to be crowded into any merely economic explanation. It is part of the universal pattern of faith shaped by experience. In the religious view of the calamity as the judgment of God on sin, there has been the spiritual experience recorded in the 107th Psalm: "Their soul melted away because of trouble. They reel to and fro like a drunken man, and are at their wits' end. Then they cry unto the Lord in their trouble."

As has been frequently observed, in times of prosperity Christians tend to become Greek in their theology; in times of adversity they again become Hebrew. The movement from Greece to Judea has assumed the proportions of a great trek. Out of experience the emphasis has shifted from the immanence of God to his transcendence; from rationalism to revelation. The process might be put into old words, that "man's extremity is God's opportunity." There has been a compulsion to find other sources of salvation than those we have looked for in the ingenuities of a secular civilization.

Today words of purely secular hope have a musty flavor. They bring little more heartening than do embossed bonds in a company which has gone bankrupt. Witness Harry Elmer Barnes's recent words: "It is too much to believe that *homo sapiens* who has brought forth a Leonardo, a Shakespeare, a Beethoven, an Einstein will allow fanatical obscurantism to plunge him after a million years into the suffering darkness of the sub-man." But *is* it too much to believe? Especially if one reads the newspapers three days in succession? For the *sapiens* part of *homo* has gone under a bit of a cloud. *Homo* has a remarkable gift for making every one of his advances into one of the world's diseases. If all our hope is in *homo sapiens,* that is nothing to sing about. Any real hope must be found in that other music: "He shall reign forever and ever."

In this spiritual pilgrimage I have shared. Where I part company with some whom I have admired and to whom I am deeply indebted is that I cannot join heartily in the presently popular Hymn of Hate to liberalism. Let it be granted freely that "liberalism" is an India-rubber word, and has been stretched to cover many different things. And thereby hangs a good deal of the present theological and religious confusion. We need a new word to cover some of the permanent values which were denoted by the word. But no single word has emerged in answer to that need.

So many people who have adopted the new orthodoxy—call it what you will: Barthian in derivation, continental theology, transcendent as opposed to immanent—have not only repudiated the old home of liberalism, but have libeled it as they have gone out. A "liberal" has been defined as "a person who holds the right views but lacks the courage and single-mindedness to do anything about them." That type of liberalism has been weighed in the balance and found wanting. We have seen the futility of political liberalism, with its will-o'-the-wisp hopes from extension of the suffrage and its fear of change in the economic structure of society. Yet, represented by the word have been and are values which have been all too lightly thrown away, values essential to any Christianity with relevance to today's need and power in it. Many have gained a so-called religious "realism" and lost at the same time a social realism.

In many who have oriented their thought to Barth as to a new planet swung into their ken, God has been made so completely transcendent and far off that it does not make much difference to humanity on earth whether he is there or not. The transcendence of God is so emphasized that it effectively removes him from human life by lifting him so high above the human struggle for righteousness, justice and peace that he does not touch it. It is a strange paradox that the extreme exaltation of God may have the practical effect of atheism. In many who have accepted Barth uncritically the Christian's native hue of resolution is sicklied o'er with the pale cast of "wholly otherness." I cannot accept at all what seems the false alternative set up between "liberalism" and the acceptance of Christianity as the supernatural revelation of God through Christ.

The disparagement of reason which has such a central place in the thinking of many adherents of the new orthodoxy seems to me nothing less than trading a great religious birthright of a faith rooted in human experience for a mess of dialectic. The reiteration of the dogmatic, "This is the word of God," seems too much like Father Divine's counsel, "Relax the conscious intelligence." To me, the basic Christian apologetic is still the capacity of the fully developed personality as an instrument of the apprehension of reality, that is, of God. A "wholly other" God is no God for me. When everything "subjective" is eliminated, the only way in which God becomes real for me, through what I can experience as something akin and not "wholly other," has been eliminated.

This sort of theology quite begs the questions which to a large part of our generation are the very ones upon the table for discussion. To the question, "How do you know this is the word of God?" there is no answer but a booming insistence, "I know because I know." Dr. Harris Franklin Rall has expressed forcibly my personal feeling:

Just what is this Word of God, just where do we find it, and how can we know it? Barth is so afraid of humanism, so anxious to assert the transcendent and sole and absolute action of God, that he cannot give satisfactory answer to these questions. Man is not to judge the Word, only to accept it. On the human side, faith is just a "vacuum," an empty space, and when Barth sets forth the meaning of this Word, it becomes under his hand the traditional creeds, the Augustinian-Calvinistic system of theology in extreme form, with its absolute election and predestination, often too highly abstract and even speculative, with matters constantly settled in the old way by appeal to the letter of the Bible.

I feel most strongly the social inadequacy of this preoccupation with "classic" theology. Is it not fair to say that to a large extent our present economic system, which is the real challenge to the Christian religion today, was built up by people who believed in the classic theology, much the same thing that we are asked to accept as a new revelation? Writing about Barth's book, *Trouble and Promise in the Struggle of the Church in Germany,* Professor Burton Scott Easton asks a sharp question at this very point. "Perverse though its methods have been, nazism has really tried to do something for a distressed nation. Has Dr. Barth's insistence that religion moves in a realm above humanitarianism helped or hindered in winning respect for Christianity?"

More strongly than ten years ago I feel the urgency of the compulsions to attempt social and economic change which are in the Christian conception of God. The permanent values in the whole group of attitudes roughly called liberalism seem to me to be expressed with a timeless worth in Walter Rauschenbusch's little book, *Dare We Be Christians?* His contention there will never be "dated." Starting from the conviction that love is the central thing in Christianity, he argues that the task of Christians is to organize their whole life and the life of society upon the basis and by the power of love. This has been lost sight of by many who have been confused by a false syllogism after this order: "Superficial optimism is a bad thing. Many liberals were superficially optimistic. Therefore, liberalism was a bad thing."

The world is confronted today by a tragic "or else." We use the phrase frequently, usually in the form of a threat, "You do this, or else—" It is a divine phrase as well. Sounding out through the explosion of bombs and scores of bitter conflicts is the command: "Get your life organized on the endurable foundation of Christ—or else." As someone has convincingly put it, contemporary history is shouting, "Learn to live like brothers or you cannot live at all."

Here in the United States, for instance, we are hearing much talk about the need of "dramatizing democracy." It is a timely word. But the effective dramatization of democracy will never be made by learning to sing "The Star Spangled Banner" as well as the Nazis sing the Horst Wessel song, or by loud shouting about the glories of democracy. It will only be done by making democracy work as a foundation for broad human welfare. Unless democracy can carry through the social changes which will reduce unemployment on a large scale, all the paeans of praise will be futile. Germany and Italy turned to dictators under the pressure of unemployment, hunger, insecurity, frightful economic conditions. The same conditions in the United States will produce a similar result.

Some outlines of the future picture begin to come clear. Up to the present the United States has been able to deal at least partially with unemployment and the need for relief by borrowing against the future. That cannot go on forever. What then, little man? Taxation! That will be greeted by loud howls and savage opposition from the holding classes. The temptation to take the easy fascist solution of force and work camps will gather strength. Where will the church be in that struggle? There is a great danger that it will be on the side of reaction, that, blinded by middle class interests and prejudices, it will fail to see where the moral and spiritual compulsions lie. Democracy must be not only political but economic as well. It must go on from a half-hearted political democracy to a genuine social democracy.

Amid all the tocsins sounding for a war to save democracy again, my mind remains unimpressed. I still believe in the futility of war. In that respect there has been a tremendous change since twenty years ago; none since ten years ago. Just twenty years ago I committed—that is the right word for it, for it was a sin—a book with the title, *The Christian Crusade for World Democracy,* in which I showed that the World War was a logical and inescapable extension of the New Testament. It was used as a mission study textbook but, thank God, it has been long out of print. But I still keep a copy for my sins, and read occasionally the chapter which emits a trumpet call to load the guns for Jesus. We loaded the guns, but it is hard for me to see that it did very much for Jesus. Any argument that I have yet read in favor of having the United States go to war to throttle fascism appears to me to be just as specious and deluded as that vicious book of mine of twenty years ago. Consequently I am not moved by the shrill music of the fife and drum corps now tuning up on the theological right—and on the left. I still believe that the only way to avoid a "peace" treaty as bad as Versailles, or worse, is to avoid a war that inevitably leads to it.

There are no words hurled today by religious realists who are willing to go to war more loaded with contempt than the epithet "romantic optimists." Those words have become the ultimate anathema. Yet I fail to see any group in our present world more deserving of the name "romantic optimists" than the hard-headed realists who believe that through the means of another carnival of slaughter we can ever arrive at a Christian end. We tried it once. Are we never to learn from experience? And with whom are we to march off to God's Holy War? Are we to go over the top with Chamberlain and Bonnet, those valiant defenders of democracy, freshly crowned with the laurels of the betrayal of democracy in Czechoslovakia and Spain? If that is "realism," I'm a romantic! And there is no hope of my conversion to a more "practical" view.

One thing more. We are greatly concerned for the doctrinal authority of Christianity. But in this century the ethical failure of the churches has greatly weakened the doctrinal authority. More ethical failure in dealing with these social issues of livelihood and mass slaughter will weaken it still more.

PERSISTING SOCIAL IDEALISM

For Henry Adams in 1870, nothing had so discredited theories of moral evolution as America's "progress" from Washington to Grant. For the new realists of the 1930's, nothing so discredited liberal social strategies as the further "progress" from Grant to Hitler. As totalitarianism abroad widened into aggression, the neo-orthodox social critique came increasingly to be directed against pacifism, a principle to which the liberal community had made especially strong commitments during the twenties. In their pacifism, more than in any other area of social concern, liberals had trusted in the sufficiency of an ethic of love; and it was here, consequently, that events of the age appeared to do the most palpable damage.

After Pearl Harbor, defections from the creed of non-violence were enormous, not merely among the post-Versailles pacifists but even within the "historic peace churches." Among men of draft age in the Church of the Brethren and the Society of Friends, there were more combatants than conscientious objectors. Estimates from within the American Friends Service Committee put Quaker participation as high as eighty percent.

Religious leaders who continued to preach non-violence, either as a national or as a personal policy, varied greatly in their willingness to deal with the moral ambiguity of a stance that seemingly allowed madmen to murder whomever they pleased. D. Elton Trueblood, a Quaker leader then serving as Chaplain at Stanford University, did face this dilemma squarely. Responding in November, 1941, to an invitation from the interventionist *Christianity and Crisis,* Trueblood held tenaciously to that square foot of ground that had to be preserved for the irreducible rights of conscience. But he also went beyond this, consulting society's interest in terms that recalled the Emersonian defense of radical Transcendentalism. "It may not be without its advantage," Emerson had urged, "that we should now and then encounter rare and gifted men, to compare the points of our spiritual compass, and verify our bearings from superior chronometers." Trueblood suggested that the singular talents and sensitivities of the nonviolent would be indispensable in the struggle to prevent a third World War.

~ 20 ~
VOCATIONAL CHRISTIAN PACIFISM
by D. Elton Trueblood

It is fair to assume that every thoughtful Christian is trying desperately to know what position he should take in regard to the world crisis. This task is so difficult and so important that we need all the help we can get from one another in these dark days. Because I have been aided by the honest efforts of others, I am glad to accept the invitation of the editorial board of *Christianity and Crisis* to state my own position, a position to which I have come with intense effort and which I hold with humility. No doubt the chief reason for my being asked to contribute an article is the fact that, being a life-long Quaker, I have sought to approach various problems in the light of accumulated Quaker experience and insight. I am conscious, of course, that neither I nor anyone else can speak for the Society of Friends as a whole, but, at the same time, the position which now gives me a modicum of mental peace is by no means a merely individual one. It is rooted in our history.

The historic Quaker position in regard to war, first enunciated by George Fox in the middle of the seventeenth century, and quickly supported by others, is the rejection of all war as a way not open to the true Friend. Time and again Friends have refused to participate in wars, in spite of the moral issues sometimes at stake. For the most part, this has been done, not as a blind adherence to a tradition nor a slavish obedience to the letter of Scripture, but as a moral insight rooted in religious experience. Friends have felt that they were called to a type of life which is incompatible with all carnal warfare.

Now the modern man who has learned to appreciate this tradition, knowing how often the early Friends were right in their fundamental insights, has a great reluctance to depart from their

SOURCE: *Christianity and Crisis, 1* (November 3, 1941), 2–5. Reprinted by permission of the author.

precepts and example. Part of this reluctance comes from the conviction that the pacifist position, so well formulated in the seventeenth century, represents a faithful adherence to the teaching of Christ. Even if the rationality of such a course is not entirely clear, the thoughtful person will be very slow to abandon it, for fear something precious might be lost. But in the present world crisis the position is peculiarly hard to maintain, so hard, indeed, that many sincere pacifists find it impossible to arrive at a satisfactory solution of their problem.

It is important to show why the historic Christian pacifist position is hard to maintain, since great misunderstanding is possible at this point. *It is not hard because of persecution.* In fact, quite the contrary is true. Part of the misgiving felt by the sincere Christian pacifist arises from the double fact that pacifists and Quakers are immensely popular in our present society, whereas the Christian interventionist is an object of continuous abuse. Some few Friends, indeed, still talk about taking up their cross and doing the hard thing in spite of public censure, but this is almost wholly vestigial, with little reference to the current situation. The interventionist, on the other hand, is denounced as a traitor, a turncoat, one who cannot abide the rigors of the Christian position. This kind of persecution has little to do with numbers, since it is the good opinion of his fellow Christians which a Christian leader naturally most covets.

This alteration in the pattern of persecution gives the pacifist pause, for he knows how often the one who is called the coward is really the brave man. The misgiving which he feels is increased by consideration of the kind of people he appears to oppose if he remains true to his historic position. As between isolationists and interventionists, he finds that almost all his sympathies are with the latter. The pacifist is sobered when he reads the list of names of those sponsoring *Christianity and Crisis;* these are the men with whom he has worked shoulder to shoulder for idealistic causes; these are the men whose moral judgment he has had reason to trust in other areas. On the other hand, he is revolted by the narrow nationalism and incipient fascism of the isolationists. He is likewise embarrassed by the admiration of these people. The Christian pacifist is always an internationalist; *his reasons for rejection of war are not geographical.*

The fundamental difficulty which the contemporary pacifist faces is not the fear of persecution, but the fear of being wrong. What if, with the best of motives, and the best of backgrounds, we should be found to be working against the light? There is no doubt that the Nazis have considered the pacifist movements of England and America as factors favorable to themselves. The pacifist, if he is really honest, must often put to himself the following question: What if all people who cherish the free way of life should refuse, as I refuse, to participate in war? Would not the Nazis overrun Great Britain tomorrow and America next week? Would there not be fastened on the world, as by a strange hold, the will of a self-perpetuating group of men who believe fanatically that they represent a master race? These men would have such full control of technical instruments as to make successful revolt impossible. The kind of life we cherish, of which the generous recognition of conscientious objection to war is one item, would be utterly destroyed. All this might not happen, but humanly speaking, there seems nothing to prevent it. Much as they hate war and reject the war method, most pacifists are honest enough to admit that it is only the British armed forces that have kept such a wave of destruction from spreading beyond the borders of continental Europe. Apart from the British army, navy and air force, the Gestapo would now rule unchecked in the British Isles, the ancient universities would be closed, the German refugees would be returned to the hell of continental concentration camps, and London would be a larger Prague.

This can be put another way by saying that the pacifist, if he is frank, knows as well as anyone else that *it makes a difference who wins*. It may make a difference, as Hitler has so truly said, for a thousand years. The Christian pacifist can hardly be so blind as to fail to see that there are genuine moral distinctions in the present upheaval. This is still true no matter how greatly we stress the iniquity of the Treaty of Versailles and no matter how carefully we point out the sins of democratic countries. Moral distinctions are not eliminated by the fact that no side is perfect. The person who maintains the pretense of neutrality is either naive, dishonest or morally undeveloped.

The issue is further complicated by the fact that the present struggle is really not a war at all. Those who love to speak of it as a "foreign war" are incorrect not only in their adjective, but also in their noun. The old-fashioned "war" now seems a relatively decent affair, an affair in which most of those killed were in the army and in which psychological warfare was not the dominant phase. We are now in the midst of a revolution produced by a combination of forces, ideological, psychological and technological, which have given us a new problem. Since the combination of forces never existed before, the present situation has no true counterpart in history.

It is the new methods of aggression which make the adjective "foreign" inept and the noun "war" equivocal. Inasmuch as the chief method is the psychological one of the creation of the impression of invincibility, thus making actual use of physical coercion unnecessary, it is clear that America is already in the struggle, though no nation has declared war on us and no alien soldiers have landed on the New Jersey beaches. The struggle for American public opinion is probably the most important single current operation, from the aggressor's point of view, and the aggressor is greatly aided by those Americans who argue for non-participation on the ground of Nazi invincibility. Their reason for objecting to war is so different from the Christian pacifist objection that the two hardly belong to the same universe of discourse.

Considerations such as those just mentioned cannot but fill the soul of the Christian pacifist with perplexity. Anyone who is not perplexed is merely simple minded. There is no easy answer; there are competing strains; there is a necessary agony of spirit. The person who has no agony of spirit, no doubts about the rightness of his own position, has not begun to understand the nature of the issues involved. This holds true for militarist and pacifist alike. *But there is a grace of perplexity.* There is spiritual gain in a frank recognition of complexity in the moral order, and the fruit of this recognition is intellectual humility.

The problem we face is the problem of aggression, a problem which once seemed academic, but is so no longer. Whether we are of draft age or not we cannot avoid making up our minds on this question: What should the citizens of a nation do which finds itself attacked? Since by attack is meant the effort to destroy a nation's way of life, whether this is done at long range or short range makes no essential difference. To be specific, we may take China's struggle as an example.

China is faced by an aggressive foe with little or no moral scruples: What should the nation do? There are three ways in which the aggression can be faced. First, the nation can follow a pacifist technique of disciplined love and active good will. Second, it can do nothing, and consequently submit to the will of the aggressor. Third, it can fight the aggressor to the limit of its powers.

Of these three ways, only the second is reasonably certain as to outcome. It means degradation both physical and spiritual. The first and the third are ventures which may succeed and may fail, the main contingent factors being the degree of preparation in each case and the strength of ruthlessness of the invader. There is no insurance in these matters, and the success of one way is not indicated by pointing to the failure of the other. Of all three ways, the first is probably the ideal best. It might fail, just as military defense sometimes fails, but in the long run it must be the way of overcoming evil, *overcoming* and not merely *hindering*. But, though this is the ideal best, no modern nation is in any degree prepared to follow it. No nation and no considerable group within a nation has the requisite discipline even to begin such an enterprise. Therefore to ask a modern nation, made up of millions of people who do not even make any pretense of loyalty to the Christian ethic to adopt this policy is fatuous in the extreme.

Since a modern national state does not have the requisite discipline or faith for the pacifist way of meeting an invader, only two ways are left: to do nothing or to use military measures. Between these it is easy to choose, since the negative way means certain degradation and the military way means possible salvage of something precious, providing the external danger can be eliminated without introducing equal or similar internal dangers. There was a time when many of us argued that war, meaning military resistance, was worse than any possible alternative. There are few who argue that way now. The world has before it numerous striking object lessons of a condition worse than any war we have ever known. When the unobstructed invader proceeds to take over all the means of communication and of education, so that even the children of the invaded country can be taught to oppose and despise their parents, when the presence of secret agents produces constant fear of reprisals against one's loved ones, what is there about war that could be worse? The greatest evil of war is not the actual physical death, but the poisoning of spirits. The peace of the prison-house has all of this poisoning, without the hope of release. Thus, it follows, that there are situations in which a Christian, no matter how much of a pacifist he may be personally, cannot honestly escape the conclusion that it is better for the nation, *as a nation, and not a Christian society,* to try to defend itself by the means it possesses rather than by the means it does not possess.

The task of a nation and the task of a Christian individual or a Christian society may, however, be vastly different. While the nation may be in a position where it has no real alternative except to fight, the individual Christian or the separated group may be ethically and spiritually required to follow another way. But the point is that the separated group can follow another way without denouncing the government for failure to follow it also. Here is where the long pacifist experience of the Society of Friends can be of great value to the general pacifist movement of today. It is instructive to note that the two most distinguished of the intellectual leaders of early Quakerism found a working solution of the pacifist problem which was already implicit in the teaching of George Fox. These were Isaac Penington and Robert Barclay. These devout and scholarly men, who have, more than any others, set the standard of Quakerism, so far as intellectual formulation is concerned, stressed the great difference which exists between a "mixed" company and special company of Christians called to uphold a special position. The pacifism which Penington and Barclay, as well as many later Quakers, represent is *vocational* pacifism, which holds that there are situations in which it is right for the state to defend itself by arms, but it is not right for some members of the state to share in this enterprise.

To many people it seems that there is something inconsistent about the position which the vocational pacifist maintains. The question turns largely on what is needed in our society, if we are concerned with both the long view and the short view. In modern England it is undoubtedly necessary that a great many persons should give their services to make possible the actual defense of the approaches to the island. But it is also necessary that there should be some who, even in the midst of strife and terror, keep alive a different conception of how the world may be ordered. The pacifist who keeps alive this different conception is contributing to the future welfare of his people by providing a balance to the extremes of hatred which arise, and by holding aloft the principles of ultimate peace which might otherwise be forgotten. He is keeping a humble fire burning, to light the new fires which must burn again after the storm is over. If he understands his position rightly he accords his government the same courtesies which he expects. That is, the government grants him a measure of recognition of his conscientious objection and he, in his turn, does not try to embarrass the government. It is for this reason that some of the recognized leaders of English Quakerdom have refused to sign a petition asking the government to sue for peace now. As one of the younger Friends has put it, we are not merely concerned with overcoming *this* war, but with overcoming *war*. To sue for peace now might jeopardize the success of the ultimate effort. Those who understand and champion this position are firm and uncompromising in regard to their own efforts, but they do not try to make the government's task of defense more difficult.

No doubt many of those who suppose the position of the vocational pacifist is inconsistent are thinking, in some way or other, of Kant's Categorical Imperative. The proper answer to this is that the formal rule which seeks to universalize a maxim needs something else to give it concreteness. In short, what is our maxim? It is that each group, whatever it may be, must be true to its vocation and that there are differences of vocation. When we ask what our vocation is we are helped by turning to a principle enunciated by a philosopher of the generation just gone, the philosopher who held that nearly all ethical answers are summed up in the phrase "My Station and its Duties." If I really know what my station is, including my responsibilities and my connections, I may not always be clear about what I have to do, but I am far more nearly clear than before. In short, we are better prepared philosophically for our task if we read Bradley as well as Kant.

The religious pacifist, if he understands rightly his station and its duties, cannot look upon himself as one who tends his little individualistic fires of conscience. On the contrary he has an exciting social responsibility, and the fewness of his numbers makes the responsibility the greater. If the number of religious pacifists were to become a dominant majority, that would be cause for rejoicing. Though there would still be the risk of martyrdom for a whole people, we should be willing to take the risk, since there would be an excellent chance of real success in positive peace making. The individual religious pacifist would not, however, be as important then as he is now. Now he is sufficiently rare that each is greatly needed.

I do not wish to underestimate the gravity of the present danger, and I honor the men who are following their consciences in the encouragement of resistance to tyranny, but it is evident that military resistance is a palliative at best. *It is no cure.* And there ought to be people in the world who concentrate on the cure *at all times.* Military power may succeed in stopping wanton aggression and in setting the oppressed free, but it will not change the hearts of the aggressors. It will not, in the phrase of George Fox, take away the "occasion" of war.

There is a magnificent opportunity ahead for those who are drawn to religious pacifism as a way of life. Those who separate themselves from the war effort (while they do not obstruct it), are in a splendid position to try to overcome the growing hatred of the *people* of Axis nations. And when the actual fighting is over, those who have followed this way may be expected to have the easiest entrance into the lives of "enemy" peoples. The fundamental task is the task of overcoming wars before they start, and this is the task to which the vocational pacifist seeks to be loyal.

We tried to avoid the present horror before it began. We failed. Now our job is chiefly to stop the next one, and the one after that, so that when our little ones are men and women, they will not still know the horror of cities that are bombed and young men who are killed by the millions. Success in this sacred undertaking is more probable if there are men and women who go the whole way *now.*

THEOLOGICAL REBUILDING

As the *Christian Century* series repeatedly confirmed, neo-liberalism (or, in the abject phrase of the time, "chastened liberalism") was still, in 1939, a patchwork position at best. By the later 1940's, however, religious liberals had gained greater perspective. Like such secular scholars as Morton White, they undertook appraisals of liberalism that represented real synthesis and gave promise of liberal reconstruction.

Daniel Day Williams, then of the University of Chicago, made outstanding contributions of this kind. His study of the *Andover Liberals* in 1941 had qualified him as one of the few critics of the older religious liberalism who could work from a detailed knowledge of that movement. The following essay of 1945, which reported his reflections on certain enduring strengths of liberal theology, was to appear later, in much expanded form, as his book *God's Grace and Man's Hope* (1949).

~ 21 ~
THE PERPLEXITY AND THE OPPORTUNITY OF THE LIBERAL THEOLOGY
by Daniel Day Williams

The Christian man lives by the faith that life has its source in the goodness of the Eternal God and by the assurance that life's ultimate outcome must be the victory of that goodness—the accomplishment of the redemption of the world. The victory has its tragic side. The way to life's fulfilment is dark with suffering, sacrifice, and death. Redemption lies on the other side of judgment, and there are the lost who make their beds in hell. Yet against this

SOURCE: "The Perplexity and the Opportunity of the Liberal Theology in America," *Journal of Religion*, 25 (July 1945), 168–71, 175–8. Reprinted by permission of the University of Chicago Press. Footnotes abridged.

darkness the mercy of God shines only the more brightly. The peril of lostness makes more real and more urgent the hope of finding salvation. That hope remains when all about is shattered.

At the present moment in human history the Christian gospel can again bring to disheartened humanity the revitalizing message of hope. True, no age ever needed more to hear the powerful criticism which the gospel brings against our wrongness, but such criticism can lead only to despair unless we can also be led to see the rightness which is in and above all things and which is not shaken. To give witness to that rightness without sentimentality, to know the evil in the world and in ourselves to the last bitter fact, and still to know that we are laid hold upon by the redemptive power of God— this the Christian gospel can mean to our time.

What has come to be termed the "liberal tradition" in American theology was nothing if not hopeful.[1] It believed there were few evils in human life which could not be overcome through the loyal and intelligent cooperation of men with the work of the Living God. We might expect that the liberal theology today would be bringing hope to mankind with more compelling power than ever before. Such happens not to be the case. Those of us who stand in the liberal tradition find ourselves in perplexity of mind and spirit. It is the cause of that perplexity and our attitude toward it which I wish to examine.

The plight of the liberal tradition in theology is this: at the moment when its gospel of hope for the world is most desperately needed, it has become uncertain about the soundness of its doctrine of redemption. It is in the position of the man hearing the storms beat upon his house who is suddenly assailed by doubts as to whether it was solid rock or shifting sand upon which he had built the house. We know that liberalism gave a special interpretation to the traditional Christian conception of God's work in history. Did it get entirely off the right track?

[1] The term "liberal theology," especially as used by its critics, is too often undefined. In this paper I am concerned with theological issues rather than with schools of thought, and therefore I may be permitted to let the term stand for that movement in modern theology which sought to bring Christian doctrine into organic relation with the scientific knowledge, the evolutionary world view, and the movement for ethical and social reconstruction of the nineteenth century.

If one believes, as the writer does, that liberalism developed a permanently valid and indispensable insight within the Christian faith, then the present perplexity is also opportunity. Through critical self-examination the heirs of the liberal faith must deepen their grasp of man's need and God's grace, but this without discarding the truth which liberalism discovered. Only a theology with the freedom won by liberalism can state the Christian message in forms which will convey it powerfully to contemporary minds. Only a theology which keeps its faith in man while it deepens its faith in God can avoid the defeatism in Christian social action which looms today on the theological horizon.

The heart of the Christian gospel is its assertion of the need and the fact of redemption. The fulfilment of life and its restoration to wholeness are accomplished in God's eternal Kingdom. I propose to begin by asking the question: What was the liberal theology's interpretation of the doctrine of redemption, and why has this doctrine been so radically called into question?

In the Bible man's life in relation to God is described in a series of events which constitute a "history of the work of redemption." This history includes all the acts of God in creating and saving his world. The creation of the world and of man, the sin of man, the covenants with Israel and its deliverance from bondage, the word of the prophets, the incarnation of Christ, his crucifixion and resurrection, the growth of the church in the world, the prospective return of Christ, the last judgment, the establishment of God's Kingdom—all this relates what God has done, is doing, and will do for the accomplishment of the reign of his love over all things.

What the liberal theology did was to reinterpret this history of redemption. Most of its elements were retained, but they were seen in a new perspective. The new version began with the fundamental assertion that the world is the subject of the divine working. But, in the light of the new knowledge available in the nineteenth century, Christians began to think in a new way about the course of world history in relation to the history of redemption. Looking through the eyes of nineteenth century science and philosophy, they saw the cosmos emerging from an infinitely remote chaos by gradual stages. They saw the slow heave and surge of the process of evolution out of which life, mind, and spirit emerge. They saw man coming from animal beginnings through savagery and barbarism to civilization. All this they saw fulfilled in the appearance of Jesus and transformed by him, for in his life and death and the experience of his resurrection new moral and spiritual power was released among men, making them co-workers with God in the task of making the world good.

Liberalism is sometimes characterized as having "flattened out" the Christian world view into a thin and colorless triviality. Quite the contrary. It was a stupendous drama which this theology described, ranking fully in grandeur and awesome wonder with the visions of Augustine and Milton. It conceived of creation and redemption as continuing aspects of the same process in which the good is cumulatively achieved. The progressive fulfilment of the possibilities of life constitutes the gradual attainment of the Kingdom of God.

It is true that there was a shift of attention here from redemption as meaning primarily a fulfilment in a future life to redemption as the realization of the good in this life. Yet the liberal theology did not ignore the eternal for the sake of the temporal. It rather conceived the eternal love of God as being disclosed within the temporal realm. Most liberal theology looked, as Christian theology has always looked, beyond death for the consummation of redemption. This was emphasized in the doctrine of immortality as a continuation and completion of man's life with God.

If God's work can be interpreted in this way, there are two consequences, both of which were stressed by the liberal theology. The first relates to the practical question of Christian action. Here is the Christian businessman, homemaker, soldier, politician, minister. How is he to think of himself in what he has to do in the world's life? The liberal answer was this: In so far as the Christian is pursuing the ideal of making the world into a brotherhood of man, he is a co-worker with God in the building of his Kingdom. The Christian is an imperfect person in an imperfect but dynamic world. God is working against imperfection. The Christian cooperates with God by using all his human capacities to bring himself and the world more completely into harmony with God's will. Christian liberalism was not humanism. No human achievement is possible without

God's power and presence. No one was more clear on this point than Walter Rauschenbusch. "By accepting the Kingdom as a task we experience it as a gift."[2]

The second consequence of this standpoint is the increased hope that Christian action for the transformation of the world will be effective. The Kingdom which God is achieving certainly includes the making of this world good, whatever more it may mean. Therefore none of the evils which stand across God's path, the inertia of nature, the stupidity and rebellion of men, intrenched social injustice, cruelty, and war—none of these need be accepted as ineradicable from human life. God works against them—so should man, with hope.

It is commonplace now to say that liberalism fell into incautious and extravagant expressions of its hope for the world's perfection. There did creep in a romantic and utopian element borrowed from the secular rather than from the Christian mind. But the liberal theology never really depended upon a utopian view of the future of this world as its primary faith. The significant conviction was that, whatever the limitations of this earthly existence, it is the field of God's working, and it is not for man to set limitations upon what God can accomplish. It is a fair judgment, I think, that this belief in God's transforming power lay side by side in the liberal mind with a romantic utopianism and that the two were never wholly compatible or reconciled. A well-nigh perfect expression of this divided mind can be found in the closing pages of Walter Rauschenbusch's *Christianity and the Social Crisis,* written in 1907. As he comes to his final paragraphs, he states explicitly the objections to thinking of the world as gradually achieving freedom from evil. He predicts that "the strong will always have the impulse to exert their strength, and no system can be devised which can keep them from crowding and jostling the weaker." Yet he voices the "hot hope that perhaps the long and slow climb may be ending" and closes with the suggestion that if men can rally sufficient religious faith and moral strength, the "day of the Lord" for which the prophets waited will soon arrive.[3]

[2] *A Theology for the Social Gospel* (New York: The Macmillan Co., 1917), p. 141.
[3] *Christianity and the Social Crisis* (New York: The Macmillan Co., 1907), pp. 420-22.

When critics of liberalism have rejected this "romantic optimism," they have often forgotten that the question still remains as to what the Christian does have a right to hope for in the improvement of this world. God is the Lord of his creation, and he seeks a world in which personal life is fulfilled in creative expression and fellowship. The Christian has a right to believe that efforts toward such an outcome are neither misguided nor hopeless. Without the continued struggle to release the possibilities of this life, human existence and all its value must sink to nothing. If God is not at work creatively in this tremendous scheme of things, who is? And if his working in history be not a part of his work of redemption, what possible meaning could redemption have?

The ideas we have outlined were the common sense of liberal theology. As so often happens, the common sense of one age has become the perplexity of the next. In the reaction against liberalism, it is now charged that this theology missed the essential insight of Christianity when it tended to equate the realization of the possibilities of this life with the achievement of the Kingdom of God, that is, with redemption.

* * *

The raising of these issues has already led to a fruitful theological renaissance. Some liberals react defensively, choosing to stand where they are. Some have departed for other theological camps. But there are those who believe that Christian truth can also be served by a creative movement from within the liberal tradition. I believe that such a movement is possible. It calls for radical self-criticism and the capacity to make structural alterations in past modes of thought. But the theology for which we must labor will have a deeper grasp of the nature of man's need, while it includes the truth for which the liberal theology contended.

I wish to suggest the following formula for the reconstruction of the doctrine of redemption: The divine work of redemption to which Christianity bears witness cannot be identified with the perfecting of this world and our human life—so far the liberal doctrine will not hold; but the work of redemption *includes as an integral aspect* whatever perfecting of this world and human life is possible —so far liberalism is right.

In concluding this paper I wish briefly to indicate why the two assertions in this formula are necessary.

We cannot identify redemption with the progressive realization of the possibilities of life, even though that life include a continuing existence beyond death, because the very nature of human existence involves our need for something which is more and other than infinite self-realization. This something more is twofold. On one side it is our need for the knowledge that we have found the Eternal God to whom we can intrust our lives absolutely, and on the other side it means a reconciliation with God, from whom both the conditions of our life and our own sin separate us. Only a forgiving love which restores us to fellowship with our Creator, only a divine mercy which takes the fragments of our human achievements and failures and gives them an enduring meaning, can make life truly whole and release us to live it confidently and creatively. The chaplain who said that on the eve of battle he discovered that his liberal theology was not enough was, I think, simply testifying to the discovery which many today are making that, when we come to see some things in our lives for what they are, the evangelical message of redemption through the suffering love of God becomes our one sure defense.

But there is no redemption without creation, and God's creative work is related to his redemptive work somewhat on the analogy of the part to the whole. In the light of what we now know about the world, creation is a continuing process. It includes the continuous career of a dynamic unfolding life. God has given man capacity to guide and transform the processes of existence, within limits, to be sure, but with the possibility of exercising some control over the conditions under which life is lived. Christian theology must hold that the redemption of the world includes the development of the possibilities of this temporal existence.

It is fair to say, I think, that what troubles many about the neo-Reformation theologies is their apparent disregard of the significance of a patient, intelligent, working through of the processes of existence to discover the conditions under which the persons about whom God cares can have life and have it more abundantly. The scientist, artist, educator, and legislator are always in a position either to increase or to decrease the opportunities for persons to find the ultimate meaning of life in the service of God. Even if it be admitted that every particular value and every concrete decision in human experience involves evil as well as good, this must never obscure the fact that some ways of life must be judged more wholesome than others. The Christian gospel does not relieve man of the necessity of making the wisest moral choices he can.

Specifically, the theology which will bring the Christian message most powerfully to our time must include three basic insights in its doctrine of redemption.

1. The Kingdom of God, which is the Christian name for the fulfilment of life in fellowship with God, includes the temporal values' of human existence, however it may transcend them. The supreme good to which Christianity points is not a negation of the worth of this life. Wherever there is anything in the whole realm of nature which contributes to the growth and creative expression of this world's creatures, there is a good which is to be cherished not only for our sake but for the sake of the Kingdom itself. That Kingdom is the fulfilled and transfigured life of *this* world, not some other world.

It can be said that to bring the Kingdom into relation with human possibilities is to lose the transcendent vantage point from which Christianity can pronounce its ethical criticism against the world. But any prophetic criticism which has a cutting edge must possess a basis of judgment which stands in direct relation to the choices we have to make here and now. Valid criticism depends upon a relevant standard of criticism.

There are signs that the schools of contemporary Protestant theology are moving toward a deeper mutual understanding of the problem of Christian social ethics. American liberalism is achieving a clearer conception of the transcendence of the Kingdom without sacrificing its relevance, while Continental theologians like Emil Brunner and W. A. Visser t'Hooft are emphasizing the necessity for Christianity to play a creative role in all forms of human culture. Dr. Visser t'Hooft, for example, in a recent article analyzing the cultural problem, points to the unique opportunity for the proclamation of the Christian message and adds: "It goes without saying that its message must be proclaimed in relation to the great problems of today, the thirst of a true freedom, a true justice, and a real security."[4]

2. The doctrine of the work of redemption must take account of the elemental fact that human existence is a dynamic process. The concept of process was among the most significant contributions of the nineteenth century to man's knowledge. The notion was often and erroneously identified with that of progress, which it does not necessarily imply. It means that time is of the essence of our existence, that a gradual, connected development in which specific conditions lead to specific consequences is a fundamental aspect of individual and social life. The significance of this concept for Christian living is that a respect for the patient study and direction of the *becoming* of life is a part of Christian wisdom.

The scientific analysis of the processes of existence has yielded a large part of the measure of control over the conditions of life which man now may exercise. Only a theology which brings such an understanding within the meaning of religious living can be relevant to the work of science, education, and statecraft. The deeper grasp in Christian thought today of the truth that man realizes his life only through being brought to a personal encounter with God ought to be an added stimulus toward the empirical task of discovering and dealing wisely with everything which influences personal growth.

If the concept of process deserves the emphasis I have placed upon it, then the present enthusiasm for Kierkegaard's thought deserves more critical and objective analysis than it is receiving. There is no "process" in Kierkegaard's world. For all his concern with the "existential" situation, he leaves out one of the most obvious facts about that situation—the fact that man has his life in a social process. Kierkegaard's man is a solitary individual. All his significant decisions take place in the vertical dimension between himself and the eternal. Kierkegaard criticizes the Hegelian conception of the process of world history on the ground that for

[4] "Social and Political Forces of Tomorrow," *Student World, 37,* No. 3 (1944), 217. The reference to Brunner is to *The Divine Imperative* (Philadelphia: Westminster Press, 1947) and also to his recent development of the concept of Christian natural law.

Hegel it is all a shadow play, there is no real becoming. But Kierkegaard's man, in spite of his profound experience, many sides of which are so superbly delineated, never really changes anything in himself or his world. His life is a becoming in which nothing ever happens. The approach to human nature of the religious education movement, with its emphasis upon the social process, represents a necessary criticism and supplementation of the Kierkegaardian standpoint.

3. A third conception is already implied in the first two. The form of this world is not absolutely fixed. The transformation for the better of the conditions of human existence is possible. The service of the Kingdom of God therefore includes whatever constructive development of the conditions of personal life we can achieve.

The new theology can learn from the Reformation doctrine of the orders that there are always given structural factors in human life which are what they are and which set the conditions under which the Christian life must be lived. But the new theology will also know that any a priori fixing of the limits of the possible transformation of the orders is unwarranted. The long testimony of history is against the notion that anything in human nature or society or perhaps even in physical nature is absolutely fixed. God is creator at every moment of time. In some degree, which it is not given our minds to delimit, his world is becoming new.

This need not lead us to romantic illusions. There are, indeed, limits to the possible transformation of the world. The sober language of Christian realism will not forget the vast mystery of evil and death. It will confess the resistance to God's way in the soul of man. But no real good can come in history unless men are willing to do what they can with human problems. Hopelessness produces helplessness. Aristotle and Aquinas argued that human slavery belonged to the natural order of things. How simple to accept this, especially if one owns slaves. Nature is full of the struggle for life. How easy to refuse the effort to organize the world for peace on the ground that warfare must forever lay waste to human life. But we cannot know the limits of peace among men until we try to find them. The spirit of moral adventure is of the essence of the Christian life.

The doctrine of redemption can be stated in a theology which recognizes both the possibilities and the tragedy of God's creative task. This is a world in which Christ the Redeemer can appear. It is subject to his transforming power. But this is also a world in which Christ is crucified, and his redemption involves the word of divine forgiveness which is spoken from his cross. A theology which holds these two truths together can keep alive the common earthly hopes of men for freedom, justice, and the good life, while it gives these hopes their one sure foundation in the knowledge of the living God.

CREEDS AND THE LEAVEN OF LIBERALISM

By the 1960's, the continuing influence of liberalism was apparent not only in what theologians were writing but in what some of the churches were doing about their confessional statements. The Northern branch of the still-divided Presbyterians, having resisted creedal revision for nearly a century, adopted in 1967 a Confession that at some points was a literal transcription of the ideas for which well-known liberals had contended in the 1870's.

To be sure, the Confession of 1967 repeatedly indicated its continuity with the evangelical tradition ("God raised [Jesus] from the dead, vindicating him as Messiah and Lord"). And it frequently attested the special influences of neo-orthodoxy ("All human virtue, when seen in the light of God's love in Jesus Christ, is found to be infected with self-interest and hostility"). But the statement was silent, just as early liberals had been, on doctrines such as Predestination that had once been thought central to a Calvinist creed. Even more strikingly, its most prominent and reiterated theme, next to the announced central one of divine-human reconciliation, was a recognition of the transience of humanly shaped creeds and institutions.

To the extent that such assertions were confessing the finitude of all human productions, their immediate parentage was neo-orthodoxy. Yet it was liberal progenitors who had fought for the unequivocal inclusion of creeds in the catalogue of human productions.

~ 22 ~

THE PRESBYTERIAN CONFESSION OF 1967

PREFACE

The church confesses its faith when it bears a present witness to God's grace in Jesus Christ.

SOURCE: *Proposed Book of Confessions* (Philadelphia: United Presbyterian Church in the U.S.A., 1967), pp. 177–9, 181, 183–4, 186.

226

In every age the church has expressed its witness in words and deeds as the need of the time required. The earliest examples of confession are found within the Scriptures. Confessional statements have taken such varied forms as hymns, liturgical formulas, doctrinal definitions, catechisms, theological systems in summary, and declarations of purpose against threatening evil.

Confessions and declarations are subordinate standards in the church, subject to the authority of Jesus Christ, the Word of God, as the Scriptures bear witness to him. No one type of confession is exclusively valid, no one statement is irreformable. Obedience to Jesus Christ alone identifies the one universal church and supplies the continuity of its tradition. This obedience is the ground of the church's duty and freedom to reform itself in life and doctrine as new occasions, in God's providence, may demand.

The United Presbyterian Church in the United States of America acknowledges itself aided in understanding the gospel by the testimony of the church from earlier ages and from many lands. More especially it is guided by the Nicene and Apostles' Creeds from the time of the early church; the Scots Confession, the Heidelberg Catechism, and the Second Helvetic Confession from the era of the Reformation; the Westminster Confession and Shorter Catechism from the seventeenth century; and the Theological Declaration of Barmen from the twentieth century.

The purpose of the Confession of 1967 is to call the church to that unity in confession and mission which is required of disciples today. This Confession is not a "system of doctrine," nor does it include all the traditional topics of theology. For example, the Trinity and the Person of Christ are not redefined but are recognized and reaffirmed as forming the basis and determining the structure of the Christian faith.

God's reconciling work in Jesus Christ and the mission of reconciliation to which he has called his church are the heart of the gospel in any age. Our generation stands in peculiar need of reconciliation in Christ. Accordingly this Confession of 1967 is built upon that theme.

THE CONFESSION

In Jesus Christ God was reconciling the world to himself. Jesus Christ is God with man. He is the eternal Son of the Father, who became man and lived among us to fulfill the work of reconciliation. He is present in the church by the power of the Holy Spirit to continue and complete his mission. This work of God, the Father, Son, and Holy Spirit, is the foundation of all confessional statements about God, man, and the world. Therefore the church calls men to be reconciled to God and to one another.

In Jesus of Nazareth true humanity was realized once for all. Jesus, a Palestinian Jew, lived among his own people and shared their needs, temptations, joys, and sorrows. He expressed the love of God in word and deed and became a brother to all kinds of sinful men. But his complete obedience led him into conflict with his people. His life and teaching judged their goodness, religious aspirations, and national hopes. Many rejected him and demanded his death. In giving himself freely for them he took upon himself the judgment under which all men stand convicted. God raised him from the dead, vindicating him as Messiah and Lord. The victim of sin became victor, and won the victory over sin and death for all men.

God's reconciling act in Jesus Christ is a mystery which the Scriptures describe in various ways. It is called the sacrifice of a lamb, a shepherd's life given for his sheep, atonement by a priest; again it is ransom of a slave, payment of debt, vicarious satisfaction of a legal penalty, and victory over the powers of evil. These are expressions of a truth which remains beyond the reach of all theory in the depths of God's love for man. They reveal the gravity, cost, and sure achievement of God's reconciling work.

The risen Christ is the savior for all men. Those joined to him by faith are set right with God and commissioned to serve as his reconciling community. Christ is head of this community, the church, which began with the apostles and continues through all generations.

The same Jesus Christ is the judge of all men. His judgment discloses the ultimate seriousness of life and gives promise of God's

final victory over the power of sin and death. To receive life from
the risen Lord is to have life eternal; to refuse life from him is to
choose the death which is separation from God. All who put their
trust in Christ face divine judgment without fear, for the judge is
their redeemer.

The reconciling act of God in Jesus Christ exposes the evil in men
as sin in the sight of God. In sin men claim mastery of their own
lives, turn against God and their fellow men, and become exploiters
and despoilers of the world. They lose their humanity in futile striving
and are left in rebellion, despair, and isolation.

Wise and virtuous men through the ages have sought the highest
good in devotion to freedom, justice, peace, truth, and beauty. Yet
all human virtue, when seen in the light of God's love in Jesus
Christ, is found to be infected by self-interest and hostility. All men,
good and bad alike, are in the wrong before God and helpless without his forgiveness. Thus all men fall under God's judgment. No
one is more subject to that judgment than the man who assumes
that he is guiltless before God or morally superior to others.

God's love never changes. Against all who oppose him, God expresses his love in wrath. In the same love God took on himself
judgment and shameful death in Jesus Christ, to bring men to repentance and new life.

God's sovereign love is a mystery beyond the reach of man's mind.
Human thought ascribes to God superlatives of power, wisdom, and
goodness. But God reveals his love in Jesus Christ by showing power
in the form of a servant, wisdom in the folly of the cross, and goodness in receiving sinful men. The power of God's love in Christ to
transform the world discloses that the Redeemer is the Lord and
Creator who made all things to serve the purpose of his love.

•   •   •

The one sufficient revelation of God is Jesus Christ, the Word of
God incarnate, to whom the Holy Spirit bears unique and authoritative witness through the Holy Scriptures, which are received and
obeyed as the word of God written. The Scriptures are not a witness
among others, but the witness without parallel. The church has re-

ceived the books of the Old and New Testaments as prophetic and apostolic testimony in which it hears the word of God and by which its faith and obedience are nourished and regulated.

The New Testament is the recorded testimony of apostles to the coming of the Messiah, Jesus of Nazareth, and the sending of the Holy Spirit to the Church. The Old Testament bears witness to God's faithfulness in his covenant with Israel and points the way to the fulfillment of his purpose in Christ. The Old Testament is indispensable to understanding the New, and is not itself fully understood without the New.

The Bible is to be interpreted in the light of its witness to God's work of reconciliation in Christ. The Scriptures, given under the guidance of the Holy Spirit, are nevertheless the words of men, conditioned by the language, thought forms, and literary fashions of the places and times at which they were written. They reflect views of life, history, and the cosmos which were then current. The church, therefore, has an obligation to approach the Scriptures with literary and historical understanding. As God has spoken his word in diverse cultural situations, the church is confident that he will continue to speak through the Scriptures in a changing world and in every form of human culture.

God's word is spoken to his church today where the Scriptures are faithfully preached and attentively read in dependence on the illumination of the Holy Spirit and with readiness to receive their truth and direction.

•　　•　　•

The church in its mission encounters the religions of men and in that encounter becomes conscious of its own human character as a religion. God's revelation to Israel, expressed within Semitic culture, gave rise to the religion of the Hebrew people. God's revelation in Jesus Christ called forth the response of Jews and Greeks and came to expression within Judaism and Hellenism as the Christian religion. The Christian religion, as distinct from God's revelation of himself, has been shaped throughout its history by the cultural forms of its environment.

The Christian finds parallels between other religions and his own and must approach all religions with openness and respect. Repeatedly God has used the insight of non-Christians to challenge the church to renewal. But the reconciling word of the gospel is God's judgment upon all forms of religion, including the Christian. The gift of God in Christ is for all men. The church, therefore, is commissioned to carry the gospel to all men whatever their religion may be and even when they profess none.

In each time and place there are particular problems and crises through which God calls the church to act. The church, guided by the Spirit, humbled by its own complicity and instructed by all attainable knowledge, seeks to discern the will of God and learn how to obey in these concrete situations. The following are particularly urgent at the present time.

a. God has created the peoples of the earth to be one universal family. In his reconciling love he overcomes the barriers between brothers and breaks down every form of discrimination based on racial or ethnic difference, real or imaginary. The church is called to bring all men to receive and uphold one another as persons in all relationships of life: in employment, housing, education, leisure, marriage, family, church, and the exercise of political rights. Therefore the church labors for the abolition of all racial discrimination and ministers to those injured by it. Congregations, individuals, or groups of Christians who exclude, dominate, or patronize their fellowmen, however subtly, resist the Spirit of God and bring contempt on the faith which they profess.

b. God's reconciliation in Jesus Christ is the ground of the peace, justice, and freedom among nations which all powers of government are called to serve and defend. The church, in its own life, is called to practice the forgiveness of enemies and to commend to the nations as practical politics the search for cooperation and peace. This requires the pursuit of fresh and responsible relations across every line of conflict, even at risk to national security, to reduce areas of strife and to broaden international understanding. Reconciliation among nations becomes peculiarly urgent as countries develop nuclear, chemical, and biological weapons, diverting their manpower and resources from constructive uses and risking the annihilation of mankind. Although nations may serve God's purposes in history, the church which identifies the sovereignty of any one nation or any one way of life with the cause of God denies the Lordship of Christ and betrays its calling.

c. The reconciliation of man through Jesus Christ makes it plain that enslaving poverty in a world of abundance is an intolerable violation of God's good creation. Because Jesus identified himself with the needy and exploited, the cause of the world's poor is the cause of his disciples. The church cannot condone poverty, whether it is the product of unjust social structures, exploitation of the defenseless, lack of national resources, absence of technological understanding, or rapid expansion of populations. The church calls every man to use his abilities, his possessions, and the fruits of technology as gifts entrusted to him by God for the maintenance of his family and the advancement of the common welfare. It encourages those forces in human society that raise men's hopes for better conditions and provide them with opportunity for a decent living. A church that is indifferent to poverty, or evades responsibility in economic affairs, or is open to one social class only, or expects gratitude for its beneficence makes a mockery of reconciliation and offers no acceptable worship to God.

d. The relationship between man and woman exemplifies in a basic way God's ordering of the interpersonal life for which he created mankind. Anarchy in sexual relationships is a symptom of man's alienation from God, his neighbor, and himself. Man's perennial confusion about the meaning of sex has been aggravated in our day by the availability of new means for birth control and the treatment of infection, by the pressures of urbanization, by the exploitation of sexual symbols in mass communication, and by world overpopulation. The church, as the household of God, is called to lead men out of this alienation into the responsible freedom of the new life in Christ. Reconciled to God, each person has joy in and respect for his own humanity and that of other persons; a man and woman are enabled to marry, to commit themselves to a mutually shared life, and to respond to each other in sensitive and lifelong concern; parents receive the grace to care for children in love and to nurture their individuality. The church comes under the judgment of God and invites rejection by man when it fails to lead men and women into the full meaning of life together, or withholds the compassion of Christ from those caught in the moral confusion of our time.

. . .

God's redeeming work in Jesus Christ embraces the whole of man's life: social and cultural, economic and political, scientific and technological, individual and corporate. It includes man's natural environment as exploited and despoiled by sin. It is the will of God that his purpose for human life shall be fulfilled under the rule of Christ and all evil be banished from his creation.

Biblical visions and images of the rule of Christ such as a heavenly city, a father's house, a new heaven and earth, a marriage feast, and an unending day culminate in the image of the kingdom. The kingdom represents the triumph of God over all that resists his will and disrupts his creation. Already God's reign is present as a ferment in the world, stirring hope in men and preparing the world to receive its ultimate judgment and redemption.

With an urgency born of this hope the church applies itself to present tasks and strives for a better world. It does not identify limited progress with the kingdom of God on earth, nor does it despair in the face of disappointment and defeat. In steadfast hope the church looks beyond all partial achievement to the final triumph of God.

"Now to him who by the power at work within us is able to do far more abundantly than all we ask or think, to him be glory in the church and in Christ Jesus to all generations, forever and ever. Amen."

THE NEW IMMANENTISM

The writers of the Presbyterian Confession of 1967, though they overcame the limits that much Crisis Theology had placed upon the church's response to culture, showed no inclination toward wholesale questioning of Christian or theistic terminology. But the "radical theology" of the 1960's did take this further step, either by stressing the futility of using terms like "God" and "Father" in reference to a truly transcendent being; or by suggesting that a transcendent being simply does not exist.

These ventures into "radical immanence," often accompanied by reassertions of humanist optimism and by perceptions of the religious meaning of the profane or secular, constituted the clearest resurgence to date of the leading themes of liberalism. Professor Paul Van Buren of Temple University, whose *Secular Meaning of the Gospel* was important to the new critique of religious language, took a position that was reminiscent especially of that brand of liberalism that had moved away from philosophical Idealism. Though he thought "the death of God" a poor phrase for expressing it, Van Buren eloquently supported the argument that modern man has ceased to assume the existence of an Absolute, a principle of cosmic unity.

When Van Buren hinted, in this connection, that William James's pluralistic universe should be called a "polyverse," the suggestion was more than semantic pedantry. The innovators of the sixties, like every other generation of new reformers, were demanding that old reformers, dead or living, accept the consequences of their own principles.

~ 23 ~
THE DISSOLUTION OF THE ABSOLUTE
by Paul M. Van Buren

The world in which I live, and apparently not alone, is a world which I should like to describe as following upon, or in the late stages of, a major socio-psychological shift in our culture, which I shall label "The Dissolution of the Absolute." It seems to have been the case, prior to this shift, that thoughtful men spoke not infrequently, and as though they had no thought of not being understood by their peers, of the Absolute, the Highest Good, or of Reality (with a capital R). This characteristic of language and thought has become increasingly difficult to maintain or recapture. The change has come about, so far as I can see, not as a result of a frontal assault on the idea of the Absolute, but by a process of dissolution or decay. The Absolute was not murdered, *Zarathustra* not withstanding; it died of neglect.

The dissolution of the Absolute, the passing of a world view and a habit of thought, or its quiet displacement by another and different habit of thought, is a phenomenon that I have called a socio-psychological fact. With that label I wish to indicate how broad and basic a shift I have in mind, and how many ways there are of exploring and describing this change. One can, for example, ask about the causes and timing of the dissolution of that pattern of thought in which differing views about the Absolute were held to be of such importance that these differences could lead to heresy trials and burnings at the stake, not to speak of wars. I take this question about the causes and timing of the change to be a historical question which it is the proper business of the historian of Western culture to explore. Setting dates for this sort of cultural shift is a rather

SOURCE: "The Dissolution of the Absolute," *Religion in Life, 34* (Summer, 1965), 335–42. Copyright © 1965 by Abingdon Press; reprinted by permission. The article was part of a symposium on "The Secular Emphasis of Our Age—Its Values and Dangers." Two prefatory paragraphs have been omitted. Also reprinted in Paul M. Van Buren, *Theological Explorations* (New York: The Macmillan Co., 1968).

arbitrary business, but let me just suggest, as an illustration of the historical aspect of the problem, that if one were to write a history of Western Christianity, it might be more accurate to locate the fundamental turning point not in the Reformation, as is so often the case with Protestant histories of Christianity, but somewhere nearer the French Revolution. After all, Luther and Calvin stand in one world with Augustine and Aquinas, no matter how they may disagree about the details; whereas none of them fit easily, if at all, into the world of the Enlightenment. The gap between the Reformers and the Scholastics is small indeed compared with the gap between them all and such men as Rousseau, Voltaire, or Jefferson.

One can also ask about the extent of the dissolution, to what extent it is the case that people no longer seem to operate on the assumption of an absolute. This is a question which the sociologist might be in as good a position as any to explore. Or, if they were willing to study our society with the penetration shown in their study of some other societies, perhaps cultural anthropologists could help us to see the extent to which our values, attitudes, and patterns of thought betray a departure from those in which words such as "God," "providence," "destiny," and "absolute" seemed to function powerfully. The social sciences could help us see to what extent the Absolute has been dissolved out of our operative images of life and the world.

Or one can ask about the shape of this changed situation, how it looks when the dissolution has taken place. This can be opened up to some extent by the social sciences, but it can also be exposed by the works of writers, poets, and artists. The question of shape is in part an aesthetic question, and insofar as a quantifiable answer seems to fall short of satisfying our questions, the artists, writers, literary and art critics, and aestheticians can help us to see where we are today.

Further, there is a task of clarifying the dissolution and the logic of our new situation, which is, from one point of view, a philosophical question. Metaphysics I take to be not some sort of superscience which might provide us with new information about the universe or "Reality" of a rather esoteric or subtle kind. I know that there are theologians who speak as if ontology were some sort of penetration of the "structure of being," but I gather that few if any philosophers are impressed by this. A metaphysics or ontology, as I gather it would be taken by most philosophers today, consists rather of a proposal, one might say an invitation, to see what we already know in a particular way. Metaphysics does not give us something new to see (such as "being itself" or "the ground of being") in any other way than by giving us a new way to see what we have been looking at all along.

From this point of view, then, to speak of the dissolution of the Absolute is one way of indicating a shift which has occurred in our metaphysical assumptions. At this point, however, I find that philosophers seem to withdraw from what I take to be a serious and worthwhile enterprise: the attempt to formulate and clarify the logic of the commonsense metaphysics of our society. They say, quite correctly, that a major piece of this job is not their business: namely, the careful empirical study of what people in our society think and the way in which they think. That would properly be the business of the behavioral and social sciences to discover. Yet when it comes to the task of formulating and analyzing the workings of our commonsense attitudes, it would seem to me that the philosopher need not be so retiring. The disdainful remark that the common sense of today is only the poor leavings of the best thinking of yesterday and beneath the dignity of philosophical investigation, which I have heard from several philosophers, bothers me a bit. After all, the common sense of today is the pattern of thinking in which we do our major arguing and debating of the great issues of our society. I notice that philosophers appear just about as frequently as theologians among the lists of those thinkers called upon by government and industry to assist in dealing with the major issues of our time. Could it be that philosophers as well as theologians, admittedly for different reasons, have simply opted out of the society of common sense? If theologians are the more irrelevant to life today, it is because they have been even more disdainful of the realm of ordinary language and ordinary common sense. Be that as it may, I would still wish to urge that there is a philosophical task to be performed in our attempts to get clear about the commonsense understandings of our time, and if this task is not well done by competent philosophers, then it will be poorly and sloppily done by others.

The dissolution of the Absolute, then, is a broad cultural shift which may be investigated and documented from a number of angles. It is a change that has affected our thought and language in ways so fundamental that they are not always noticed. Few have taken as little account of this shift as have the theologically inclined, although it should be evident that religion and theology are as much or more touched by the dissolution of the Absolute as any area of human activity. One consequence of failing to see this change that has taken place has been a certain degree of linguistic and logical confusion, resulting from attempting to operate in a world without absolutes while using ideas and languages drawn from a world in which the idea of the Absolute had an important place. The confusion is not unlike that of the substitute player in a football game rushing onto the field firmly clutching a baseball bat.

A prime example of this sort of confusion may be seen in the use of the word "reality." Now on any showing, this is a tricky word, an odd sort of noun, like "sadness" or "beauty," which is derived from a reasonably clear usage in the adjectival form of the world. That is to say, we do not seem to have much difficulty when we use the word "real." There is little difficulty knowing what we mean when we say that a mirage, the appearance of water on the road ahead on a hot summer day, is not real. Or in doing an elementary experiment in refraction, we may see that a stick half immersed in water looks bent; but we know, or so we say without confusion, that the stick is really straight, in spite of appearances. In these cases the words "real" and "really" serve the purpose of touching base in or reminding us of a commonly agreed frame of reference. Empirically minded though we may be, we are also aware of the limitations of sense experience. Our senses are not infallible, we say. Things are not always what they seem; skim milk masquerades as cream. But we do have words such as "seem," "appear," and "masquerade," and we do have the working distinction between the uses of these words and the use of the word "real," because we do have that common network of ground rules to which we are able to appeal with the word "real." If this, then, is how we use the word "real," what would be the meaning of "reality"? Well, in a great many cases "reality" is a word that refers to the whole of our understandings of how things are according to this same network of ground rules. So we might say that a man who is insane is a man who has "lost touch with reality." We mean that he no longer plays life's game according to the common rules. Or we say that a hypothesis seems "to conform to reality," by which we mean that it seems to fit fairly well into how we take things to be according to our commonly held understandings.

So far so good. That is, nothing is at all airtight about any of this, but we get along all right; we understand each other fairly well. Now along comes the knight of faith and speaks of "reality breaking in upon us!" Or he speaks to us in the name of "absolute reality," or, even more confusing, his faith is placed in "an objective reality." And here I would suggest that language has gone on a wild binge, which I think we should properly call a lost weekend.

This knight of faith is presumably speaking English, and so we take him to be using words which we have learned how to use. Only see what he does with them. "Reality," which is ordinarily used to call our attention once more to our agreements about how things are, is used now to refer to what the knight of faith must surely want to say is radically the opposite of all of our ordinary understandings. Why not better say, "Unreality is breaking in upon us"?

I think we can say something about what has gone wrong here. There was a time when the Absolute, God, was taken to be the cause of a great deal of what we would today call quite real phenomena, from rain and hail to death and disease. God was part of what people took to be the network of forces and factors of everyday existence, as real and as objective as the thunderbolts he produced. But today we no longer have the same reference for the word "reality." The network of understandings to which the word points has undergone important changes. The word "reality" has taken on an empirical coloration which makes it now a bit confusing to speak of "reality breaking in upon us," unless we are referring to, for example, a sudden and unexpected visit from the police or a mother-in-law.

There is, however, another source of unclarity or confusion here, and that is the very fact of the dissolution of the Absolute itself. In the eleventh century the great theologian Anselm of Canterbury wrote a little essay containing an argument for the existence of God which continues to this day to occupy philosophers and theologians. I do not intend to explore Anselm's argument, but there is one contextual aspect of it which bears on our problem. Anselm was asking a certain question, the question about God, in such a way that he understood himself to be asking the one question which included and summed up every human question. And when he arrived at his answer, it was, as he conceived it, the discovery which was in some sense at once the answer to every human question. Indeed, I believe that this observation is true for all of the great traditional arguments for the existence of God. Those arguments were not trying to make a case for simply one entity, namely God, but for that which was the basis for and foundation of everything that is. Take away this frame of reference, this approach to these arguments, and they all become a bit silly.

Now the reason why most people today do regard these arguments as silly, the reason why we have difficulty accepting the answers or conclusions of these arguments, is because we simply do not know how to ask Anselm's question. We do not conceive it possible that there could be one answer which would entail and provide the answer to every question man can ask, in such diverse areas as, for example, politics, physics, mathematics, and aesthetics; so we are unable to ask after "God" in the way in which Anselm could. That being the case, we find it hard to accept his, or any of the arguments for the existence of God, as being persuasive. To speak of Absolute Reality is to speak in Anselm's world, not ours, both with respect to the word "Absolute" and to the word "Reality."

The change which I have called the dissolution of the Absolute has led to a pluralistic society and a pluralism of values and understandings. We are not in this world in one way; we live in our world in many ways, and it hardly seems to make sense to try to pull everything together under one heading. The sociologists call this differentiation, I believe, and another way of putting it would be to say that we have become relativists as well as pluralists. I am not saying, however, that we think everything is of the same or equal importance, or that we inhabit our various worlds or parts thereof in always the same and equal ways. Plurality does not entail equality of all the parts. It does mean, however, that life and the world are for us many different things, and that when we talk in a manner which convinces ourselves, we talk about "the whole" of life by talking in more detail or with more care about the various parts.

I touched on this in connection with Anselm's question and our inability to ask his question. The fact that Anselm and his world are part of our past may be taken as a clue to what I would call our monistic hangover, which, when it is particularly acute, makes our pluralist waking an agony. The monistic images of our past haunt us in the most unexpected and sometimes unwanted places. We may find, for example, when we try to think or speak of the universe, that we do not honestly want to spell "universe" with a capital "U." If we are asked about the extent of our small "u" universe, we may mention the rule of thumb which gives it a radius twice the range of the most powerful telescope, under the assumption that any presumed sources of light beyond that range are moving away from us at so nearly the speed of light that for all practical purposes (and isn't that a revealing phrase!) we can ignore them. And if we come closer to home, it is only out of habit that we speak of a "universe" at all. It really depends on how you approach it, we might say, for the "universe" of one discipline is but the background or a detail for another. All things considered, it appears to be more appropriate to speak of a polyverse.

But then that old monistic hangover begins to creep over us and tempts us to ask if there is not something fundamental to the human mind which leads us to keep on trying to pull things together, to see everything in some sort of interrelatedness, to devise laws and hypotheses in the hope of seeing how it all fits together into one whole. Perhaps at this point we need a bit of aspirin. Does the human mind actually do this, or is it more accurate to say that the human mind indeed tended to do this in the past out of which we have come? Perhaps we need to recall, for example, that historical study is one way of going at things, and it has developed and continues to develop its own methods. And physics is another way of going at things, with its own methods. And literary critics and biologists and painters also have their appropriate ways of exploring the world. Do we honestly think we shall come to understand any one of these ways, with its results, or indeed the whole of life, by somehow pulling them all together into one great system? When human knowledge was conceived of hierarchically—say on the model of a Gothic arch—it made sense to build comprehensive systems, and there could also be one queen of the sciences. But since the Gothic arch has been displaced by the marketplace as a model for human understanding, comprehensive systems have become strangely out of place, just as royalty finds itself out of a job in the context of the marketplace.

Pluralism means that we have granted that there are many ways of looking and seeing, many points of orientation, and that attempts to pull these all together into one grand scheme do not bring us closer to understanding how things are. The generalist has been displaced by the specialist in our society, in area after area of our common life. Insofar as this is true, insofar as this is how we think, we lose interest in Anselm's answer because we are not convinced he was asking the right question.

Relativism means that we appear to be coming more and more to a consensus that there is more than one way to look at any matter, and that what is said can be called true or false only in the terms provided by the particular point of reference. The student of art, for example, is encouraged to look at a given work of art in the light of the problems which the artist set for himself or were set for him by his situation. It is not a serious question for the student of art to ask what is the single greatest painting of all time.

Pluralism and relativism do not mean, however, that there are no distinctions to be made. One may have reasons for preferring one scale of values to another, one way of looking at a problem to another. But it is, I think we should agree, a mark of education and good sense to refrain from dogmatic statements which necessarily deny all merit to all other positions and points of view. One can hold serious commitments without universalizing them and without insisting that all who disagree are either knaves or fools. If relativism has an unpleasant sound, then let us call it tolerance. By whatever name, it is an important feature of the (secular) spirit of our age; and when we run into its denial, as in McCarthyism or Goldwaterism, most of us are at least uncomfortable. Somehow extremism has lost status, and if at moments it seems to make headway again, I think most of us regard this as a step backward, as a betrayal of what little progress civilization has made.

To ask theology and religion to accept the dissolution of the Absolute, to open their eyes to the world in which they live, is admittedly to ask much. It means that religion must not only become much more guarded in speaking of God (if not give this up altogether); it means also that more care be exercised in speaking of

"unique revelation," "absolute commitment," and some single "ultimate concern." It is to ask of the life of faith that it be lived as a
certain posture, involving commitments, but held in balance with
many other commitments; a certain willingness to see things in a
certain way without feeling obliged to say that this is the only way
in which they can be seen. The question may fairly be asked whether
theology and faith can survive this shift of focus; whether Christianity, for example, which has for so long proclaimed a monistic
view of the universe, a single and unique point of reference as the
only valid one, with a single and unique revelation of this truth,
can learn to live in a world from which the Absolute has been dissolved. However one may choose to answer this in theory, we are in
fact in the actual process of finding this out, for living when we do
and as we are is not exactly a matter of choice. What are the values
and dangers of this? Well, what are the values and dangers of being
alive? They are the values and dangers of being who we are.